D1045630

Learning With the Community

Concepts and Models
for Service-Learning
in **Teacher Education**

Joseph A. Erickson and Jeffrey B. Anderson, volume editors

Edward Zlotkowski, series editor

A PUBLICATION OF THE

AMERICAN ASSOCIATION
FOR HIGHER EDUCATION

Published in cooperation with the American Association of Colleges for Teacher Education

Acknowledgments

This monograph was published in cooperation with:

American Association of
Colleges for Teacher Education
One Dupont Circle, Suite 610
Washington, DC 20036-1186
202/293-2450
www.aacte.org

Learning With the Community: Concepts and Models for Service-Learning in Teacher Education
(AAHE's Series on Service-Learning in the Disciplines)
Joseph A. Erickson and Jeffrey B. Anderson, *volume editors*
Edward Zlotkowski, *series editor*

ISBN 1-56377-011-3
ISBN (set) 1-56377-005-0

Contents

Annotated Bibliography

Appendix

About This Series

by Edward Zlotkowski

The following volume, *Learning With the Community: Concepts and Models for Service-Learning in Teacher Education,* represents the third in a series of monographs on service-learning and the individual academic disciplines. Ever since the early 1990s, educators interested in reconnecting higher education not only with neighboring communities but also with the American tradition of education for service have recognized the critical importance of winning faculty support for this work. Faculty, however, tend to define themselves and their responsibilities largely in terms of the academic disciplines/interdisciplinary areas in which they have been trained. Hence, the logic of the present series.

The idea for this series first surfaced approximately three years ago at a meeting convened by Campus Compact to explore the feasibility of developing a national network of service-learning educators. At that meeting, it quickly became clear that some of those assembled saw the primary value of such a network in its ability to provide concrete resources to faculty working in or wishing to explore service-learning. Out of that meeting there developed, under the auspices of Campus Compact, a new national group of educators called the Invisible College, and it was within the Invisible College that the monograph project was first conceived. Indeed, a review of both the editors and contributors responsible for many of the volumes in this series would reveal significant representation by faculty associated with the Invisible College.

If Campus Compact helped supply the initial financial backing and impulse for the Invisible College and for this series, it was the American Association for Higher Education (AAHE) that made completion of the project feasible. Thanks to its reputation for innovative work, AAHE was not only able to obtain the funding needed to support the project up through actual publication, it was also able to assist in attracting many of the teacher-scholars who participated as writers and editors.

Three individuals in particular deserve to be singled out for their contributions. Sandra Enos, former Campus Compact project director for Integrating Service and Academic Study, has been shepherd to the Invisible College project. John Wallace, professor of philosophy at the University of Minnesota, has been the driving force behind the creation of the Invisible College. Without his vision and faith in the possibility of such an undertaking, assembling the human resources needed for this series would have been very difficult. Third, AAHE's endorsement — and all that followed in its wake

— was due largely to AAHE vice president Lou Albert. Lou's enthusiasm for the monograph project and his determination to see it adequately supported have been critical to its success. It is to Sandra, John, and Lou that the monograph series as a whole must be dedicated.

Other individuals to whom the series owes a special note of thanks include Matt Bliss, who, as my graduate assistant, helped set up many of the communications mechanisms that got the project started, and Jeannette MacInnes, coordinator of student programs at the Bentley Service-Learning Center, who has served as a reliable source of both practical and moral support.

The Rationale Behind the Series

A few words should be said at this point about the makeup of both the general series and the individual volumes. Although teacher education may seem a natural choice of disciplines with which to link service-learning, being intrinsically concerned with the work of public schools and the communities they serve, "natural fit" has not, in fact, been a determinant factor in deciding which disciplines/interdisciplinary areas the series should include. Far more important have been considerations related to the overall range of disciplines represented. Since experience has shown that there is probably no disciplinary area — from architecture to zoology — where service-learning cannot be fruitfully employed to strengthen students' abilities to become active learners as well as responsible citizens, a primary goal in putting the series together has been to demonstrate this fact. Thus, some rather natural choices for inclusion — disciplines such as anthropology, geography, and religious studies — have been passed over in favor of other, sometimes less obvious selections from the business disciplines and natural sciences as well as several important interdisciplinary areas. Should the present series of volumes prove useful and well received, we can then consider filling in the many gaps we have left this first time around.

If a concern for variety has helped shape the series as a whole, a concern for legitimacy has been central to the design of the individual volumes. To this end, each volume has been both written by and aimed primarily at academics working in a particular disciplinary/interdisciplinary area. Many individual volumes have, in fact, been produced with the encouragement and active support of relevant discipline-specific national societies. For this volume on teacher education, in fact, we owe thanks to the American Association of Colleges for Teacher Education.

Furthermore, each volume has been designed to include its own appropriate theoretical, pedagogical, and bibliographical material. Especially with regard to theoretical and bibliographical material, this design has resulted in considerable variation both in quantity and in level of discourse. Thus, for example, a volume such as Accounting contains more introductory and less bibliographical material than does Composition — simply because there is less written on and less familiarity with service-learning in accounting. However, no volume is meant to provide an extended introduction to service-learning as a *generic concept*. For material of this nature, the reader is referred to such texts as Kendall's *Combining Service and Learning: A Resource Book for Community and Public Service* (NSIEE, 1990) and Jacoby's *Service-Learning in Higher Education* (Jossey-Bass, 1996).

I would like to conclude with a note of special thanks to Jeffrey Anderson and Joseph Erickson, coeditors of the teacher education monograph. Not only have they demonstrated great skill and resourcefulness in putting it together, they have also maintained throughout the entire process a welcome flexibility and patience. I would also like to acknowledge the generous assistance of Arden Moon of Michigan State University, who provided valuable feedback on the manuscript.

April 1997

Foreword

by Vito Perrone

There has been, in the past decade, a revival of interest in service-learning in schools and colleges, even though the call to service-learning has long been embedded within the society. This revival has many roots: concerns about a growing age stratification, a youth culture that has too few connections to civic life, feelings among youth of having no critical and acknowledged place in the society, disturbing voting patterns in the 18- to 24-year-old population, growing school-work transitional difficulties, deterioration of communities as settings for social growth, and a belief that schooling isn't powerful enough to evoke deep commitments to learning, among others.

The early efforts to make service important focused on the establishment of modest requirements for graduation — 15 hours per year, 60 hours over four years, and the like. In such circumstances, it became an add-on, not a set of activities or a philosophical-moral stance integral to the life of the schools or connected sufficiently to genuine community needs.

I have long been attracted to service-learning as a means of revitalizing schools and their connections to communities, as an important means of fully engaging students, pushing what is done in and around schools toward the use of knowledge and not just the possession of information, and as a process directed toward the full integration of all persons, young and old, into the civic and economic aspects of life in their various communities. To think in these terms is to go beyond the view of service as another requirement, another course, another one-time event.

Currently, children and young people tend to describe their school learning as having very little to do with their lives beyond school. When students speak of the "remoteness" of school, and they do, they are really talking about the lack of connection between school and world outside. They are essentially acknowledging what Alfred North Whitehead noted — that most of what is taught in school is not about life "as it is known in the midst of living it."

Students see, for example, homelessness and poverty in the streets around them. They know about immigration as they hear so many languages being spoken. They are aware of racial discord, community violence, drugs, war, famine, and environmental degradation. That schools do not explore such issues deeply, for the most part even ignoring them, reinforces for students that the schools are about something other than the realities of the world. This is unfortunate.

Further, the content of schools seldom relates to what people in a particular community are worried about or care deeply about. For example, the schools do not often make the local community architecture, its historical and cultural roots or its economic and political structures, a focus of study. The community's storytellers, craftspersons, builders, day-care and health providers are not common visitors. The literature that is read has generally not been selected because it illuminates the life that students see day in and day out beyond the school, or because it helps them assume a larger sense of responsibility for some aspect of the social good or makes it possible for them to engage a nonschool mentor more productively or assist a person in need. This disconnectedness trivializes much of what students are asked to learn.

Most of us who work in and around schools know this intuitively. This knowledge causes many in schools to make occasional forays into the community — a walk to the park in relation to a science project, going to the local library so every student will get a library card, inviting in a couple of persons each year to share some aspect of their experience, having a cultural awareness day related to the special ethnic origins of a dominant community group, having students go sporadically to a senior citizens center or read to children in a lower grade level. Such efforts tend to be viewed as special events surrounding the real work of the school. This is the case even as teachers and their students often view these efforts as the highlights of the school year. The real work could, of course, be centered a good deal more on aspects of and interaction with the local setting. That could be the principal starting point of learning.

Those in the schools talk a great deal about preparing their students for social and civic responsibility, but the opportunities to gain experience in these directions are limited, if they exist at all. It is possible for students to complete their schooling and never be involved deeply, in or outside the school, in any service-oriented activity such as tutoring younger children or classmates, working with the elderly, constructing or maintaining a playground, monitoring a public hearing, completing a community survey, or teaching at a Boys' Club or Y. The lack of connections is large. Teaching for social responsibility and active citizenship is in most settings merely rhetoric.

But children from their very early years have a disposition toward outwardness, a need to learn about the world and participate actively in its ongoing life. They have a natural desire to engage others, to be helpful. And if nurtured in the home and in the schools, such a disposition can develop into a fuller form of social and civic responsibility.

Some of the wonderful remembrances of teens I have talked with are of particular trees they planted as children and that now bring so much pleasure to communities. The trees stand as visible reminders of their earlier service.

How do schools become powerful centers for community service, settings in which service is an integral part of the curriculum, something students and teachers see as critical to their lives, their ongoing learning? Answering that question is an important purpose of this book, *Learning With the Community*.

While making clear the importance of service-learning, Joseph Erickson and Jeffrey Anderson, veteran teacher educators and the editors of this book, have directed much of their attention to making service-learning integral to teacher preparation programs. They argue convincingly that service-learning will not become potent enough in schools and communities, able to transform the educational experiences of children and young people as well as help teachers themselves see service-learning as a democratizing force within schools, unless it becomes a more central element of teacher preparation. With this in mind, they have brought together an impressive array of contributions from classroom teachers, teacher educators, and teacher education students that not only address the power of service-learning but also provide inspiring examples of how service-learning has been integrated into teacher education courses at various colleges and universities. Importantly, the volume includes detailed descriptions of courses giving attention to service-learning as models for other teacher educators to emulate.

As I read the various contributions to this book, I find myself asking, Why isn't service-learning integrated into most courses that students take in college? My hope would be that this book is read by college and university faculty beyond teacher education. If service-learning becomes something broadly encouraged, we may yet have the democratic society that our public language has long supported.

Introduction

by Joseph A. Erickson and Jeffrey B. Anderson

Progressive teacher educators face a pair of daunting yet crucial tasks. New teachers must be prepared to function successfully in schools as they exist today and also be educated to take a leadership role in the improvement and reculturing of K-12 education to more fully meet the needs of individual students and resolve societal problems. One approach that can address both these tasks is the integration of service-learning experiences into teacher preparation programs.

Definition and Examples

What is service-learning? Service-learning is most often defined as a pedagogical technique for combining authentic community service with integrated academic outcomes. A growing body of research indicates that well-designed, well-managed service-learning can contribute to students' learning and growth while also helping to meet real community needs. (See "School-Based Service: A Review of Research for Teacher Educators," beginning on p. 42, for a further discussion of conceptions of service-learning and a review of research on service-learning in K-12 and teacher education.)

Examples of service-learning in K-12 schools are numerous. One case illustrates how integrated and impactful a service-learning project can become. In Minneapolis, former teacher Mary J. Syfax Noble (now a K-12 administrator, whose comments on an administrator's role in promoting service-learning begin on p. 134) developed an elaborate multilayered service-based learning unit that started with her fifth graders' visiting a local high-rise for senior citizens. The students' initial task was to meet and query the seniors regarding what (if anything) they would like from the youngsters. This initial inquiry led to the development of a formal paper-and-pencil survey that the fifth graders wrote, disseminated, collected, tabulated, and analyzed. The results of the survey indicated a wish on the part of the older people to laugh. The students set about addressing this need by writing limericks and funny stories. The students' written pieces went through several drafts until students felt prepared to deliver the results of their work to their elders. Finally, the students then engaged in limerick-reading sessions for the senior citizens. Even a casual task analysis of this project would note specific learning activities in writing, reading, decision making, mathematics, and public speaking.

Service-learning projects aimed at developing beginning or advanced teachers' competence are also numerous. At Kentucky State University in Frankfort, Kentucky, Carole A. Cobb integrates service-learning into her Introduction to Teaching course (see p. 155ff.). Students are placed as tutors and coaches in preschool and elementary classrooms, where they examine the nature and critical issues of the teaching profession via 20-hour service placements. These placements resemble traditional clinical placements with their emphases on community involvement in schools and society and opportunities for critical reflection and skill-building practice.

At California State University in San Marcos, Joseph F. Keating assists his San Diego–area secondary education students to critically examine important social issues through self-selected community service projects. One example (see p. 186ff.) was a Spanish language preservice teacher who chose to work with a tutoring organization developed for non-English-speaking parents at a local secondary school. The student learned that some of the grandparents of the secondary students with whom she worked actually had day-to-day responsibility for the students yet knew little English, so they could not work effectively with the school. In response to this need, the student developed a weekly seminar for these grandparents to learn basic English. Her lesson plans were broadened to include her upper-level Spanish class (whom she was student teaching) in tutoring with the grandparents. The preservice teacher provided needed community service that not only connected directly with her curriculum but also developed her leadership skills.

Theory and Principles of Service-Learning

The application of the specific pedagogical technique we call "service-learning" is relatively recent, but its roots are very old. Many religious and cultural traditions have attempted to impress upon their adherents a service ethic, from the common-good value of Native American cultures to the Good Samaritan story in the Christian tradition (Olszewski and Bussler 1993). Each of these traditions has held in high regard the importance of education for the common good. Field-based experience aimed at addressing *the common good* characterizes much of the theoretical basis of service-learning (e.g., Barber 1992; Cohen and Kinsey 1994; Giles 1988; Hutchings and Wutzdorff 1988; National Commission on Youth 1980; Newmann 1985).

The theoretical groundwork for service-learning's approach to learning has generally been provided by traditional experiential learning theory. Kurt Lewin's experiential learning cycle, as adapted and elaborated by Kolb (1984), gave the field a practical tool for analyzing the manner in which we introduce students to new ideas and the ways students integrate this new knowledge into their lives. This four-part cycle — concrete experience, reflective observation, abstract conceptualization, and active experimentation — is utilized in the field as a means to structure learning activities and to provide a structure for their assessment.

One way to classify the multiple theoretical threads of service-learning is to sort the various approaches into five camps (Anderson and Guest 1995): experiential learning (Dewey 1938; Kolb 1984), transformational or social reconstructionist theory (Allam and Zerkin 1993; Miller 1988), multicultural education approaches (Sleeter and Grant 1987), critical reflection (Sparks-Langer et al. 1990; Sullivan 1991), and education as preparation for civic responsibility (Coleman 1974; Martin 1976; National Committee on Secondary Education 1972). This analysis helps to identify the various competing movements that have motivated and continue to motivate the service-learning movement.

While much of the work at developing a theoretical and philosophical base for service-learning has emphasized either the common good or the role of experience on learning and cognition, few theorists have studied both. Many advocates emphasize *service*-learning, while others appear to accentuate service-*learning* (Littlefield 1996; Sigmon 1994).

A promising new attempt at simultaneously addressing *both* service and learning issues is found in Liu's recent discussion (1995; see also the Philosophy volume of this monograph series). In this paper, Liu structures an argument that service-learning's epistemology is distinct from and incompatible with the traditional view of learning as observed in most higher education institutions. He then builds a case for a new interactional base for learning that embeds the values of community, diversity, and engagement. By doing so, his argument takes a completely different tack that avoids the familiar service-or-learning dichotomy.

Connections to Other Educational Reform Movements

During the past 20 years, calls for educational reform at the K-12 and post-secondary levels have often included community service as one method for producing accelerated learning outcomes in both the cognitive and attitudinal domains (Boyer 1983, 1995; Goodlad 1984, 1990, 1994; Sizer 1992). Service-learning is philosophically in line with other educational reform initiatives, such as authentic assessment, cooperative learning, school-to-career experiences, site-based management, and teacher empowerment. Teacher educators have connected service-learning with professional development schools, Goals 2000 projects, integrated curriculum, and constructivist teaching as well. Service-learning can be a convenient and practical vehicle for implementing many of these reforms. For example, when conducting a well-planned service-learning project, preserve teachers and K-

12 students assume leadership roles through engaging in higher-order thinking, problem solving, collaborative decision making, and the application of numerous academic and career skills, all within the context of addressing authentic community needs (Wade and Anderson 1996).

Several recent reports on educational reform have also advocated for youth service initiatives, including the Carnegie Council on Adolescent Development (1989), Sarason (1991), and the William T. Grant Foundation (1991). Prominent educational organizations such as the Association for Supervision and Curriculum Development, the Council of Chief State School Officers, and the National Association of Secondary School Principals have strongly endorsed service-learning. In addition, the Corporation for National Service has provided hundreds of millions of dollars of federal funding for service-learning in K-12 and higher education programs since being established in 1993 by the Federal National and Community Service Trust Act. With the reelection of President Clinton in 1996, it is likely that this level of funding will continue through this decade. Given this ground swell of interest in service-learning, it is not surprising that all across America teacher educators are taking strides to ensure new teachers have the knowledge and experiences necessary to utilize service-learning as a teaching method with their K-12 students. Service-learning is now poised to move from the margins into the mainstream of K-12 and teacher education.

Purpose of the Monograph

While service-learning is compatible with other national educational reform movements, we contend it represents a powerful and unique philosophical and ethical stance regarding the role of youth and community in the learning process. This monograph is an attempt to bring together the best recent work in the field to assist teacher educators in developing successful service-learning in their programs and to promote policies and procedures that will foster successful service-learning activities at the local, state, and national levels.

To achieve these goals, the monograph is organized beginning with more theoretical and research-oriented essays, then progressing to discussions of some of the practical challenges involved in preparing teachers to effectively employ service-learning. This is followed by perspectives of individuals in diverse roles in service-learning teacher education sharing their experiences. Part 3 of the monograph presents detailed descriptions of 14 models of teacher education courses and programs that integrate service-learning. The monograph concludes with an annotated bibliography of frequently cited resources and a listing of helpful organizations in service-learning.

It is our position, as editors, that this monograph could best serve teacher educators interested in service-learning by dealing directly with practical models and issues in the field, and placing these issues in a theoretical and research framework. As a result, this monograph does not include a primary focus on issues in K-12 service-learning (other than Sue Root's review of K-12 service-learning research, beginning on p. 42). Due to space limitations, several of the theoretical rationales for the use of service-learning, such as citizenship education, community cohesion, school-to-career education, character education, and moral development, have been referenced but not discussed in depth. Readers are encouraged to examine the annotated bibliography to obtain additional resources in these areas.

Integrating Service-Learning Into Teacher Education: Critical Issues

Based on our personal experiences integrating service-learning in our teacher education programs, we would like to raise several important issues and provide suggestions regarding possible solutions and improvements in the practice of service-learning in teacher preparation. While we believe it is imperative that individuals licensed to be K-12 teachers through our teacher education programs should have the competence and desire to pursue such learning activities in their classrooms, there are real deterrents. Teacher educators commonly provide one or more of the following three reasons why they do not incorporate service-learning preparation into their pre-service programs:

1. Service-learning is experiential. Teachers learn it just by doing it; therefore, explicit preparation is unnecessary.

2. Preparation in the use of service-learning is not productive until after teachers have resolved many of the challenges faced by novice teachers; therefore, it is not useful in preservice teacher education programs.

3. There is no room in our program for anything else. If we added service-learning, what would we take out?

Each of these concerns requires a thoughtful response. Regarding the first issue, our experience suggests that service-learning preparation is a necessary component of preservice programs if our goal is to have graduates who engage their students in high-quality experiences involving learning through service. Many teachers who are "self-taught" tend to engage their students in community service rather than service-learning projects. While frequently addressing real community needs, community service projects fail to capitalize on the numerous opportunities to enhance student learning that pop up frequently throughout most service experiences. These teachers may neglect to incorporate reflection activities before, during, and after students' service experiences, thereby reducing the educational value of the service. Instruction and experience in how to utilize reflection with service projects and how to tie service to the academic curriculum would strengthen the learning component of these valuable community service efforts.

In response to the second issue, service-learning can be used effectively in preservice teacher education programs. Preparation in the use of service-learning as a teaching method has resulted in many preservice teachers' employing service-learning during their student teaching experience. The academic gains and personal growth experienced by their K-12 students who participated in service-learning projects has stimulated interest in service-learning in experienced cooperating teachers and helped novice teachers begin to incorporate service-learning into their schema of what teaching, learning, and schools are all about. We have also found that approximately 25 percent of our graduates utilize authentic service-learning with their K-12 students during their first year of teaching (Anderson et al. 1996). What is needed to facilitate these teachers' use of service-learning is not the elimination of preservice preparation but rather the addition of inservice technical assistance, mentoring, funding, increased scheduling flexibility, and administrative support. In most cases, these types of support have been extremely limited or nonexistent.

There are at least two responses to the third issue, "What should we take out of our program in order to make room for service-learning?" One response is don't take anything out but rather use service-learning experiences as a method to teach current course content. For example, service-learning has been successfully used to enhance students' understanding of motivation theory, authentic assessment, the meaning of active citizenship, interdisciplinary units, and cooperative learning. It can also be effective in influencing preservice teachers' awareness of multicultural issues, individual differences, and the realities of issues of educational reform and collaboration.

The second response involves a recognition that integration of service-learning into teacher education implies work in two areas: (1) using service-learning as a pedagogical technique in the postsecondary setting, and (2) teaching licensure-seeking students how to integrate service-learning into their own repertoire of teaching techniques for use with K-12 students. This instruction would include not only principles of effective service-learning practice (how to do it) but also background in the theoretical underpinnings and history of service in education (why we do it). For this to occur, it is likely that something would have to be removed from the existing teacher preparation curriculum. Although never easy to do, this choice is easier to make once teacher educators have experienced the powerful potential of service by themselves participating in a service-learning project.

The choice to alter the amount of instructional time on other topics is also made clearer after learning the responses of K-12 and teacher education students who have had in-depth, meaningful learning experiences through service-learning. In one case, a teacher education program chose not to eliminate but rather to reduce time spent on classroom management, motivation theory, assessment, and lesson planning in order to make time for service-learning. Ironically, each of these four areas frequently resurfaces in service-learning reflection sessions as preservice teachers address them as challenges at their service-learning sites. Direct instruction provided in these areas at this time (when students' interest has been heightened through seeing a practical use for the information) has proven to take less time and be more beneficial to students. (See "Teacher Education and Service-Learning: A Critical Perspective" on p. 113ff. for additional discussion of this issue.)

Suggestions for Integrating Service-Learning Into Teacher Education

We would also like to offer several suggestions to those considering the implementation of a service-learning component in their teacher education program. First, spend time with both teacher education students and K-12 teachers to develop an understanding of key principles of effective service-learning practice. In particular, focus on the distinctions among service-learning, service, internships, and field education (Furco 1996). This is an area of continuing confusion.

Traditional student teaching placements are most often not service-learning experiences. The "service" provided by teacher education students often doesn't address a real need of the K-12 teachers and students with whom they work. (If the student teachers were making significant contributions to the schools in which they are placed, there would be a waiting list of teachers requesting our students' services. This is not the case in most teacher education programs.)

Also, student teachers usually are not given much input into determining the specifics of their placement. Effective service-learning includes providing the students involved with decision-making authority regarding the service they provide. If in some cases student teachers have input into determining where their placement will be, they frequently have less voice in deciding the curriculum they will teach and the methods used for instruction.

In addition, successful service-learning involves an emphasis on "service" — the importance of helping others and problem solving as an essential component of full citizenship. Most student teaching placements are set in a context of experiential learning but not one that highlights the creation of an ethos of service.

Second, we have found the experiential component of service-learning courses essential for preservice teachers to gain the knowledge and skills necessary to implement service-learning projects. Teacher education students retain little of what they learn from textbooks and lectures in their education courses (Kennedy 1991).

Providing preservice teachers with the opportunity to be "service-learners" themselves can be a successful teaching method to help students in learning course content. It can also serve as an effective model of how to employ service-learning as a teaching approach. However, for teacher education students to make optimal use of service-learning's potential, they need to have instruction and experiences involving the use of service-learning as a pedagogy to employ with their future K-12 students.

Third, seek out K-12 and community partners who receive support and technical assistance from organizations such as the Corporation for National Service or the National Youth Leadership Council. The confluence of energy and commitment to quality service-learning created when these partners work together is greater than that achieved with isolated, unsupported schools.

Fourth, integrate service-learning throughout a variety of courses in the teacher preparation program. Service-learning conducted in this fashion can result in a positive experience for preservice teachers (Wade 1995). For example, service-learning is now a part of four different courses in the Seattle University Master in Teaching program: (1) an educational psychology course, (2) the service leadership course, (3) an action research project, and (4) the student teaching experience (described on p. 221ff). (A similar sequence of integration at the undergraduate level is proposed by Olson and O'Connor in the Augsburg College model described on p. 203ff.) This helps ensure that prospective teachers receive a solid grounding in both service-learning knowledge and experience; it also allows students to experience a model of integrated service-learning rather than an "add-on."

Fifth, work to create service-learning field placements in K-12 schools that extend over a substantial period of time. High-quality service-learning projects take time to plan and carry out, and relationships among teachers, students, and community members take time to blossom. These long-term community-based relationships will also assist teacher education programs in demonstrating outreach and collaboration to accreditation bodies that demand these sorts of ongoing partnerships (e.g., the National Council for

Accreditation of Teacher Education (NCATE) or the state board of teaching).

Sixth, service-learning field placement sites do not need to be practicing ideal models of fully developed service-learning projects. In fact, most students tell us they learn more about service-learning in new service-learning projects where teachers are still grappling with start-up issues. This may be because teachers in new projects provide students with tasks to complete that are crucial to the success of the service project. In well-established service-learning programs, students are sometimes seen as teacher aides and given more routine, less challenging tasks to perform.

Seventh, prospective teachers need to be encouraged to "start small, but jump in" with regard to beginning new service-learning projects during their student teaching or first year of employment. They sometimes are overwhelmed with the number of components that need to be integrated into a fully successful service project and the time needed to facilitate this process. As a result, they choose to do nothing at all. We explain to them that the integration into their curriculum is a developmental process and that they can begin with a small project — perhaps one that doesn't require leaving the school site — such as cross-age tutoring, a school garden, or writing letters to soldiers.

Eighth, and last, we have found it is essential to support beginning teachers in their use of service-learning. It is not enough to give them a solid base of knowledge and experience with service-learning during their pre-service education. If we want them to integrate service-learning into a new, complex environment when they have just started to teach, we must provide them with resources, technical assistance, and moral support.

Important Areas for Further Investigation

As the use of service-learning in teacher education programs continues to grow, there is a pressing need for research on a myriad of issues in the area. What experiences do preservice and inservice teachers find most valuable in helping them employ service-learning with their students? What are their reasons for using service-learning? What are the rewards and challenges of service-learning involvement? How crucial is peer and administrative support? What are the characteristics of teachers most and least likely to engage in service-learning projects? Research is under way to answer these and other questions, but more knowledge in the field is needed urgently. We encourage all who work in the field of service-learning teacher education to benefit themselves and others by systematically examining their service-learning program features and outcomes.

There is also a need for a set of standards or principles of best practice in service-learning teacher education to help guide practitioners in designing high-quality preservice and inservice programs. With a rapidly expanding number of teacher educators in this field and many research efforts currently under way, it is our hope that the knowledge of successful practices will soon be sufficient to create such a set of guiding principles.

Although the integration of service-learning into teacher education programs takes a considerable investment of time and effort, the results we have seen in terms of benefits to the community, academic and personal gains for K-12 students, and the pedagogical growth in both preservice and experienced teachers make a commitment to service-learning very worthwhile. Working with teachers, students, and community agencies in the design and implementation of service-learning projects provides fertile ground for the seeds of commitment to service to grow. Prospective teachers can learn that, although full of challenges, service-learning can be done successfully and that they can make it a part of their approach to teaching. By helping to develop an ethos of service and caring in K-12 students and teachers, preservice teachers simultaneously gain leadership skills, enhance the academic and social education of their students, and serve as agents of educational reform — all prior to obtaining their first paid teaching position.

References

Allam, C., and B. Zerkin. (1993). "The Case for Integrating Service-Learning Into Teacher Preparation Programs." *Generator* 13(1): 11-13.

Anderson, J., and K. Guest. (1995). "Linking Campus and Community: Service Leadership in Teacher Education at Seattle University." In *Integrating Service Learning Into Teacher Education: Why and How?* pp. 11-30. Washington, DC: Council of Chief State School Officers.

Anderson, J., D. Hathaway, R. Dolbec, L. Scovie, D. Schaack, and H. Martin. (April 1996). "A Quantitative Study of Beginning Teachers' Use of Service-Learning." Paper presented at the National Service-Learning Conference, Detroit, MI.

Barber, B. (1992). *An Aristocracy of Everyone: The Politics of Education and the Future of America*. New York, NY: Ballantine Books.

Boyer, E. (1983). *High School: A Report on Secondary Education in America*. New York, NY: Harper & Row.

————. (1995). *The Basic School: A Community for Learning*. Princeton, NJ: Carnegie Foundation for the Advancement of Teaching.

Carnegie Council on Adolescent Development. (1989). *Turning Points: Preparing American Youth for the 21st Century*. Washington, DC: Carnegie Corporation of New York.

Cohen, J., and D. Kinsey. (Winter 1994). "'Doing Good' and Scholarship: A Service-Learning Study." *Journalism Educator* 48(4):4-14.

Coleman, J. (1974). *Youth: Transition to Adulthood*. Chicago, IL: University of Chicago Press.

Dewey, J. (1938). *Experience and Education*. New York, NY: Collier Books.

Furco, A. (1996). "Service-Learning: A Balanced Approach to Experiential Education." In *Expanding Boundaries: Service and Learning*, edited by B. Taylor, pp. 2-6. Columbia, MD: Cooperative Education Association.

Giles, D.E. (1988). "Dewey's Theory of Experience: Implications for Service-Learning." *Experiential Education* 13(5):3-10.

Goodlad, J. (1984). *A Place Called School: Prospects for the Future*. New York, NY: McGraw-Hill.

————. (1990). *Teachers for Our Nation's Schools*. San Francisco, CA: Jossey-Bass.

————. (1994). *Educational Renewal: Better Teachers, Better Schools*. San Francisco, CA: Jossey-Bass.

Hutchings, P., and A. Wutzdorff, eds. (1988). *Knowing and Doing: Learning Through Experience*. San Francisco, CA: Jossey-Bass.

Kennedy, M. (1991). "Some Surprising Findings on How Teachers Learn to Teach." *Educational Leadership* 94(3): 14-17.

Kolb, D. (1984). *Experiential Learning: Experience as the Source of Learning and Development*. Englewood Cliffs, NJ: Prentice-Hall.

Littlefield, V. (1996). *Community Service Learning at Augsburg College: A Handbook for Instructors*. Version 2.0. Minneapolis, MN: Augsburg College. [Available from the Augsburg College Center for Faculty Development, C.B. #97, 2211 Riverside Avenue, Minneapolis, MN 55454, ph 612/330-1229, littlefi@augsburg.edu.]

Liu, G. (Fall 1995). "Knowledge, Foundations, and Discourse: Philosophical Support for Service-Learning." *Michigan Journal of Community Service Learning* 2: 5-18.

Martin, J. (1976). *The Education of Adolescents*. Washington, DC: National Panel on High School and Adolescent Education.

Miller, K. (1988). *The Holistic Curriculum*. Toronto, ON: Ontario Institute for Studies in Education.

National Commission on Youth. (1980). *The Transition of Youth to Adulthood: A Bridge Too Far*. Boulder, CO: Westview.

National Committee on Secondary Education. (1972). *American Youth in the Mid-Seventies*. Reston, VA: National Committee of Secondary School Principals.

Newmann, F. (1985). *Higher Education and the American Resurgence*. Princeton, NJ: Carnegie Foundation for the Advancement of Teaching.

Olszewski, W., and D. Bussler. (1993). *Learning to Serve — Serving to Learn*. Washington, DC: ERIC Documents.

Sarason, S.B. (1991). *The Predictable Failure of Educational Reform.* San Francisco, CA: Jossey-Bass.

Sigmon, R. (1994). *Linking Service With Learning.* Washington, DC: Council of Independent Colleges.

Sizer, T. (1992). *Horace's School: Redesigning the American High School.* Boston, MA: Houghton Mifflin.

Sleeter, C., and C. Grant. (1987). "An Analysis of Multi-Cultural Education in the United States." *Harvard Educational Review* 57(4): 421-444.

Sparks-Langer, G., J. Simmons, M. Pasch, A. Colton, and A. Starks. (1990). "Reflective Pedagogical Thinking: How Can We Promote It and Measure It?" *Journal of Teacher Education* 41(5): 23-32.

Sullivan, R. (February 1991). "The Role of Service-Learning in Restructuring Teacher Education." Paper presented at the annual meeting of the Association of Teacher Educators, New Orleans, LA.

Wade, R. (May/June 1995). "Developing Active Citizens: Community Service-Learning in Social Studies Teacher Education." *The Social Studies* 86(3):122-128.

———— , and J. Anderson. (1996). "Community Service-Learning: A Strategy for Preparing Human Service Oriented Teachers." *Teacher Education Quarterly* 23(4): 59-74.

William T. Grant Foundation. (1991). *States and Communities on the Move: Policy Initiatives to Build a First-Class Workforce.* Washington, DC: William T. Grant Foundation.

Service-Learning: An Essential Process for Preparing Teachers as Transformational Leaders in the Reform of Public Education

by Carol Myers and Terry Pickeral

There is growing evidence that integrating youth service with the curriculum contributes to the motivation, growth, and achievement of students. [See Root, beginning on p. 42, for a summary of research on learner outcomes associated with service-learning.] Students come to appreciate the talents and perspectives of their classmates as they work side by side to have an impact on a community issue. Students develop collaboration, critical-thinking, and problem-solving skills needed to be successful learners and contributing citizens in the 21st century.

Teachers who employ service-learning pedagogy can also make unique contributions to the reform of public education. Those who incorporate service-learning develop the skills and perspectives needed to implement other instructional strategies known to enhance student learning. Engagement in the service-learning process prompts teachers to both support and inspire needed changes in school structure (i.e., use of time, scheduling, staff/student relationships, decision making). Teachers who work alongside their students, parents, and community members find that this form of learning brings life to the learning community and helps to shape a positive climate within the school. Making improvements within each of these elements of instructional practice, school structure, and school climate is essential if schools are to meet the challenges and needs of our society and economy.

Higher education faculty who include service-learning as a pedagogy for teacher preparation provide their graduates with a dynamic instructional strategy that engages students in meaningful learning and empowers teachers with the skills needed to contribute significantly to broad-based school reform. K-12 teachers who incorporate service-learning bring to their classrooms and schools an instructional strategy that influences all dimensions of school reform. For these reasons, service-learning should be included as a central process within teacher preparation programs in order to increase the ability of students to be successful teachers and leaders in the reform of public education.

This essay places service-learning within the context of national school-reform efforts in public education and teacher preparation. The reader will have a deepened understanding of the potential contributions made by educators who design and integrate service into the curriculum. The essay begins by exploring the need for reform of public education and presents a framework for thinking about the critical dimensions of school reform. Service-learning is presented as a process that contributes to each area of the school-reform framework. Service-learning is then explored within the parameters of reform initiatives under way within teacher preparation programs and higher education. The chapter concludes by examining the notion of a K–higher education (seamless) system of education. The reader is challenged to identify ways in which service-learning through teacher preparation can help to shape such a vision and contribute to the reform of teacher preparation and public schooling in America.

K-12 Educational Reform and Service-Learning

The Pressure Is on Because the Goals Have Changed

Those who accept the challenge to teach enter public education at a time like no other in our nation's history. The demands on the public schoolhouse, as the only primary institution that contributes to the lives of all youth in America, are at an all-time high. The purpose of public education has always been to contribute to the development of productive citizens. School success has been equated with a person's being able to contribute to the economic base and life of his/her community. Our historical model of education was successful in moving young people into a larger society where conformity and the abilities to produce and follow directions were central to agricultural and industrial productivity.

Schools today must prepare young people to access information that has not yet been created, to be effective problem solvers for problems that have not yet been identified, and to work effectively with others in jobs that do not yet exist. To contribute to the economy, students today must leave school with effective writing, reading, and communication skills. Graduates must be creative and effective problem solvers. They must have strong interpersonal skills. Students need to be self-directed learners and researchers in accessing, understanding, and applying knowledge to the problems and possibilities they face. Without these abilities, many of our youth are destined to minimum-wage imprisonment on the fringes of an economic system they can impact only through illegal means.

The Pressure Is on Because Society Has Changed

Our progress as a nation within the global marketplace is diminished by our inability to care for and support our children. Each fall, teachers greet more and more children who are missing the basic nutrition, health services, and emotional support needed to grow and learn. As of 1993, 22.7 percent of our nation's children were living in poverty (Erickson 1995). Surveys by the federal Department of Health and Human Services show that the number of abused or neglected children has more than doubled in the last decade to 2.9 million annually. Abuse and neglect were cited as the leading causes of death among children younger than 4 and accounted for 2,000 fatalities a year among children of all ages during 1995 (Pear 1996). The violence in society has carried over into the schoolhouse, as evidenced in a recent Centers for Disease Control study. The study reports that nearly 20 percent of all high school students carry a weapon and 5 percent carry a firearm at least once a month (Banach 1994). "This very day almost 200,000 American youngsters will stay home from school because they're afraid to go" (32).

The positive modeling of adults in families and neighborhoods, the dialogue and coaching on porch steps or in the classroom, has been lost for many of our youth. On average, children have 7.5 minutes of conversation with a significant adult each day (Nelson et al. 1993). The loss of sustained positive relationships with significant adults has left many youth without the self-perceptions and skills needed to be successful learners and productive citizens (Nelson et al. 1993). As we scan the nation across rural, suburban, and urban communities, the statistics reflect the increasing needs of our youth, the struggles of our schools in supporting their academic and social development, and the resulting manifestations within a society that is failing its youth.

This disconnection between youth and adults extends to the larger community as well. Robert Putnam, in his 1995 article "Bowling Alone," identifies the current state of "civic disengagement," that is, a lack of social connectedness in our nation that leads to a reduction in social capital. He calls for deliberate attempts to reconnect through social organizations. The disconnection between K-12 and higher education is consistent with the lack of connections between societal institutions.

Putnam, in a discussion with Russ Edgerton, then president of the American Association for Higher Education, states, "The first step is to recognize the character of the problem, to acknowledge that connections matter. Without connections, it's not just that people don't feel warm and cuddly toward one another. It's that our schools don't work as well . . ." (AAHE 1995: 6).

And so it is that in schools across America today, teachers receive more children who are living in at-risk environments. Children and young people come to school with limited adult guidance in supporting their development. Students come to school missing the experiences and encouragement to support their social and academic development within the classroom. The children who enter the classroom still have the right to an education that will allow them to be lifelong learners and contributing citizens. Those who choose to teach are challenged to accelerate the learning of all children while helping them develop the perceptions and skills needed to become contributing and productive citizens.

What Should Our Students Know, Understand, and Be Able to Do?

The historical system of equating student learning with time and credit is giving way to public and governmental demands for results. Landmark legislation at the federal and state levels related to Goals 2000 and workforce development begs the question. What should a student know and be able to do? What does it take to be prepared for highly skilled and highly paid careers? What does it take to be prepared for postsecondary education and lifelong learning? What does it take to be prepared for active citizenship?

Nationally recognized school-reform initiatives such as Comer's School Development Program (Squires and Kranyik 1995-1996) and Sizer's Coalition of Essential Schools (Sizer 1992) place these questions on the table for students, parents, school staff, and community members to explore. The answers drive the instruction, school structure, and climate changes needed to meet the desired learner outcomes. The coalition's tenets of "student as worker" and "less is more" speak both to the ways in which students learn and to the need for deepened understandings and applications of knowledge, skills, and behaviors related to life beyond the classroom.

Service-Learning as an Effective Strategy to Accomplish Five Outcomes

National Learner Outcomes Established

In 1989, governors throughout the nation met and developed six national education goals to be achieved by the year 2000. These goals were incorporated into federal policy in 1994 with the Goals 2000, Educate America Act. The goals of the act address early childhood education, graduation rates, teacher preparation, adult literacy, the school environment, and partnerships with parents that promote the emotional, social, and academic growth of children. Two specific goals within this national agenda speak to desired learner outcomes:

> *Goal 3: American students will leave grades four, eight, and twelve having demonstrated competency over challenging subject matter, including English, mathematics, science, foreign languages, civics and government, economics, art history, and geography; and every school in America will ensure that all students learn to use their minds well, so they may be prepared for responsible citizenship, further learning, and productive employ-*

ment in our nation's modern economy.

Goal 4: American students will be first in the world of science and mathematics achievement. (as quoted in Erickson 1995: 7)

Learner Outcomes Related to Employment

Learner outcomes identified by the Secretary's Commission on Achieving Necessary Skills, Foundational Skills, and Competencies (SCANS) have been developed for various types of jobs. Basic to all areas of employment are competencies, basic skills and thinking skills, and personal qualities. The SCANS *five competencies* include having future employees who can:

• identify, organize, plan, and allocate resources of time, money, materials, facilities, and people;

• work with others, participate as a member of a team, teach skills to others, exercise leadership, negotiate and work toward agreements, and work well with people from diverse backgrounds;

• acquire, evaluate, organize, maintain, interpret, and communicate information, and use computers to process information;

• understand complex interrelationships, know how social, organizational, and technological systems work, and operate effectively with them;

• work with a variety of technologies, choosing procedures, applying technology to tasks, and maintaining equipment and troubleshooting.

The SCANS *basic skills* include reading, writing, performing mathematical operations, listening, and speaking. SCANS *thinking skills* include creative thinking, decision making, problem solving, visualizing, reasoning, and knowing how to learn. The *personal qualities* identified in SCANS include responsibility, self-esteem, sociability, self-management, integrity, and honesty. Many states, communities, and individual school teams undertaking school-to-work initiatives use the SCANS outcomes as the basis for their identified learner outcomes.

One of the unique outcomes of service-learning that applies to employment-related outcomes is the value of citizenship. Students, through service-learning, become familiar with the world of work and understand the integral role citizenship plays in that arena.

Learner Outcomes Related to Critical-Thinking Skills

Ensuring that students obtain higher-order thinking skills has been seen as a necessity in meeting global and economic conditions of the future. Study after study indicates that, while American students grasp certain areas of content and can execute well-defined tasks similar to those practiced in the classroom, they do not demonstrate the ability to analyze information and assess and apply knowledge and processes to new situations or problems that they encounter. The development of critical-thinking skills requires significant changes in the mode of instruction and in desired learner outcomes. Paul et al. (1995) have identified the elements of reasoning and systematic strategies to help students attain the outcomes associated with critical thinking:

> The elements of reasoning include developing a clear purpose, goal, or objective for undertaking the thinking; having a question at issue/problem to be explored; obtaining information (data, facts, observations, and experiences related to the question); making interpretations and inferences and drawing conclusions or solutions based on the information, developing concepts (theories, definitions, axioms, laws, principles, models) from the knowledge evaluated; identifying assumptions (presuppositions, notions being taken for granted); arriving at implications and consequences given the new understandings; presenting points of view (frame of reference, perspective, orientation) to the topic. (11)

Paul et al. believe that students can best master content in a deep and thoughtful way when they use their own thinking as a major tool of learning.

Learner Outcomes for Active Citizenship

A historical goal of public education has been to prepare young people for active citizenship in their communities. What was once an assumed outcome has taken on a new level of challenge and urgency. As Boyte and Farr (1997) indicate in "The Work of Citizenship and the Problem of Service-Learning," societal conditions and attitudes make education for active citizenship an imperative for schools. In a society where two-thirds of the public are distrustful of others, only 8 percent express "a great deal of confidence" in American institutions, and 58 percent of those polled believe that people like themselves "had little to say about what the government did," it is not surprising that we look to public education for creating caring and concerned citizens who will contribute to the public good. Boyte and Farr suggest that citizens are "practical agents of a civic world who work together in public ways and spaces to engage the tasks and try to solve the problems that they collectively face" (37). They challenge those in public education to think of young people as "citizens-in-the-making who have serious public work to do" (43).

Learner Outcomes Related to Personal Perceptions and Skills

The last area of learner outcomes pushing the reform of public education is associated with students' developing the self-perceptions and skills to be successful learners. The call comes from inside the schoolhouse and from those outside who work with youth in at-risk environments. All students need to develop perceptions of personal significance and belonging, personal capability and mastery, and personal influence and generosity. Students need skills associated with self-understanding, self-control, and self-discipline. Students need skills to communicate their feelings and ideas and to listen effectively to others. Students need to develop skills that will help them solve conflicts peacefully. The words may differ, but the challenge made by Nelson et al. (1993) in *Positive Discipline in the Classroom,* Brendtro et al. (1990) in *Youth at Risk: Our Hope for the Future,* and Kuykendall (1992) in *From Rage to Hope: Strategies for Reclaiming Black and Hispanic Students* is the same: How do we put the positive development of people at the center of public education?

The learner outcomes from Goals 2000 and workforce development — critical thinking, active citizenship, and personal development of America's youth — present clearly the challenge before public education. It is no longer enough for young people to leave school with the basic skills and competencies associated with traditional schooling (i.e., reading, writing, mathematics, science, economics, history, the arts). Responsible citizenship, further learning, and productive employment for the 21st century require that students graduate from high school with skills to work effectively with others, understand and negotiate complex systems, and access and utilize information and technology. High school students must graduate with positive self-perceptions and skills to take responsibility for their actions and to influence their world. Graduates of public education need skills to systematically plan, implement, and evaluate their efforts, to effectively utilize resources and processes in solving problems and creating new possibilities for society. Student achievement in these terms requires nothing less than the transformation of learning and teaching as we have come to know it.

What kinds of instructional strategies, school structures, and school climates foster these new aspects of student growth and development? How can teachers be equipped and prepared to support these changes? What does service-learning contribute to these dimensions of school reform and student achievement for the 21st century?

Instructional Strategies That Assist All Students in Achieving the New Learner Outcomes for the 21st Century

One can identify a number of strategies that have been associated with efforts to increase student motivation and achievement. Service-learning, cooperative learning, project-based learning, whole-language development, experiential learning, thematic instruction, and problem-based learning are seen as strategies that can maximize student engagement and development of higher-order thinking skills. Teachers who effectively utilize these strategies draw upon the experiences and backgrounds of their students, create a supportive environment for learners, and bring meaning and understanding to the knowledge and skills to be developed.

Until recently, these instructional strategies have been utilized primarily with students in gifted and talented programs. It has been assumed that students who are missing basic skills are not prepared for advanced work with higher-order thinking skills. As the number of students from at-risk environments has grown to more than one-third of the student population (Levin 1994), so has the gap in student achievement. Educators face the challenge of educating all students in ways that will both develop basic skills and enhance higher-order thinking skills.

The research of Knapp et al. (1995) suggests that teachers who teach for meaning or understanding help their students develop higher-order thinking skills without lessening their acquisition of basic skills. The authors studied 140 elementary school classrooms serving large numbers of children from low-income families. Three aspects of instruction were observed: teaching for meaning, managing the academic learning environment, and responding to student diversity. Teaching for meaning or understanding was defined as:

• instruction that helps students perceive the relationship of parts (discrete skills) to wholes (application of skills to communicate, comprehend, or reason);

• instruction that provides students with the tools to construct meaning in their encounters with academic tasks and in the world in which they live;

• instruction that makes explicit connections between one subject area and the next and between what is learned in school and children's home lives.

Comparisons were made in student scores for basic skills and higher levels of achievement in mathematical understanding, problem-solving ability, reading comprehension, and competence in written expression. The researchers compared the scores of classrooms that experienced the highest levels of meaningful instruction with the classrooms that received the lowest levels of meaningful instruction. There was clear evidence that students exposed to instruction emphasizing meaning are likely to demonstrate a greater grasp of advanced skills at the end of the school year without impeding the mastery of basic skills. The authors found that meaning-oriented practices work at least as well for low-performing students as high-performing students.

The work of Knapp et al. suggests that students from at-risk environments can develop higher-order thinking skills through challenging instructional strategies that apply content and skill development to students' lives and experiences outside school. The authors do not suggest that conventional practices be abandoned but that teachers view traditional forms of instruction (skill and drill) within a larger framework of meaning-oriented instruction. The authors conclude that "learning to teach for meaning effectively is difficult; mastering and sustaining the process in the classroom demands a lot of teachers and of the policy environment in which they work." While teaching for meaning is not a "formula for the future," it does "belong in the repertoires of teachers who work in high-poverty elementary schools" (Knapp et al. 1995: 776).

Fullan (1993b) describes three things that can change when teachers change the way they teach: curriculum materials, new behavior/practices, and new beliefs/understandings. Sustaining a change in teaching takes time and practice in developing new behaviors and practices needed to implement a specific pedagogy. New beliefs and understandings about teaching and learning come only as teachers internalize and understand the rationale for the innovation and can make judgments about its use and needed situational adaptations. It is clear from reviewing a variety of authentic instructional strategies that there are common elements among these strategies that contribute to student learning and require certain skills and beliefs from the teacher. It follows that teachers who are able to successfully implement any one of these instructional strategies will have developed skills and beliefs that will support them in implementing other innovative forms of instruction. Those who choose to teach for meaning and authentic learning need to develop abilities to:

- create a trusting, respectful climate with students;
- assist students in creating and carrying out plans;
- help students solve problems collaboratively and make effective decisions;
- facilitate group discussions;
- identify and draw upon community resources;
- implement reflective thinking processes with students;
- define and describe desired learner outcomes and ways to assess and demonstrate desired competencies;
- assist students in accessing, analyzing, and synthesizing information.

Palmer (1990) has stated that "people seldom think their way into new ways of acting, more often they act their way into new ways of thinking." And so it is with the development of beliefs and understanding about teaching and learning. The sustained incorporation of meaningful and authentic instruction through the practices and skills identified above leads teachers to new understandings about what it means to teach and learn. Teachers no longer believe that textbooks should drive what is taught. They seek essential questions, problems, and student interests to motivate and frame instruction and utilize basic instruction to support meaningful learning.

Teachers as facilitators of learning cultivate new beliefs about the capabilities and responsibilities of students. Those who effectively create trusting learning environments develop new understandings about the importance of learning as a social activity.

Service-learning supports authentic learning and can help teachers to develop skills and beliefs needed to implement other effective forms of instruction. Teachers who initially try out service-learning often see the act of service as the central element of learning for students. As they incorporate elements of student investigation, assessment, planning, decision making, preparation, and reflection in meeting real community needs, teachers develop new skills and discover new levels of student motivation and achievement. Standards of quality for service-learning that include these elements and others have been developed by the Alliance for Service-Learning in Education Reform (ASLER). (The complete list of ASLER Standards follows this essay on p. 41.)

Service-learning engages the hearts of teachers as they see students develop self-confidence, concern for others, intrapersonal and interpersonal skills, problem-solving skills, and new enthusiasm for learning. When teachers experience the struggles associated with trying new strategies (Fullan 1993b), they are able to draw upon the power of student experiences to sustain their efforts. Those who continue to develop the service-learning process gain skills and beliefs needed to implement other forms of authentic instruction. Teachers who incorporate service and public work as a central focus for learning also create new visions of teaching and learning for the 21st century.

> Imagine . . . a school where the betterment of the community is the focus of academic study, and students are active producers of goods, services, and new information. Imagine a school where young people study, research, and serve their own communities through such projects as community surveys, newspapers, history projects, and photographic documentation. Imagine a school that focuses on "sustaining communities: shelter, food, and good work." Students at this school might build low-cost solar-heated houses and rehabilitate existing homes, operate greenhouses and aquaculture projects, design and conduct health inventories, test water, and create and run local businesses. Imagine a school where students build parks, put on plays, perform musical programs that feature local musical traditions, and establish the bonds of common purpose and mutual enjoyment. (Hass and Lambert 1995: 138)

This vision places public work at the center of learning. Students engage in meaningful learning that addresses community concerns and provides opportunities for active participation in civic life. Teachers facilitate learning within changed school structures and climates that are created in partnership with the community. This is the challenge for schooling in America.

Structures of Schools That Contribute to Meaningful Instruction and Authentic Learning for All Students

Recent federal and state legislation has placed the responsibility for schooling largely within the control of local districts and site-based decision-making management (SBDM) teams at individual schools. At the least, SBDM teams provide approval for changes and improvements that build ownership but do little to improve upon teaching and learning. With greater intentionality and development, SBDM teams provide a vehicle for continuous inquiry, problem solving, action planning, celebration, and self-assessment focused on the growth and development of children and adults.

The most significant improvements (in student behavior, attendance, and achievement) have been found in schools that have incorporated site-based management within the larger framework of sustained school-reform efforts. Nationally recognized school-reform models (such as Levin's Accelerated Schools, Sizer's Coalition of Essential Schools, Comer's School Development Program, and the PACERS collaborative) support school staffs in building a shared commitment among stakeholders to common principles that guide planning and inform decisions impacting the future of the school community. This new decision-making structure and planning process finds many staff in need of basic group-process and decision-making skills. As Henry Levin (1996) indicates, "School staff need experiences in working together, with special attention to group processes and participation, sharing of information, and working toward decisions. In addition, they need exposure to inquiry-oriented processes that help to identify and define challenges, to look for alternative solutions, and to implement these solutions" (23).

The service-learning process provides numerous opportunities for teachers to practice and improve upon skills needed to contribute to site-based decision making and sustained action-planning processes. Teachers serve as facilitators with their students in identifying issues, obtaining information, seeking alternative solutions, and determining the most effective and feasible course of action. Implementation plans are developed that include identifying measurable goals, available resources, preparation needs, time lines, responsibilities, forms of evaluation, and celebration. Teachers learn to modify and adapt to changing conditions, to provide motivation in the midst of difficulties, and to draw upon the strengths of their students in providing meaningful service.

Teachers who lead service-learning processes develop new understandings about collaboration as they work in partnership with community members at service sites. They are able to bring an experience base to school-wide planning efforts that draws upon relationships developed with businesses and local community groups. Teachers are better prepared to include various stakeholders as they recognize the contributions that can be made by students and community members. Above all, teachers who actively facilitate the service-learning process have images of meaningful and authentic learning. Their stories of student growth and discovery can motivate and inspire visions of what can occur for all students!

Once the structures for school-wide planning and decision making are established, school staffs focus attention on changing the structures of time, relationships, and location of learning and partnerships to support new visions of teaching and learning. The impact of these structural changes will be limited unless they are aligned with the broader school vision and goals for student learning. The chart "Structures of Schooling" (see box) presents the types and purposes of structural changes that impact teaching and learning.

Teachers who employ service-learning often become change agents in advocating for structural changes associated with time, professional development, relationships, locations of learning, and partnerships. As old structures get in the way of implementing the service-learning process, teachers question practices and policies that inhibit meaningful learning opportunities for students. Often requests associated with a specific service-learning project innocently propel structural changes within a school. This point is illustrated by the following stories.

Susan, a seventh grade science teacher, incorporated service-learning within her class to help her students experience and understand the scientific method. She needed help in supervising them as they conducted a neighborhood needs assessment. As a result of her search for supervisory assistance from other teachers, an interdisciplinary partnership was formed that eventually established flexible scheduling and off-site learning for this team.

J.D., a sixth grade teacher, worked with his team to develop an interdisciplinary unit on walls. This led to the participation of 150 sixth graders, who painted a wall at a neighborhood housing complex. This initial relationship has evolved into a sustained partnership with area residents. Today one sees neighbors at home in the school, where they serve as tutors to individual students, share responsibilities for developing a school/community garden, and serve on a school/community advisory board.

These examples suggest that the service-learning process encourages teachers to change school structures that impede student learning. While

Structures of Schooling

Structure	Rationale

Time/Scheduling:

Block Scheduling
- Allows for extended learning opportunities

Flexible Scheduling
- Allows for changing needs of instruction

Intensive/Terms
- Allows for in-depth, short-term topics and projects, e.g., winter term, one- to four-week term

Professional Development:

Common Planning
- Allows for daily working time among grade levels, interdisciplinary teams, etc.

Extended Days
- Allows for banking of time for concentrated total staff work, e.g, three hours per week, one day per month

Relationships/Grouping of Students:

Teaming
- Allows core group of staff to work with same group of students; focus can be academic and/or social growth and development

Looping
- Allows teachers to move with students from one grade level to the next in order to extend relationships and support learning over time

Multi-Age
- Allows students to develop relationships with "elders" and "youngsters" and have sustained relationships with teachers over two or more years

Family
- Allows students and staff to be a part of an identified "family" unit throughout student's life at school in order to support student outside of academic realm

Locations of Learning:

Independent Study or Contracts
- Allows students to learn within a time frame and environment most conducive to the student and development of desired learner outcomes

Community-Based
- Allows individual students or classes to utilize community as classroom; i.e., learning may take place at a laboratory, a neighborhood park, library, senior citizens center, hospital, bank

Pods
- Allows for separate time and space to group students in learning communities around specific topics of mutual interest

Partnerships:

Learning Sites
- Allows access on a sustained basis to people, resources, and opportunities needed for student learning

Social/Human Services
- Allows outside personnel and social service resources structured access to students and/or their families through the school

Businesses
- Allows for sustained relationships with organizations and businesses that provide apprenticeship opportunities within or outside the school day; may also allow for sustained employee/parent participation within the school

people may resist changing structures from an objectified distance, they are more willing to support structural changes one decision at a time, especially when encouraged by their colleagues "up close and personal."

Types of School Cultures That Cultivate Meaningful and Authentic Learning for All Students

Perhaps the most difficult challenge facing public education is changing the school culture. Many (e.g., Malen et al. 1989; Ogawa and White 1994; Sidener 1994; Squires and Kranyik 1995-1996) believe that failures in implementing site-based management and effective instructional practices are embedded within the failure to change school cultures. While individual teachers, building administrators, and SBDM teams can implement improvement strategies, they run a high risk of failure without a culture in place that embraces new ideas, encourages risk taking, and includes the entire community in ongoing reflection and action.

Each of the successful national school-reform projects described previously shares the process of transforming culture. At the heart of this process is the development of collegiality. Transforming the culture of schooling requires:

• new levels of inclusion for all those connected to school (students, parents, teachers, support staff, administrators, neighbors, and community members);

• sustained opportunities for conversation and dialogue about "what matters" within an atmosphere of mutual trust and respect;

• having problem-solving and decision-making processes in place that include participation of all voices in the school community (with perspectives changing from "blaming" and "defending" to identifying and solving problems and seeing "problems as our friend") (Fullan 1993b);

• commonly agreed-upon goals that everyone understands, supports, and works toward individually and as a whole, goals that drive conversation and decisions and break down the balkanization (Fullan 1993b) and personality conflicts that isolate and divide people;

• continuous opportunities for learning and experimentation that are encouraged, supported, and rewarded within the structure of the school community;

• recognition of the school as community with rituals, events, communications, and celebrations that reinforce common values, goals, and accomplishments of the community.

Teachers experienced in the pedagogy of service-learning are a resource for creating a positive school culture and learning community. Those who effectively facilitate the service-learning process with groups of students are experienced in creating learning communities. By definition, the service-learning process engages people in identifying a common concern, investigating the issue, proposing solutions, and deciding as a group on actions to take. Participants have meaningful conversations and opportunities to reflect on their efforts, the process, and what they have learned or need to learn. Forms of celebration are built into the process to recognize effort and results of the work. An underlying condition that must be somewhat present and developed throughout the service-learning process is the mutual trust and respect of all. Teachers need to model, teach, and affirm positive behaviors to cultivate students' abilities to be trustworthy and to be respectful in their interactions with one another and with people they meet and serve in the community. These elements of the service-learning process support the common elements just described for transforming school cultures. Teachers who employ service-learning can contribute significantly to building the type of collaborative and collegial environment needed to transform the culture of schools.

K-12 Summary

We believe that teachers who employ the pedagogy of service-learning bring to their classroom authentic learning experiences that capture the interests and talents of their students. Students work longer and try harder to accomplish tasks and develop skills when there are real-life purposes and consequences connected to learning. As teachers gain more experience with the service-learning process, they develop the skills and beliefs needed to implement other innovative instructional practices. In extending learning beyond the classroom, teachers become trailblazers by calling into question many of the structures and policies that inhibit teaching and learning. Teachers are able to apply their service-learning experiences to ongoing planning processes involved with site-based management and significant school-reform initiatives. Teachers who facilitate service-learning recognize the importance of creating effective and empowering learning communities. Their experiences in building collaborative working groups become an asset to transforming the culture within their own schools.

Above all, those who engage in service-learning bring new life to their classrooms and hope to themselves, their schools, and their communities. Service-learning allows everyone to contribute in meaningful ways to the greater good. Students have an opportunity to develop the personal perceptions and skills that they so desperately need. They become resources to themselves and others and discover the power of public work and civic action. For teachers, it is like coming home to that place of struggle, joy, and true understanding of what it means to teach and learn. As students and teachers work together to address concerns that affect their lives, they come to know each other as human beings on a common journey. They stumble along the road, sometimes get lost as they look for answers, and draw courage to act. As they continue their quest, they come to know that success in learning and life is the quality of the journey. With new tools, deepened relationships, and a little more wisdom about life, they thank each other and part ways. This is the gift that service-learning brings.

Need for Reform in Teacher Preparation

With the recognition that college-based teacher preparation programs provide new teachers for the K-12 system, it follows that these programs need to be aware of and integrate new expectations for teachers in their programs. Earlier in this chapter, we discussed how national attention is paid to K-12 educational reform. While the public calls for reform of higher education are less frequent, the need for reform in both educational arenas is warranted if we are to prepare today's youth and retrain adults. The rationale for K-12 educational reform also applies to higher education, where changes are sought to increase students' knowledge and skills in areas of effective problem solving, writing, interpersonal communication, self-directed learning, global awareness, and civic action.

Reforming higher education will:

• increase the contribution colleges and universities make to communities through research and service;
• produce graduates skilled in liberal arts as well as specific disciplines;
• connect learning with the world of work;
• develop more effective systems of education;
• enhance the articulation between K-12 and higher education;
• better prepare graduates for active citizenship.

According to Haycock (1996), connecting K-12 and higher education "strives for coherence all the way up and down the line: If we believe that all students can learn to high standards, then we must organize our classrooms around that goal and reorder district and state policies accordingly" (15). Haycock goes on to identify eight tasks for higher education as it responds to K-12 systemic reform. Among the eight tasks are two relevant to our discussion: teacher professional development and preservice preparation.

To meet the first task for higher education, we must assist teachers in mastering content areas and staying current within their fields. "We need to cooperate with K-12 schools, school districts, teacher associations, and the like to build an infrastructure capable of boosting the professional development of all our teachers. Like other professionals, teachers need regular means to stay abreast of developments in their fields and ongoing support for improving their practice" (Haycock 1996: 17). Concerning preservice preparation, Haycock challenges higher education to align the preparation of new teachers as closely as possible with the imperatives of systemic K-12 educational reform.

If higher education is responsible for developing K-12 teachers, it seems logical to align teacher preparation curricula and preservice teacher experiences to changes in K-12 schools. If K-12 educational reform is successful and substantial, and positive changes occur in learning outcomes, teaching strategies, school structure, and climate and culture, how appropriately prepared are future teachers for that system if they have been trained for K-12 schools "the way they were"?

Social and institutional change is much more effective if all stakeholders are involved in development as well as implementation. To that end, educational reform should focus on "simultaneous renewal," as suggested by Goodlad (1990), connecting the two dimensions of education (K-12 and higher education). Therefore, as one system changes, the other aligns with the "new" system and/or operation.

More strongly stated by Benson and Harkavy (1995):

> To transform conventional public schools into innovative community schools, we have painfully discovered, requires (at minimum) two different types of "revolutions": (1) a revolution in the highly bureaucratic, highly dysfunctional, American public school system for which American universities in general, and [education schools] in particular, bear such heavy responsibility; (2) a revolution in the universities. . . . (88)

There is opportunity offered to higher education to step up and play an integral role to ensure educational reform is given its fair chance to succeed. Higher education benefits from educational reform because more students complete K-12 education successfully. There is also a greater pool of students who are prepared to enter postsecondary education. The other obvious benefit is the wellness and safety of our communities, resulting in the educational success of more of America's youth.

The National Council for Accreditation of Teacher Education (NCATE) is an organization that has developed initiatives for reform within departments/colleges that prepare future teachers. NCATE is a coalition of 27 national organizations of teachers, teacher educators, policymakers, and school specialists committed to quality teaching. "The goal of the National Council for Accreditation of Teacher Education," according to a council document published in 1994, "is rigorous teacher preparation so that all America's children are taught by teachers who are prepared to teach them effectively."

NCATE advocates educational reform and states: "The reform of education [that] does not include reform of teacher education will not accomplish national education goals." To that end, it has developed several initiatives that support K-12 and higher education partnerships for teacher preservice and inservice training. They include the Professional Development School Standard Project, where teachers learn to practice in a restructured setting, and the New Professional Teacher Project, which is designed to complement state reform efforts and enhance the performance of the teaching profession.

Recently, NCATE developed standards that emphasize performance:

NCATE expects schools of education to ensure that prospective teachers have the knowledge and skills they need to work effectively with all children. Further, NCATE standards require the school of education to monitor and evaluate the progress of teacher candidates throughout their program of study, and to use performance assessments as part of the evaluations. These performance-oriented standards are new and make the NCATE system stronger than ever before. (Wise 1994: 4).

The most recent Holmes Group report (1995) identifies the current state of teacher education and offers a view of what tomorrow's schools of education should look like. They report, among their findings, that (1) K-12 and higher education cultures clash easily, (2) there is often a lack of opportunities for students to connect their classroom learning to K-12 applications, and (3) the lack of substantive change in teacher preparation programs is a function of too few faculty willing to change and lack of institutional alliances to other educational and community systems.

They encourage the reform of education preparation programs through more appropriate reward systems and career opportunities for teaching, along with changes in certification processes. They encourage education programs to link theory and research to improve K-12 schools.

Learner Outcomes for Future Teachers

What skills, experiences, and proficiencies do we require new teachers to possess? During their collegiate years, future teachers are expected to acquire skills necessary to succeed as educators within educational settings. As educational reform takes root and schooling and schools change, the anticipated outcomes of teachers likewise change.

Along with acquiring traditional subject-area skills, this new generation of teachers must also demonstrate proficiency in the following areas:
- team teaching
- interdisciplinary curriculum development and implementation
- use of technology

- strategies that engage students in meaningful activities
- authentic assessment.

The Council of Chief State School Officers (1992) has developed Model Standards for Beginning Teacher Licensing and Development, which include the following 10 principles:

- Principle 1: The teacher understands the central concepts, tools of inquiry, and structures of the discipline(s) he or she teaches and can create learning experiences that make these aspects of subject matter meaningful for students.
- Principle 2: The teacher understands how children learn and develop, and can provide learning opportunities that support their intellectual, social, and personal development.
- Principle 3: The teacher understands how students differ in their approaches to learning and creates instructional opportunities that are adapted to diverse learners.
- Principle 4: The teacher understands and uses a variety of instructional strategies to encourage students' development of critical-thinking, problem-solving, and performance skills.
- Principle 5: The teacher uses an understanding of individual and group motivation and behavior to create a learning environment that encourages positive social interaction, active engagement in learning, and self-motivation.
- Principle 6: The teacher uses knowledge of effective verbal, nonverbal, and media communication techniques to foster active inquiry, collaboration, and supportive interaction in the classroom.
- Principle 7: The teacher plans instruction based upon knowledge of subject matter, students, the community, and curriculum goals.
- Principle 8: The teacher understands and uses formal and informal assessment strategies to evaluate and ensure the continuous intellectual, social, and physical development of the learner.
- Principle 9: The teacher is a reflective practitioner who continually evaluates the effects of his/her choices and actions on others (students, parents, and other professionals in the learning community) and who actively seeks out opportunities to grow professionally.
- Principle 10: The teacher fosters relationships with school colleagues, parents, and agencies in the larger community to support students' learning and well-being.

The principles developed by the Council of Chief State School Officers provide an image of model standards for a beginning teacher. The notions of continuous reflection and self-improvement are evident within these principles. Notions of collaboration to improve instruction are also described. As noted earlier in this chapter, it is not enough, however, to change and improve upon learner outcomes and instructional strategies. Teachers must become active participants in developing the culture, climate, and structures of the total school community in order to maximize opportunities for meaningful learning.

Fullan (1993a) and education faculty at the University of Toronto have extended the image of teaching to include skills of change agentry. They believe that there is a moral purpose that draws people to teaching who want to make a difference in the lives of others. While preservice teachers may develop the visions and skills for making a difference in the classroom and in the lives of individual children, they begin teaching without the capabilities to impact on the overall school organization. Fullan suggests that teacher preparation programs need to develop students' change capacities to help future teachers to simultaneously improve upon their classroom practice and impact upon the development of their schools as organizations.

The University of Toronto faculty have reengineered the entire teacher preparation program to include learner outcomes associated with change agentry. These change capacities include personal vision building, inquiry, mastery, and collaboration. Fullan (1993a) challenges education faculty to "design their programs to focus directly on developing the beginners' knowledge base for effective teaching and the knowledge base for changing the conditions that affect teaching" (12).

Engaging college students in the service-learning process as an integral part of their preservice preparation can further the development of each of the identified change capacities. The service-learning process challenges future teachers to develop personal visions of what "can be" as goals are set for service, and students experience authentic instruction and meaningful learning. K-12 students build skills of inquiry as they learn more about an issue, explore avenues for addressing it, and continually reflect upon their work.

Carrying out service can require new areas of skill development. As K-12 students continue their involvement in service and gain practice and feedback, they experience the notion of mastery and increased motivation to seek continuous development of skills that impact directly on the lives of those they serve. K-12 students build skills of collaboration when they plan together, secure community resources, and establish or extend partnerships with the individuals and organizations with whom they work. Preservice teachers who engage in the service-learning process within their formal coursework develop images of teaching and learning and new change capacities that will better prepare them as change agents within their classrooms and schools.

Root (1994) reviews various rationales for integrating service-learning into teacher preparation programs, including the alignment of service-learning strategies with K-12 educational reform, preparation of students as productive citizens, and that "participation in service-learning experiences [that] are focused on the needs of children may prepare prospective teachers to participate in a learner-centered educational system in ways that reflect a caring ethic" (96).

We encourage colleges of education to consider the NCATE standards, the challenges offered by Fullan (1993b) and Root (1994), and the need for reforming instruction and leadership in K-12 schools as they identify the outcomes desired for teachers. We caution against paying attention to only the learner outcomes of future teachers. The other dimensions of teacher education should also be considered: teaching strategies, structure, and climate and culture.

Teaching Strategies in Teacher Preparation Programs

How do we ensure high-quality opportunities for preservice teachers to acquire and enhance requisite skills, experiences, and proficiencies? Education faculty, like K-12 teachers, are challenged to modify not only their course objectives but also their teaching methods. Teaching someone how to engage students in meaningful activities solely through standard classroom lectures is ineffective. This paradox must change.

Faculty need to model the teaching strategies they encourage their students to acquire; if engaging models of learning work, they too should be utilized. Faculty need to demonstrate how to develop learning communities and provide high-quality opportunities for future teachers to learn by doing (much as K-12 classrooms will do). Fullan (1993a) articulates this well: "Faculties of education should not advocate things for teachers or schools that they are not capable of practicing themselves" (12).

Teaching strategies such as team teaching, effective use of technology, and interdisciplinary approaches to teaching align with the outcomes of educational reform efforts. Service-learning as pedagogy is a strategy that has particular promise in preparing future teachers to motivate and educate K-12 students, because it incorporates authentic assessment and addresses many of the principles identified in the previous section on learner outcomes: teacher understanding of how children learn and develop, appropriate use of instructional strategies, instruction based on knowledge of the community, change leadership capacity, and reflective strategies to evaluate their performance and impact on students.

Service-learning encourages student decision making, effective communication, partnership development, and self-directed learning. As we have pointed out previously in this chapter, service-learning provides high-quality opportunities for students to acquire and enhance academic, social, civic, vocational, and personal skills while improving their community.

Colleges of education have demonstrated the effectiveness of service-learning teaching strategies. Many of the resulting programs are examined in Part 3 of this monograph. They do yield an empirical generalization: The more future teachers actually engage in service-learning and create lesson plans integrating this process into the curriculum, the more comfortable and competent they become using service-learning.

Teacher Preparation Program Structural Changes

We earlier made the point that as learner outcomes and teaching strategies change, the school structure must change correspondingly. We also believe this is true of teacher preparation programs.

As teacher preparation programs change preservice outcomes and the way faculty teach, they are encouraged to develop constructs that foster these skills and strategies. This notion of the relationship among time, location, and partnerships requires teacher preparation programs to consider which "time constructs" work best for examining teaching and learning processes, acquiring requisite skills, and learning which locations are most effective and which types of partnerships offer the most promise for creating knowledgeable, skilled, and caring teachers.

We suggest another strategy for participation and learning. College students have proven to be excellent service-learning coordinators, tutors, and mentors; placing preservice teachers in K-12 classrooms to fulfill corresponding responsibilities offers a win-win situation. The K-12 teachers receive assistance in developing high-quality learning opportunities for their students (either through service-learning or direct service), and the college student learns by performing a service.

There are at least two models of service-learning: (1) college students performing as tutors/mentors to serve K-12 students, and (2) college students assisting teachers to design service-learning curriculum for their K-12 classes. The latter paradigm offers more promise to future and current teachers as well as assists K-12 schools to consider and employ more effective teaching strategies. In both these cases, preservice teachers can test theories they have learned in the classroom, explore strategies that work for them and their students, assess their fit as teachers, and determine their future in education. In the second case, they can also gain experience with the design and implementation of service-learning as a pedagogy to use with their future K-12 students.

It has been suggested that service-learning as a pedagogy not be taught in preservice classes but be considered an appropriate "inservice" subject for K-12 teachers. We cannot disagree more. We believe that the more integrated service-learning is in the process of learning how to be an effective teacher, the greater the opportunity to acquire and enhance corresponding skills. Delaying K-12 future and current teachers' orientation to service-learning results in their viewing service-learning as less attached to the central components of teaching.

School structural change alone does not ensure competent teachers; schools of education must develop appropriate learner outcomes, effective teaching strategies, and a climate and culture conducive to learning.

Teacher Preparation Program Climate and Culture

Teacher preparation faculty play an integral role in creating the climate and culture of the college or academic department. As they engage their students in service-learning activities, they become learners with their students and find themselves less isolated from their community. This is true both inside and outside campus boundaries. Service-learning requires partnership development and enhancement. Teacher preparation faculty find themselves working with faculty from other departments because of the interdisciplinary nature of service-learning. They also work closely with community partners to ensure real community needs are being met. [See Wade, beginning on p. 141, for an example of a teacher education program collaborating with community partners.]

We earlier identified a variety of components of school climate and culture that nurture educational reform and service-learning. What is needed for the transformation of teacher education culture is the development of effective and empowering learning communities that foster all members as lifelong learners and contributors to school and community. This challenge can be met several ways.

First, infuse service-learning into methods and subject-area courses. Preservice teachers and faculty developing a service-learning curriculum that meets community needs and ensures the ability to meet academic objectives require a culture different from the routine of higher education courses.

Second, use learning communities as a pedagogy. Create community in the classroom through small- and large-group work, resulting in shared decision making and a habit of learning together.

Third, encourage preservice teacher input into course design through frequent reflection sessions identifying what is working and what is not. If our preservice teachers are moving between the classroom and K-12 schools, they bring back a wealth of information, questions, and concerns. Building on their experiences gives meaning to their studies.

Many teacher education programs are moving toward the elements of climate and culture outlined above. You will read about many of them in this volume. In some cases, the movement has begun from a single faculty member who embraces the pedagogy of service-learning and has significantly changed the way he or she teaches. The benefits of change have to outweigh its costs; therefore, rigorous assessment of new and improved preservice courses is critical, not only for our colleagues but for ourselves, to ensure we are making the positive differences in future teachers that we expect to make. [See Shumer, beginning on p. 73, on evaluation.]

The Challenge for Teacher Preparation Programs

Myers (1994) identifies the following opportunity for teacher preparation programs:

> Schools and colleges of education have a unique opportunity to be at the cutting edge of school-improvement efforts by preparing their students to effectively facilitate the service-learning process. Teacher educators who incorporate service-learning as a central learning approach for preparing their students to become teachers and who help their students develop the skills needed to effectively implement this instructional strategy in the classroom will find that they have also prepared their students to be major players in the transformation of public education. The skills and perceptions needed to effectively implement the service-learning process are very similar to the skills teachers need to facilitate school change and improvement. (11)

Teacher education programs need to recognize their role in educational reform and contribute to school improvement by providing the highest-quality teachers with skills, knowledge, and experiences to motivate and educate all students. Meeting this challenge through educational and community partnerships ensures the greatest opportunity for schools and students to be effective now and in the future.

K–Higher Education Connections

"K-16" is a popular concept among service-learning practitioners and others concerned with developing a more seamless K-12 and postsecondary education system. We feel most comfortable using the designation "K–higher education," as it is more inclusive of students and organizations. Programmatic focuses of this initiative include school-to-work, early-entry collegiate experiences, and vocational education programs.

We earlier explored the application of this concept in K-12 educational reform, teacher preparation, and service-learning. K–higher education constructs offer an opportunity to engage educators from different education systems in processes and activities that meet specific outcomes but also model mutually beneficial partnerships.

K–higher education partnerships have received support from several organizations outside the educational system, including from the Community Compacts for Student Success sponsored in part by the Pew Charitable Trusts, the Danforth Foundation's Schools Leaders Program, the Education–Social Work Network, the American Association of Colleges for Teacher Education's DeWitt-Wallace National Demonstration Program, and the American Association for Higher Education, as well as other partnerships formed with the support of the Hitachi, Ford, DeWitt-Wallace, Lilly, Stuart, and other foundations.

There are also many K–higher education collaborations that have grown out of mutual concerns and resource sharing. For example, the East Valley Think Tank in Arizona is made up of senior administrators in K-12, higher education, and private/public organizations to create a world-class system of education for all students.

If institutions are serious about developing effective partnerships that engage K-12 youth, future teachers, current teachers, and community members for the benefit of all, they will find that students suffer less anxiety associated with transitions between the various educational constructs. We lose many of our youth in the transition from middle school (or junior high school) to high school and from high school to postsecondary institutions. A more connected education system encourages smoother transitions encouraging success, as opposed to the traditional abrupt transitions that often lead to failure for many of our students.

Conclusions

This essay offers strategies and hope by implementing educational reform through service-learning practices that positively impact students, teachers, schools, and communities.

The need for changing the way our schools teach and operate is apparent. We offer several reasons for educational reform and identify four critical components of successful school improvement (learner outcomes, teaching strategies, school structure, and school climate and culture).

Service-learning is suggested as an effective pedagogy that encourages schools to change along all four dimensions and meet educational reform outcomes. As K-12 systems change, teacher preparation programs must respond by providing high-quality teachers with skills, knowledge, and experiences that prepare them to motivate and educate K-12 students.

There is growing evidence that service-learning is an effective pedagogy. This essay challenges us to identify ways in which service-learning through teacher preparation can help to shape a vision of effective schools and contribute to the reform of teacher preparation and public schooling in America.

"Teacher education programs must help teaching candidates to link the moral purpose that influences them with the tools that will prepare them to engage in productive change" (Fullan 1993a: 12). The service-learning process is a powerful pedagogy that brings future teachers closer to the notions of what it means to teach and learn and to collaboratively create learning communities and organizations that support lifelong learning and continuous renewal. Service-learning has a vital role to play in formatting new visions of learning at all levels throughout the K–higher education continuum.

Readers are invited to learn from the experiences of colleagues in the essays that follow and discover opportunities to integrate service-learning within their own institutions. We believe that those who accept this challenge will bring new life and possibilities to their students, themselves, their colleagues, and the institutions and communities they seek to serve.

References

American Association for Higher Education. (September 1995). "Bowling Alone: An Interview With Robert Putnam About America's Collapsing Civic Life." *AAHE Bulletin* 48(1): 3-6.

Banach, W.J. (1994). *Critical Issues Facing America's Public Schools*. Philadelphia, PA: University of Pennsylvania.

Benson, L., and I. Harkavy. (1995). "School and Community in the Global Society. A Neo-Deweyan Theory of Community Problem Solving and Cosmopolitan Neighborly Communities: Actively, Progressively, Connecting School and Community in the Global Economic and Communication Systems of the 21st Century." Discussion paper for the National Conference on Community Service and University-Assisted Community Schools: Developing and Integrating Academically Based Community Service, K-16. Philadelphia, PA: University of Pennsylvania.

Boyte, H., and J. Farr. (1997). "The Work of Citizenship and the Problem of Service-Learning." In *Experiencing Citizenship: Concepts and Models for Service-Learning in Political Science,* edited by Richard M. Battistoni and William E. Hudson, pp. 35-48. Washington, DC: American Association for Higher Education.

Brendtro, L.K., M. Brokenleg, and S. Van Bockern. (1990). *Youth at Risk: Our Hope for the Future.* Bloomington, IN: National Educational Service.

Council of Chief State School Officers, Interstate New Teacher Assessment and Support Consortium. (1992). *Model Standards for Beginning Teacher Licensing and Development: A Resource for State Dialogue.* Washington, DC: Council of Chief State School Officers.

Erickson, J.B. (1995). "Kids Count in Indiana 1995 Data Book." Indianapolis, IN: Indiana Youth Institute.

Fullan, M.G. (March 1993a). "Why Teachers Must Become Change Agents." *Educational Leadership* 51(6): 12-17.

———. (June 1993b). "Managing Change." *Restructuring Brief* (a publication of the North Coast Professional Development Consortium) 5: 1-8.

Goodlad, J.I. (1990). *Teachers for Our Nation's Schools.* San Francisco: Jossey-Bass.

Hass, T., and R. Lambert. (October 1995). "To Establish the Bonds of Common Purpose and Mutual Enjoyment." *Phi Delta Kappan* 77(2): 136-142.

Haycock, K. (January/February 1996). "Thinking Differently About School Reform: College and University Leadership for the Big Changes We Need." *Change* 28(1): 13-18.

Holmes Group. (1995). *Tomorrow's Teachers: A Report of the Holmes Group.* East Lansing, MI: Holmes Group.

Knapp, M.S., P. Shields, and B. Turnbull. (June 1995). "Academic Challenge in High-Poverty Classrooms." *Phi Delta Kappan* 76(10): 770-776.

Kuykendall, C. (1992). *From Rage to Hope: Strategies for Reclaiming Black and Hispanic Students.* Bloomington, IN: National Educational Service.

Levin, H.M. (1996). "Accelerated School After Eight Years." *Innovations in Learning: New Environments for Education,* edited by G. Schauble. Hillsdale, NJ: Erlbaum.

Malen, B.L., R.T. Ogawa, and J. Kranz. (1989). "An Analysis of Site-Based Management as an Educational Reform Strategy." Occasional policy paper. Salt Lake City, UT: Department of Educational Administration, University of Utah.

Myers, C. (1995). "Service Learning: A Teaching and Learning Strategy." In *Integrating Service-Learning Into Teacher Education: Why and How?* pp. 1-10. Washington, DC: Council of Chief State School Officers.

Nelson, J., L. Lott, and S.H. Glenn. (1993). *Positive Discipline in the Classroom.* Rocklin, CA: Prima Publishing.

Ogawa, R., and P.A. White. (1994). "School Based Management: An Overview." In *Site-Based Management: Organizing for High Performance,* edited by S.A. Mohrman and P. Wohlstettler, pp. 53-80. San Francisco, CA: Jossey-Bass.

Palmer, P. (January 1990). Speech at the North United Methodist Church. Indianapolis, IN.

Paul, R. (1995). "How to Design Instruction So That Students Master Content in a Deep and Thoughtful Way." Critical Thinking Workshop. Rohnert Park, CA: Center for Critical Thinking and the Foundation for Critical Thinking, Sonoma State University.

Pear, R. (March 17, 1996). "20 States Don't Meet Mandates on Child Welfare." *The Indianapolis Star.*

Putnam, R. (January 1995). "Bowling Alone: America's Declining Social Capital." *Journal of Democracy* 9:65-78.

Root, S. (Fall 1994). "Service-Learning in Teacher Education: A Third Rationale." *Michigan Journal of Community Service–Learning* 1(1): 94-97.

Sidener, R.P. (1994). "Site-Based Management/Shared Decision Making: A View Through the Lens of Organizational Culture." Doctoral dissertation. Teachers College, Columbia University.

Sizer, T.R. (1992). *Horace's School: Redesigning the American High School.* Boston, MA: Houghton Mifflin.

Squires, D.A., and R.D. Kranyik. (December 1995–January 1996). "The Comer Program: Changing School Culture." *Educational Leadership* 53(4): 29-32.

Wise, A.E. (1994). "NCATE's Emphasis on Performance." *NCATE Quality Teaching* 4(2): 3-4.

Standards of Quality for School-Based and Community-Based Service-Learning

I.   Effective service-learning efforts strengthen service and academic learning.

II.   Model service-learning provides concrete opportunities for youth to learn new skills, to think critically, and to test new roles in an environment that encourages risk taking and rewards competence.

III.   Preparation and reflection are essential elements in service-learning.

IV.   Youths' efforts are recognized by those served, including their peers, the school, and the community.

V.   Youth are involved in the planning.

VI.   The service students perform makes a meaningful contribution to the community.

VII.   Effective service-learning integrates systematic formative and summative evaluation.

VIII.   Service-learning connects the school or sponsoring organization and its community in new and positive ways.

IX.   Service-learning is understood and supported as an integral element in the life of a school or sponsoring organization and its community.

X.   Skilled adult guidance and supervision are essential to the success of service-learning.

XI.   Preservice training, orientation, and staff development that include the philosophy and methodology of service-learning best ensure that program quality and continuity are maintained.

Source: Alliance for Service-Learning in Education Reform, March 1995.

School-Based Service:
A Review of Research for Teacher Educators

by Susan C. Root

> *Today Sarah and I talked about our feelings on service-learning. . . . Some potential problems that we saw were: lack of parental involvement, lack of school support, too much time commitment for your classroom. . . . But then we talked about the positives and these really outweighed the negatives. I told her about my fifth grade service-learning project and how much the students were getting out of it. The students act so mature when they are interviewing their seniors, and are very sincere and respectful. The students are so proud of their writing and doing exceptional work.*
>
> *We talked about how students learn in different ways and how service-learning would benefit them all. Kinesthetic-tactile, auditory, visual learners would all gain something from this hands-on type of education. We called service-learning a "secret weapon." (excerpt from the journal of an undergraduate elementary education student in a service-learning workshop)*

Across the country, service-learning has increasingly become a part of K-12 and teacher education programs. Service-learning is recognized as a philosophy and a pedagogical approach that can promote "the simultaneous renewal of K-12 education and teacher education" (Council of Chief State School Officers 1995: 81).

The goal of this essay is to provide a review of the research on service-learning and school-based community service programs. The essay begins with a definition of terms and a brief history of the use of community service in K-12 programs. The literature on the effects of school-based service and service-learning on K-12 students is then reviewed. The paper then describes efforts by a number of teacher preparation institutions to infuse service-learning into their programs and a review of recent studies of the effects of service-learning on teacher development.

Definitions

A number of terms have been used to describe school-based service programs, including "community service" and "service-learning." Community service can be defined as programs in which students provide assistance to individuals, organizations, or communities outside of their school. The assistance can be direct (e.g., visiting a senior pen pal) or indirect (e.g., doing clerical tasks, engaging in advocacy, organizing and administering service activities). Service-learning includes community service, but that service is deliberately integrated with learning objectives.

Perhaps the most widely used definition of service-learning is that provided in the National and Community Service Act of 1990. It defines service-learning as an educational experience:

> a. *Under which students learn and develop through active participation in thoughtfully organized service experiences that meet actual community needs and that are coordinated in collaboration with school and community;*
>
> b. *That is integrated into the students' academic curriculum or provides structured time for a student to think, talk, or write about what the student did and saw during the actual service activity;*
>
> c. *That provides students with opportunities to use newly acquired skills and knowledge in real-life situations in their own communities; and*
>
> d. *That enhances what is taught in school by extending student learning beyond the classroom and into the community and helps to foster the development of a sense of caring for others.*

Since much of the research in this field has involved community service, I will use the term "school-based service" to refer both to community service programs in schools and to service-learning. [See Shumer, beginning on p. 113, for additional discussion of issues in defining service-learning.]

A Brief History of School-Based Service

The use of community service projects in the curriculum is not new. It can be traced to Dewey (1916, 1966) and the progressive education movement. Rejecting the mental discipline approach then predominant in the schools, Dewey (1938, 1972) argued that learning must be grounded in experience. True learning would develop from a curriculum of purposive activities and opportunities for social interaction that used the child's own interests as a starting point. Concerned about the inability of an emergent industrial society to instill habits of cooperation, Dewey argued that schools should be organized as democratic communities. The theme of engaging students in realistic tasks and small-group instruction was also articulated by William Kilpatrick in 1918 in his "Project Method."

In the 1920s and 1930s, the progressive education movement began to fragment, with one faction emphasizing the creation of activity-based, child-centered instruction. Other progressives continued to regard education as key to social transformation. In 1933, the Progressive Education Association issued *A Call to the Teachers of the Nation,* calling for curriculum that would include "philosophies and plans of action designed to deal with the . . . problems of the age" (Committee of the Progressive Education Association 1933: 22).

The ideals of progressive education came under attack during the 1950s. In response to the cold war and the space race, experts (e.g., Bestor 1956) called for a return to the fundamentals and the presentation of subjects in isolation. However, school-based community service again attracted the support of educators in the 1970s when several committees, such as the National Association of Secondary School Principals (1972), the Panel on Youth of the President's Science Advisory Committee (Coleman 1974), and the National Panel on High School and Adolescent Education (1976), criticized the high schools' isolation from real life and their failure to integrate adolescents into society. These panels recommended using alternative educational settings and community participation to increase the relevance of school to adolescents and ease their assumption of adult roles.

With the publication of *A Nation at Risk* (National Commission on Excellence 1983), school and teacher effectiveness became the defining concerns of the 1980s. However, some educators continued to call for school-based service. For example, in *High School,* Boyer argued that students needed opportunities to "reach beyond themselves and become more responsibly engaged" (1983: 209). In *A Place Called School,* Goodlad (1984) recommended that high schools include community service experiences.

The 1990s has been a period of renewal for school-based service. In 1990, the National and Community Service Act became law, followed, in 1993, by the National and Community Service Trust Act. The themes of active and interactive learning, meaningful roles for adolescents, and civic education continue to be sounded as justifications for youth community service. However, recent developments in cognitive psychology and indicators associated with the well-being of youth, particularly minority, disadvantaged youth, have lent new urgency to calls for service-learning in the 1990s.

For example, in cognitive psychology, the definition of learning as the acquisition and retention of declarative knowledge has been replaced by a view of learning as the construction of meaning in the context of purposeful activity and social interaction (Brown et al. 1989). Proponents of service-learning argue that because it is inherently purposeful, contextualized, and interactive, service-learning has the ability to foster meaningful learning.

Recent recommendations for service-learning have also been spurred by record levels of social pathology among youth, e.g., violence, teen pregnancy. Several authors have proposed character education curricula that would include youth service (Damon 1988; Lickona 1991; Schaps et al. 1986; Wynne and Walberg 1986). In addition, service-learning has been viewed as a vehicle for reengaging minority youth in the school learning process. For example, Keith and Horn (1994) argue that service-learning can provide urban youth with a sense of "agency," nonschool activities that can become legitimate subjects of classroom discourse, and greater accessibility to teachers.

Impacts of Service-Learning on K-12 Students: A Review of Research

In this section, I review research on the effects of school-based service on students in kindergarten to 12th grade. The studies reviewed are divided into three sections: cognitive development and academic engagement; civic, social, and moral development; and personal development. In the review, I also attempt to answer questions concerning the contextual factors that influence the outcomes of school-based service. What features of programs are important in ensuring that students benefit from community service and service-learning? How do aspects of the service experience (e.g., challenge) mediate the impacts of service? How do student characteristics such as gender and prior service influence service outcomes?

Sources of data for this review were articles, dissertations, and evaluation reports. These sources were identified using several databases: ERIC, PsyLit, Dissertation Abstracts, and the Social Science Index. I also consulted the National Information Center for Service-Learning Bibliography (Vue-Benson and Shumer 1995). Only studies that examined the effects of school-based community service and service-learning in K-12 programs were included in the review. Studies of tutoring effects or peer counseling were not reviewed, because several meta-analyses of these approaches already exist.

In the summary chart that follows on pp. 61-72, each study was summarized to include the following information: author(s) and year; age/grade level of subjects; a description of the program; design (whether the study included a control group and involved pre- and posttesting or posttesting only); student outcomes assessed; independent variables other than the program (characteristics of subjects, programs, and experience); and a description of the results. Because the focus of this review is on service impacts on K-12 students, I did not include any results for staff, the recipients of service, or others.

Cognitive Development and Academic Engagement

In the following section, the effects of school-based community service and service-learning on cognitive outcomes are described. I also discuss the influences of school-based service on variables indicative of engagement in school learning, including academic motivation, attitudes toward school, and attendance.

Cognitive development. The cognitive outcomes assessed in studies of community service have included grades, subject-matter achievement, and higher-order thinking skills such as analysis and problem solving. Three studies have examined the effects of service involvement on grades. In a study of students in ServeAmerica programs at 12 sites, Melchior and Orr (1995) found no significant impacts for service-learning on GPA. However, Shumer (1994) found that students in the Community-Based Learning Program, a drop-out prevention program that includes community service, had significantly higher grades after a year in the program. A survey of teachers of adolescents with disabilities involved in service-learning (Brill 1994) indicated that adolescents with mild disabilities demonstrated improved academic performance. These results suggest that service-learning may have its most marked impact on the grades of at-risk and disabled students. It may be that motivation to learn in these students is particularly enhanced by service projects.

In general, investigations of content knowledge pertinent to the service activity have shown stronger effects for service than studies of GPA. For example, Hamilton and Zeldin (1987) found that the students who completed internships in local government offices scored higher in their knowledge of local government than their peers in traditional classes. In a study of the effects of an international environmental project, Silcox (1993) found that both Russian and American participants showed significant gains in scientific knowledge. In a project on hunger, students who visited a food bank emerged "better informed" about the problem of hunger than students who did not (Dewsbury-White 1993). However, Waterman (1993) found that high school participants in a Literacy Corps project did not outscore their counterparts in traditional English classes on a measure of reading achievement.

One frequent argument for including service in the K-12 curriculum is that activities in which students analyze community problems and plan and implement solutions can stimulate the development of higher-order thinking skills, such as analysis, evaluation, and problem solving. Three studies have examined the effects of service projects on higher-order thinking. Conrad (1980) and Conrad and Hedin (1982) found that students in experiential learning programs, particularly community service programs, significantly outperformed comparison students in the empathy and complexity of their responses to interpersonal problems. Using Bloom's taxonomy, Schollenberger (1985) assessed the frequency with which students reported engaging in higher-order thinking during service-learning and their level of thinking in response to social problems. In addition, she examined the relationships between higher-level thinking and time spent in service-learning and students' aptitude test scores. Schollenberger found that participants in service-learning reported frequent opportunities to engage in higher-level thinking during service-learning and demonstrated high levels of thinking about social problems. However, analyses revealed no significant correlations between higher-order thinking and either time spent in service-learning or aptitude test scores.

Academic engagement. The features of service-learning tasks would seem to appeal to a broader range of motives than conventional school tasks, thus increasing students' motivation for school learning and academic engagement. For example, in service-learning, students are involved in cooperative relations with peers, teachers, and community members and may positively affect the welfare of other people, experiences that may elicit social motives (Urdan and Maehr 1995). Service-learning projects also engage students as resources in the solution of social problems, a task characteristic that may contribute to self-perceived competence and control. Several studies have attempted to document the effects of service-learning on academic motivation. Four studies utilized paper-and-pencil measures of motivational outcomes. For example, Silcox (1993) assessed the impacts of the environmental project on intrinsic motivation and students' sense of agency. While students showed no significant gains in intrinsic motivation, analyses of their written reflections revealed large increases in students' feelings of agency. Waterman (1993) found no change in Literacy Corps participants' academic motivation over the course of their project; however, their counterparts in traditional English classes experienced a decline in academic motivation. Melchior and Orr (1995) found no significant changes in ServeAmerica participants' self-perceived competence and control.

While the results for service-learning on paper-and-pencil measures of motivation have been limited, results of studies using measures of behavioral engagement, e.g., attendance and time on task, have been more positive. For example, Melchior and Orr (1995) found that high school students in the ServeAmerica program increased in attendance, while middle school students increased both in attendance and in hours doing homework. Increased attendance for service participants was also observed by Luchs (1980) and Brill (1994).

Civic, Social, and Moral Development

A primary objective of school-based service programs has been to facilitate the development of attitudes, values, and behaviors necessary for membership in a participatory democracy. Its proponents argue that school-based service can be an effective alternative or supplement to text-based civic education, whose limited effects are well established. Citizenship outcomes that have been the focus of study include attitudes and values such as social and personal responsibility, political efficacy, political trust, political interest, dogmatism, attitudes toward others, and attitudes toward cultural diversity. In addition, investigators have measured the impacts of school-based service on both the intention to become involved in the community and community involvement.

The most frequently assessed attitudinal outcome of school-based service is social and personal responsibility, and the measure most widely used is the Social and Personal Responsibility Scale (SPRS) developed by Conrad and Hedin (Conrad 1980). The SPRS consists of four subscales that measure separate dimensions of responsible social behavior, including attitudes toward responsibility (beliefs about social welfare and duty), self-perceptions of competence to behave responsibly, efficacy (i.e., students' beliefs that their actions can effect positive change in their communities), and behavior (items measuring actual positive social behaviors). Some studies have used other measures of social responsibility (e.g., Luchs 1980; Waterman 1993). Two studies (Melchior and Orr 1995; Ridgell 1995) employed the personal and social responsibility scale recently developed by the Search Institute. Although there are exceptions (e.g., Kraft et al. 1993; Ridgell 1995), most studies have demonstrated a link between service-learning and social and personal responsibility using the SPRS and other measures (Conrad 1980; Conrad and Hedin 1982; Crosman 1989; Hamilton and Fenzel 1988; Luchs 1980; Melchior and Orr 1995; Rutter and Newmann 1989; Silcox 1993; Waterman 1993; Williams 1993).

In addition to social and personal responsibility, investigators have examined the effects of school-based service programs on political efficacy. Studies of political efficacy, the belief that one can positively influence the political process, have yielded mixed results. Wilson (1974), Hamilton and Zeldin (1987), and Marks (1994) found that community service participation had positive effects on efficacy, while in studies by Marsh (1973), Rutter and Newmann (1989), and Procter (1992), students did not gain in efficacy.

Marsh (1973) examined the impacts of a service-learning social studies class on three attitudinal components of political socialization in addition to efficacy: political interest, civic tolerance, and political trust. He found a significant increase in political interest for experimental students but no changes in civic tolerance or trust. Conrad (1980) and Conrad and Hedin (1982) found that participation in experiential learning was associated with increasingly positive attitudes toward community involvement.

A central democratic value is tolerance. Tolerance may include two components, a willingness to objectively consider attitudes and values different from one's own, and an acceptance of individuals ethnically, linguistically, and economically different from oneself. Several investigators have assessed the effects of school-based service experiences on the first component of tolerance. Using the Rokeach Dogmatism Scale, Sager (1973), Wilson (1974), and Corbett (1977) found mixed results for service programs. Other investigators have assessed the effects of experiential and service-learning on the second aspect of tolerance, acceptance of others and of cultural diversity. Again, the results have been mixed. While Conrad (1980) and Conrad and Hedin (1982) found that students involved in experiential learning programs demonstrated significantly more positive attitudes toward adults and toward the recipients of service than controls, Silcox (1993) found no gains for American and Russian students in their acceptance of one another during a cooperative service experience, and Melchior and Orr (1995) found no significant gains in students' acceptance of cultural diversity as a result of the ServeAmerica program.

In addition to assessing the impacts of school-based service on democratic attitudes and values, researchers have also examined the effects of service on students' intent to become involved in the communities, and their concurrent and subsequent community participation. Conrad (1980) found that students in experiential learning programs made greater gains than control students in their intent to become involved in their communities. Using a posttest only, Marsh (1973) found that participants in a service-learning class expressed greater willingness to take political action than comparison students. Melchior and Orr (1995) found no difference between ServeAmerica participants and nonparticipants in their commitment to engage in future service; however, ServeAmerica participants anticipated participating in different types of service. Yates (1995) identified features of the service experience that might account for the differential results of research on intent to serve. She found that students' emotional engagement in service and amount and level of reflection, as well as course grades and friends involved in service, predicted their projected levels of service.

Some studies have examined the effects of school-based service on community involvement. Marsh (1973) found that students who were participating in a service-learning course reported higher levels of political activity during the class than comparison students. Melchior and Orr (1995) found that ServeAmerica students were more likely to be involved in service activities than comparison students. The results of both studies were no doubt due to students' coursework. However, two retrospective studies indicate that school-based community service programs can impact subsequent community involvement. Beane et al. (1981) and O'Connell (1983) found that individuals who had participated in community service programs in high school were more likely, as adults, to hold leadership positions in formal organizations and membership in nonformal organizations than comparison subjects.

A final social outcome of service programs is moral development. Using the Defining Issues Test (Rest 1976), several researchers have obtained significant effects for school-based service programs on level of moral reasoning (Conrad 1980; Conrad and Hedin 1982; Reck 1978; Stockhaus 1976).

Personal Development

Advocates of school-based service argue that it provides opportunities to fill significant social roles, develop realistic skills, and cultivate meaningful relationships with adults, factors that can enhance the development of self, particularly during adolescence. Several indicators of personal development have been the focus of research on school-based service, including self-esteem, identity development, and personal adjustment. While some studies have shown no effects for school-based service on self-esteem (Crosman 1989; Middleton 1993; Silcox 1993), the majority of studies have shown a relationship (Conrad and Hedin 1982; Krug 1991; Luchs 1980; Sager 1973; Waterman 1993). Yates (1995) examined the effects of a social justice course on the process of identity development. Identity development was measured in terms of the transcendence of students' written reflections (the degree to which they went beyond description to relate the experience of those served to the self or to issues of social justice). Additional dependent variables in Yates's study included students' emotional and relational engagement with the service project and projected service involvement. Yates found that students' reflections became progressively more transcendent during the service course. In addition, she observed that service was an emotionally engaging activity for many students and that emotional engagement was a prerequisite for transcendent reflection. Studies that have assessed the effects of school-based service and personal adjustment have shown little evidence of a link. Corbett (1977) obtained gains in emotional, social, and task competence only during the second year of a service program. Middleton (1993) found gains for high school participants on only one measure of socio-emotional adjustment or social skills, self-disclosure.

Effects of Student, Program, and Experiential Characteristics

Studies of school-based service have revealed that service involvement can lead to certain cognitive, civic, social, and other outcomes. However, a critical question concerns the effect that contextual variables may have in mediating the effects of service participation. In this section, I review the results of studies that have assessed variations in student outcomes as a function of characteristics of students, program attributes, and aspects of students' service experiences.

Student characteristics. Two characteristics of students have been found to be minimally associated with student gains in service programs: social class and grade point average. However, gender, age or grade level, family history of service, and prior service experience have been found to significantly relate to outcome measures. Females participate in service more frequently than males (Crosman 1989; Marks 1994). In addition, two studies (Hamilton and Fenzel 1988; Kraft et al. 1993) revealed that female participants in a volunteer program made greater gains in social responsibility than males. Several studies indicate that older students may benefit somewhat more from service programs than younger students (Conrad 1980; Conrad and Hedin 1982; Kraft et al. 1993; Melchior and Orr 1995). Students with a history of service and families involved in service are more apt to participate in service activities (Crosman 1989; Marks 1994); however, there is little evidence that these characteristics mediate the benefits of service experiences. Only one study (Corbett 1977) revealed that students with a history of voluntarism made greater gains.

Program characteristics. Programmatic features of the service experience such as the provision of a reflection seminar also mediate the impacts of service-learning experiences. Students make greater gains in programs with regular, structured opportunities for reflection (Conrad 1980; Conrad and Hedin 1982; Crosman 1989; Hamilton and Zeldin 1987; Krug 1991). Waterman (1993) has argued that various types of reflection activities (oral, written) should impact different domains of development. Crosman (1989) found some support for this suggestion; in her study, students gave the highest ratings to experiences providing written reflection and a combination of oral and written reflection.

Temporal features of service programs, such as program length and intensity (number of hours of involvement per week), have also been the focus of research. The majority of studies have shown that longer service experiences and those demanding more of the student's time produce greater gains (Conrad 1980; Conrad and Hedin 1982; Crosman 1989; Reck 1978; Williams 1993).

Several studies have shown that efforts to integrate academic content with the service experience are beneficial (Conrad and Hedin 1982; Dewsbury-White 1993; Hamilton and Zeldin 1987; Marks 1994). Higher integration is associated with gains in subject-matter knowledge (Dewsbury-White 1993; Hamilton and Zeldin 1987), problem solving (Conrad and Hedin 1982), and social conscience (Marks 1994).

Some investigators have found effects for type of service activity. Corbett (1977) found that students involved in direct service (service in which they provided personal assistance to others) made greater gains on the California Psychological Inventory than those involved in indirect service. Hamilton and Fenzel (1988) obtained a more pronounced effect for a community improvement project than for child care on social responsibility. However, some other studies (e.g., Conrad 1980; Williams 1993) have found no effect for type of service.

Characteristics of individual experience. Evidence has consistently indicated that the quality of students' service experiences has a critical impact on their development on a variety of measures. Students' perceptions that they have adult responsibilities at their sites, maintain collegial relationships with site staff, make a significant contribution, and are challenged significantly mediate the impacts of their involvement in service (Conrad 1980; Conrad and Hedin 1982; Hamilton and Zeldin 1987; Krug 1991; Melchior and Orr 1995).

Context effects on student development. Two recent studies have assessed the effects of features of the context for school service programs on student development. Procter (1992) found that type and location of school and type of service affected students' scores on social isolation and powerlessness. Service participants in an all-girl parochial school showed a pre-posttest decline in social isolation. However, suburban students involved in urban service showed increased feelings of powerlessness. Marks (1994) found that a press for cooperation in schools was positively related to service participation, citizen efficacy, and social conscience, while an individualistic orientation was negatively related to social conscience.

Summary

In summary, school-based community service activities can have positive effects on pertinent subject-matter knowledge, particularly when they are part of an integrated approach to instruction and accompanied by planned opportunities for reflection. Evidence also suggests that service activities elicit higher-order thinking and foster more empathic and complex responses to interpersonal problems. The data strongly suggest a relationship between participation in school-based service and some civic and social outcomes. Social and personal responsibility, i.e., concern about social welfare and a felt obligation to serve, is the most consistently documented outcome of school service for students. However, some studies also provide support for a relationship between school-based service and gains in moral reasoning. In addition, both concurrent community activity and adult community involvement appear to increase as a result of school-based service programs. Finally, the evidence suggests that self-esteem and identity development are positively affected by service participation.

Thus, service-learning appears to be an effective pedagogical technique for achieving many of the goals of public schooling. However, schools or teachers should be aware both of the limits of service-learning and student, program, and experiential characteristics that influence its effectiveness. The evidence strongly suggests that school-based service should be integrated with academic goals and accompanied by structured opportunities for reflection. Community service activities may have more powerful impacts if they are part of an overall program to enhance social development (see Wilson 1974). While the results of the research are inconclusive regarding the exact length and intensity of service necessary to effect changes in students, it is clear that programs need to involve a substantial time investment. Finally, the implications of research regarding the effects of quality of programs are definitive. If school-based service is to influence student academic, civic, and social development in the ways we hope for, students need to have experiences that offer autonomy, challenge, and supportive relations with adult staff.

Service-Learning in Teacher Education

The evidence discussed above on the effects of school-based service programs suggests that teachers need adequate training in the pedagogy of school-based service if students are to benefit from this approach. Recently, an increasing number of teacher education programs have incorporated service-learning in their teacher training efforts. While the objective of some programs has been to prepare teachers in the pedagogy of service-learning, several institutions have also recognized that service projects may help socialize teachers in the essential moral and civic obligations of teaching, which include teaching with "care" (Noddings 1988), fostering lifelong civic engagement, being able to adapt to the needs of learners with diverse and special needs, and being committed to advocacy for social justice and for children and families.

For example, at the University of Rhode Island, teacher preparation students have completed internships in human service agencies in order to strengthen their tendency to engage in reflection and critical inquiry of the educational system. At other institutions, service-learning has been used as a tool to enhance prospective teachers' "moral knowledge" and orientation toward care (Anderson and Guest 1993; Root and Batchelder 1994). Several programs have included service-learning to make teachers more aware of their own biases and the role of schools in perpetuating inequity, and to prepare them to teach students with diverse ethnic and social backgrounds and handicapping conditions.

Although teacher education institutions are increasingly utilizing service-learning, research on the effects of service experiences on teacher preparation students is only beginning. Wade (1995) assessed the effects of a service-learning component in the elementary social studies methods class at the University of Iowa. In this class, students complete a personal service project and assist with a service-learning project in an elementary classroom. Using multiple sources of data, including an attitude-toward-community-involvement scale, student interviews, course feedback, papers, and teacher evaluations, Wade found an increase in students' positive attitudes about community participation. Participants demonstrated gains in self-esteem and self-efficacy, increased knowledge about service and other people, and increased connections to others. Finally, students in the methods course became both more positive and more realistic about using service-learning as a pedagogical tool.

Sullivan (1991) conducted case studies of two student teachers who had previously completed community service internships as part of the University of Rhode Island's program. One, who had worked in a children's museum, had a highly successful student teaching experience characterized by significant ease in planning activities and skill at communicating with students and parents. A second student, who had worked at a residential center for delinquent adolescent males, completed her student teaching in an urban high school where her cooperating teacher praised her interpersonal skills with students.

George et al. (1995) conducted a study comparing graduates of an early model of Seattle University's service-learning program with graduates of another program. At Seattle University, master of arts in teaching candidates completed a year-long service-learning experience. After learning the principles of service-learning, students performed 25 hours of fieldwork in a human service agency and presented the results of their projects at a community internship conference. George et al. (1995) found no differences between Seattle University graduates and comparison students in their attitudes toward and implementation of service-learning during their first year of teaching. In both groups, only a small percentage (approximately 25%) of the teachers implemented service-learning. Teachers cited the extreme time demands of the first year of teaching as reasons for their inability to include service-learning. Seattle University graduates expressed a need for training focused specifically on service-learning as an instructional method.

Root and Batchelder (1994) assessed the effects of a child advocacy project on preservice teachers at Alma College. In this project, preservice teachers worked in groups to investigate a social problem affecting youth and then carried out an advocacy action. Root and Batchelder examined the effects of the project on three characteristics thought to be indicative of a caring orientation in preservice teachers: complexity of thinking in response to problems of young people, teacher efficacy, and humanistic orientation toward classroom control. They also assessed the contribution of characteristics of the service-learning experience to these indicators of care. Education students in a course taught by the first author served as the comparison group. The results showed that students who completed the advocacy project made more significant gains than comparison students on two dimensions of the complexity of thinking about a social problem of child-hood — *differentiation* (the ability to identify various subgroups affected by a problem and to propose differentiated solutions) and *information gathering* (the recognition of the need to obtain information pertinent to a problem. Several characteristics of the service-learning experience contributed significantly to students' development in problem solving, including autonomy, perceived contribution of the service activity, and instructor support.

Green and his colleagues (1994) at Ball State University conducted a pre-postevaluation of Project TEACH, a program to increase education students' interactional skill with at-risk students. In this program, secondary education students served as tutors for at-risk adolescents, while students in a traditional introductory education class emphasizing observation served as the comparison group. Green and his colleagues found that participants of TEACH made significantly greater gains in self-esteem and were more likely to retain their commitment to teaching than comparison students. TEACH participants also made greater gains in their understanding of the difficulties associated with community participation and in their willingness to critically evaluate their peers' commitment to community service. Flippo and his colleagues (1993) conducted a similar study of preservice teachers in a tutoring program and a comparison group. Participants in the program reported feeling greater concern and compassion for others and demonstrated greater commitment to teaching than nonparticipants.

Siegel (1994) examined the effects of a class on diversity (which included a community service experience) on preservice teachers' understanding of diversity, ability to apply course content, and self-awareness. Data consisted of the instructor's logs and student journals and reflection papers. Siegel found that students' journals reflected increased sensitivity to diversity. Several students became more insightful about their own responses to diverse students. Students also reported learning new pedagogical strategies, including service-learning.

Vadeboncoeur and her colleagues (1995) at the University of Colorado assessed the effects of a social foundations of education course in which students completed 12 hours of work in a human service agency. The goals of the foundations course were to increase preservice teachers' acceptance of diversity and commitment to social justice, and to engage them in critically reflecting on their own biases. Data for the project came from students' course journals, a course evaluation form, a student information questionnaire (which assessed students' goals for the course and background characteristics), a social responsibility questionnaire, and a student performance assessment, in which students answered questions pertaining to the goals of the course. Evaluation instruments and journals were analyzed for themes indicative of change. While the short course and service experience did not generate the changes in social activism hoped for by the authors, students' discussions of the meaning of democracy, racism, and causes of under-achievement became "more thoughtful and complete" throughout the semester. In addition, students became increasingly more likely to ascribe social problems to structural factors than to individuals.

Conclusion

K-12 programs and institutions of teacher education are increasingly includ-ing service-learning within their curricula. Educators argue that service-learning allows for the provision of learning experiences that are meaning-ful, i.e., active, integrated, and embedded in sociocultural contexts. Additionally, school-based service is viewed as an effective means for instill-ing attitudes and skills basic to future adjustment and responsible citizen-ship. A large number of studies have established moderate but positive rela-tionships between school-based service and some of these outcomes, including subject-matter achievement, behavioral indicators of academic involvement, social and personal responsibility, moral reasoning, and self-esteem. Research on school-based service has also revealed the critical influence of program and experiential features on student development. Structured opportunities for reflection, integration with academic content, and experiences of sufficient length and intensity play a determining role in mediating service impacts, as do characteristics of the service experience, such as autonomy and relations with site personnel.

In part because of service-learning's promise for K-12 learners, teacher education institutions have sought to provide preservice and inservice teachers with training in service-learning. Several programs have also viewed service experiences as a way to foster the development of the pro-fessional values and habits essential for ethically grounded, effective teach-ing. Early investigations suggest that service-learning is associated with gains for preservice teachers on some desired dimensions. However, there is a clear need for additional research. Investigators need to examine the effects of training and of specific features of training (e.g., mentoring, sus-tained support) on teachers' subsequent interest in and ability to create high-quality service-learning experiences. There is a need to identify char-acteristics of teachers, schools, and communities that support or impede service-learning practice. If service-learning is to be accepted as a way to enhance teachers' commitment to principles of care, social justice, and civic education, instruments to measure these outcomes must be developed. Similarly, there is a need for instruments that can document the effects of service-learning on teachers awareness of bias and sensitivity to and skill at instructing diverse learners.

References

Anderson, J., and K. Guest. (1993). "Linking Campus and Community: Seattle University's Community Service Internship for Preservice Teachers." Paper presented at the National Service Learning Conference, Minneapolis, MN.

Beane, J., J. Turner, D. Jones, and R. Lipka. (1981). "Long-Term Effects of Community Service Programs." *Curriculum Inquiry* 11(2): 143-155.

Bestor, A. (1956). *The Restoration of Learning*. New York: Knopf.

Bourgeois, M. (1978). "Experiential Citizen Education for Early Adolescents: A Model." Unpublished doctoral dissertation, University of North Carolina, Greensboro.

Boyer, E. (1983). *High School: A Report on Secondary Education in America*. New York: Harper & Row.

Brill, C. (1994). "The Effects of Participation in Service-Learning on Adolescents With Disabilities." *Journal of Adolescence* 17(4): 369-380.

Brown, J., A. Collins, and P. Duguid. (1989). "Situated Cognition and the Culture of Learning." *Educational Researcher* 18(1): 32-42.

Calabrese, R., and H. Schumer. (1986). "The Effects of Service Activities on Adolescent Alienation." *Adolescence* 21(83): 675-687.

Coleman, J. (1974). *Youth: Transition to Adulthood*. A Report of the Panel on Youth of the President's Science Advisory Committee. Chicago: University of Chicago Press.

Committee of the Progressive Education Association on Social and Economic Problems. (1933). *A Call to the Teachers of the Nation*. New York: John Day Company.

Conrad, D. (1980). "The Differential Impact of Experiential Learning Programs on Secondary School Students." Unpublished doctoral dissertation, University of Minnesota.

———, and D. Hedin. (1982). "The Impact of Experiential Education on Adolescent Development." In *Youth Participation and Experiential Education,* edited by D. Conrad and D. Hedin. New York: Haworth Press.

Corbett, R. (1977). "The Community Involvement Program: Social Service as a Factor in Adolescent Moral and Psychological Development." Unpublished doctoral dissertation, University of Toronto.

Council of Chief State School Officers. (1995). *Integrating Service Learning Into Teacher Education: Why and How?* Washington, DC: CCSSO.

Crosman, M. (1989). "The Effects of Required Community Service on the Development of Self-Esteem, Personal and Social Responsibility of High School Students in a Friends School." Unpublished doctoral dissertation, Lancaster Theological Seminary.

Damon, W. (1988). *The Moral Child*. New York: The Free Press.

Dewey, J. (1916/1966). *Democracy and Education*. New York: The Free Press.

———. (1938/1972). *Experience and Education*. New York: Collier Books.

Dewsbury-White, K. (1993). "The Relationship of Service-Learning Project Models to the Subject Matter Achievement of Middle School Students." Unpublished doctoral dissertation, Michigan State University.

Fertman, C., I. Buchen, and J. Long. (1993). *The Pennsylvania Serve-America Grant: Implementation and Impact: Year One*. Pittsburgh, PA: The Pennsylvania Service-Learning Research and Evaluation Network, University of Pittsburgh.

Flippo, R.F., C. Hetzel, D. Gribonski, and L.A. Armstrong. (1993). "Literacy, Multicultural, Sociocultural Considerations: Student Literacy Corps and the Community." Paper presented at the Annual Meeting of the International Reading Association, San Antonio.

George, N., S. Hunt, D. Nixon, R. Ortiz, and J. Anderson. (1995). "Beginning Teachers' Perceptions and Use of Community Service Learning as a Teaching Method." Paper presented at the National Service Learning Conference, Philadelphia, PA.

Goodlad, J. (1984). *A Place Called School*. New York: McGraw-Hill.

Green, J., R. Dalton, and B. Wilson. (1994). "Implementation and Evaluation of TEACH: A Service-Learning Program for Teacher Education." Paper presented at the annual meeting of the Association of Teacher Educators, Atlanta, GA.

Hamilton, S., and M. Fenzel. (1988). "The Impact of Volunteering Experience on Adolescent Social Development: Evidence of Program Effects." *Journal of Adolescent Research* 3(1): 65-80.

Hamilton, S., and S. Zeldin. (1987). "Learning Civics in the Community." *Curriculum Inquiry* 17: 408-420.

Keith, N., and N. Horn. (1994). "Community Service and the Rebuilding of Community: Exploring the Potential of Service Learning in Urban Schools." Paper presented at the annual meeting of the American Educational Research Association, New Orleans.

Kilpatrick, W. (1918). "The Project Method." *Teachers College Record* 19: 320.

Kraft, R., M. Goldwasser, M. Swadener, and M. Timmons. (1993). *First Annual Report: Preliminary Evaluation: Service Learning–Colorado*. Boulder, CO: University of Colorado School of Education.

Krug, J. (1991). "Select Changes in High School Students' Self-Esteem and Attitudes Toward Their School and Community by Their Participation in Service Learning Activities at a Rocky Mountain High School." Unpublished doctoral dissertation, University of Colorado-Boulder.

Lickona, T. (1991). *Educating for Character*. New York: Bantam Books.

Luchs, K. (1980). "Selected Changes in Urban High School Students After Participation in Community-Based Learning and Service Activities." Unpublished doctoral dissertation, University of Maryland.

Marks, H. (1994). "The Effect of Participation in School-Sponsored Community Service Programs on Student Attitudes Toward Social Responsibility." Unpublished doctoral dissertation, University of Michigan.

Marsh, D. (1973). "Education for Political Involvement: A Pilot Study of Twelfth Graders." Unpublished doctoral dissertation, University of Wisconsin.

Melchior, A., and L. Orr. (1995). *Final Report: National Evaluation of Serve-America.* Cambridge, MA: Abt Associates.

Middleton, E. (1993). "The Psychological and Social Effects of Community Service Tasks on Adolescents." Unpublished doctoral dissertation, Purdue University.

National Association of Secondary School Principals. (1972). *American Youth in the Mid-Seventies* (Conference Report). Reston, VA: NASSP.

National Commission on Excellence in Education. (1983). *A Nation at Risk: The Imperative for Educational Reform.* Washington, DC: U.S. Government Printing Office.

National Panel on High School and Adolescent Education. (1976). *The Education of Adolescents: The Final Report and Recommendations of the National Panel on High School and Adolescent Education.* Washington, DC: U.S. Department of Health, Education, and Welfare, Office of Education.

Noddings, N. (1988). "An Ethic of Caring and Its Implications for Instructional Arrangements." *American Journal of Education* 96(2): 215-230.

O'Connell, B. (1983). "Long Term Effects of School-Community Service Projects." Unpublished doctoral dissertation, State University of New York at Buffalo.

Patterson, E. (1987). "The Effects of Participation in Required and Not Required Community Service Programs on the Process of Self-Actualization in High School Students." Unpublished doctoral dissertation, University of Florida.

Procter, D. (1992). "School-Based Community Service: A Descriptive Analysis of Four High School Programs." Unpublished doctoral dissertation, West Virginia University.

Reck, C. (1978). "A Study of the Relationship Between Participation in School Service Programs and Moral Development." Unpublished doctoral dissertation, St. Louis University.

Rest, J. (1976). "New Approaches in the Assessment of Moral Judgment." In *Moral Development and Behavior,* edited by T. Lickona. New York: Holt, Rinehart & Winston.

Ridgell, E. (1995). "Student Perceptions Before and After Service-Learning." Unpublished doctoral dissertation, University of Maryland.

Root, S., and T. Batchelder. (1994). "The Impact of Service-Learning on Preservice Teachers' Development." Paper presented at the annual meeting of the American Educational Research Association, San Francisco.

Rutter, R., and F. Newmann. (1989). "The Potential of Community Service to Enhance Civic Responsibility." *Social Education* 53(6): 371-374.

Sager, W. (1973). "A Study of Changes in Attitudes, Values, and Self-Concepts of Senior High Youth While Working as Full-Time Volunteers With Institutionally Mentally Retarded People." Unpublished doctoral dissertation, United States International University.

Schaps, E., D. Solomon, and M. Watson. (1986). "A Program That Combines Character

Development and Academic Achievement." *Educational Leadership* 43(4): 32-35.

Schollenberger, J. (1985). "Opportunities for Higher Level Thinking as They Occur in Service-Learning." Unpublished doctoral dissertation, University of Michigan.

Shumer, R. (1994). "Community-Based Learning: Humanizing Education." *Journal of Adolescence* 17: 357-367.

——— . (1995). "The University of Minnesota, Education, and Service-Learning." In *Integrating Service-Learning Into Teacher Education: Why and How?* pp. 55-61. Washington, DC: Council of Chief State School Officers.

Siegel, S. (1994). "Community Service Learning: A Component to Strengthen Multicultural Teacher Education." Paper presented at the annual meeting of the American Educational Research Association, New Orleans.

Silcox, H. (1993). "Experiential Environmental Education in Russia: A Study in Community Service Learning." *Phi Delta Kappan* 74(9): 706-709

Stockhaus, S. (1976). "The Effects of a Community Involvement Program on Adolescent Students' Citizenship Attitudes." Unpublished doctoral dissertation, University of Minnesota.

Sullivan, R. (1991). "The Role of Service-Learning in Restructuring Teacher Education." Paper presented at the annual meeting of the Association of Teacher Educators, New Orleans.

Urdan, T., and M. Maehr. (1995). "Beyond a Two-Goal Theory of Motivation and Achievement: A Case for Social Goals." *Review of Educational Research* 65(3): 213-244.

Vadeboncoeur, J., J. Rahm, D. Aguilera, and M. LeCompte. (1995). "Learning in the Service of Citizenship: The Limitations of Service Learning." Paper presented at the annual meeting of the American Educational Research Association, San Francisco.

Vue-Benson, R., and R. Shumer. (1995). *Impacts and Effect of Service Topic Bibliography.* St. Paul, MN: National Information Center for Service-Learning.

Wade, R. (May/June 1995). "Developing Active Citizens: Community Service Learning in Social Studies Teacher Education." *The Social Studies* 85: 122-128

Waterman, A. (1993). "Conducting Research on Reflective Activities in Service Learning." In *A How To Guide to Reflection: Adding Cognitive Learning to Community Service Programs,* edited by H. Silcox, pp. 90-99. Philadelphia, PA. Brighton Press.

Williams, R. (1993). "The Effects of Required Community Service on the Process of Developing Responsibility in Suburban Youth." Unpublished doctoral dissertation, University of Nebraska-Lincoln.

Wilson, T. (1974). "An Alternative Community-Based Secondary School Education Program and Student Political Development." Unpublished doctoral dissertation, University of Southern California.

Wynne, E., and H. Walberg. (1986). "The Complementary Goals of Character Development and Academic Excellence." *Educational Leadership* 43(4): 15-18.

Yates, M. (1995). "Community Service and Identity Development in Adolescence." Unpublished doctoral dissertation, Catholic University of America.

K-12 Community Service and Service-Learning Impacts

Author	Age/Grade Level of Subjects	Program Description	Design	Outcomes Assessed	Subject, Program, Experience Variables	Results
Sager (1973)	H.S.	9-week volunteer experience assisting mentally retarded persons	E P/P	Self-esteem, values; dogmatism; acceptance of self and others; affect; purpose in life; attitudes toward self, recipients, institutions		Significant gains in self-esteem. Improved attitudes toward self, peers, recipients of service.
Marsh (1973)	H.S.	Experimental class with community participation component	E,C P	Political activity; political efficacy; political interest; political trust; civic tolerance; willingness to get involved	Political issue and level of risk of involvement	Significant gains in political participation and interest. Significant gains in willingness to become involved in political issue regardless of perceived risk.
Wilson (1974)	H.S.	Alternative high school emphasizing open-mindedness, political efficacy, affect, school-as-community, and community-based learning	E, C, C P/P	Open-mindedness (dogmatism); political efficacy; students' ratings of schools		Significant gains in open-mindedness and political efficacy. Experimental students rated school significantly higher than one control group.

Design Key: E=experimental group only. C=control group(s). P=posttest only. P/P=pre- and posttests.

Study	Level	Program	Design	Outcomes Measured	Variables	Results
Stockhaus (1976)	H.S.	20 hours work in social service agencies	E,C P/P	Self-esteem; political efficacy; social and community responsibility; involvement efficacy; altruism		Significant gains in social and community responsibility and altruism after adjustment for background characteristics.
Corbett (1977)	H.S.	2-year community involvement program	E,C,C P/P	Social responsibility; personal values; philosophy of human nature; dogmatism; moral reasoning; intolerance of ambiguity; California Psy. Inventory; self-reported development	History of volunteer experience; type of service experience	No significant effects for first year of program. Second year: significant gains on aspects of California Psychological Inventory, including social competence, task competence, and emotional competence. History of voluntarism and involvement in direct helping predicted gains.
Reck (1978)	H.S.	3-school service program	E,C P/P	Moral reasoning	Characteristics, including entering level of moral reasoning; duration of program	Participants in programs more than 42 hours: significant gains in moral reasoning. Lower initial moral reasoning scores predicted greater progress.
Bourgeois (1978)	Jr. H.S.	7-week citizenship education program; included community service and community awareness, training in communication skills, guidance and counseling	E P	Civic competence and democratic development		Data as a whole indicated enhanced civic competence and democratic values.

Study		Program	Design	Outcomes Measured	Results
Conrad (1980)	H.S.	11 experiential learning programs (including community service)	E,C P/P	Moral reasoning; self-esteem; social and personal responsibility; career exploration; attitudes toward adults, recipients of service, and community participation; problem solving; knowledge of community	Students' background characteristics and characteristics of experience (Characteristics of Experience Checklist) and student evaluations
					Significant gains in moral reasoning; self-esteem; social and personal responsibility; career development; attitudes toward adults, recipients of service, and community participation; empathy-complexity dimension of social problem solving. Aspects of program and experience (e.g., reflection seminar, autonomy) mediated effects; duration and intensity of experience had less powerful effects.
Luchs (1980)	H.S.	Community involvement program	E,C P/P	Self-esteem; career exploration; personal and social responsibility; attendance; disciplinary referrals	Significant gains in self-esteem, career exploration, and responsible attitudes. Significant gains in attendance; decreased disciplinary referrals .
Beane, Turner, Jones & Lipka (1981)	Adult	Retrospective study of long-term effects of 1940s city planning, involving community study and service	E,C,C P	Later adult leadership in formal organizations; participation in nonformal community organizations; attitudes toward school-based service	Participants significantly more likely than controls to have held leadership positions and been involved in nonformal organizations as adults. Mixed results on attitude measure.

Conrad & Hedin (1982)	H.S.	Examined effects of four types of experiential learning programs (community service, internships, adventured education, and community study); 27 programs included in study	E,C	Self-esteem, moral reasoning, social and personal responsibility, social problem solving, attitudes toward adults and others and toward involvement in the community, career planning, knowledge of community issues and resources	Student characteristics: age, grade, region, GPA, and social class Program features: formal seminar, program length and intensity; also characteristics of the experience, including autonomy, and relationship with field site personnel	Significant gains in self-esteem, moral reasoning (for community service groups), social and personal responsibility, and empathy-complexity dimension of problem solving. Significant gains in positive attitudes toward adults, others, and community involvement. Trend toward higher levels of career planning. Significant effect for age, with older students gaining more. Presence of formal seminar, length, and intensity of program influenced outcomes. Characteristics of individuals' experiences most important mediating factor, particularly autonomy and collegial relationship with site personnel.
O'Connell (1983)	Adult	Retrospective study of impacts of school community projects	E,C	Adult community leadership and involvement	Focus of community service (community improvement or preparation for work)	Adults who had participated in school community service more apt to assume leadership positions as adults. Experience in community improvement projects more influential than in work-related placements.
Schollenberger (1985)	H.S.	"Project Action" (high school service-learning program)	E P	Self-reported frequency of higher-level thinking in service-learning; level of thinking (in structured logs); correlations between higher-level thinking and scores on standardized aptitude tests	Duration and intensity of service-learning	Students in service-learning reported frequent opportunities for higher levels of thinking and demonstrated high proportions of higher-order thinking. No significant relationship between duration or intensity of service-learning and higher-level thinking. Standardized aptitude test scores not significantly correlated with study measures of thinking.

Study	Level	Program	Design	Measures	Characteristics	Findings
Calabrese & Schumer (1986)	9th Gr.	Community service project	E1, E2, C Pre, Post1 Post2	Alienation, disciplinary referrals, attendance, GPA		Significantly lower alienation and fewer disciplinary referrals for experimental groups immediately following participation.
Hamilton & Zeldin (1987)	H.S.	4 local government internship programs	E,C P/P	Knowledge of local government; political efficacy; attitudes toward local government	Interns and supervisors perceptions of qualitative features of program	Significant gains on political efficacy and knowledge of local government compared with controls. Frequency of seminar, seminar quality, and opportunity for involvement at site mediated effects.
Patterson (1987)	H.S.	Community service programs in 10 high schools	E	Self-actualization (Personal Orientation Inventory) and attitudes toward community service	Program characteristics: length of experience, required vs. nonrequired service Student characteristics: family voluntarism level, gender	Fewer than 20 hours service had minimal impact; more than 20 hours required service had negative effect on self-actualization. Family voluntarism not significantly related to self-actualization or attitudes toward community service. Effects differed for males and females.

Study	Sample	Program	Design	Measures	Variables	Results
Hamilton & Fenzel (1988)	11- to 17-yr.-olds	Two types of volunteer experience: community improvement, child care	E1, E2 P/P	Social and personal responsibility; participant and supervisor comments	Gender; age; type of service	Significant gains in social responsibility subscale. Participants reported numerous learning outcomes and high satisfaction. Females -- greater gains in social responsibility. Community improvement program -- stronger effects on social responsibility than child-care program.
Crosman (1989)	H.S.	Friends school required service program	E P/P	Self-esteem; social and personal responsibility; student satisfaction; scores on Characteristics of Experience Checklist	Gender; family service; religious background Types of supervision (faculty, independent, or mixed); intensity of experience; type of reflection (oral, written, combination)	Significant gains in social and personal responsibility. Several characteristics of experience correlated significantly with overall satisfaction (e.g., adult responsibilities, contribution). Students who selected independent projects rated them higher than faculty-supervised students and mixed-supervised. Students rated intensive experiences and experiences combining written and oral reflection higher. Family service and religious background predicted prior service involvement.

Study	Level	Program	Design	Measures	Analysis	Findings
Rutter & Newmann (1989)	H.S.	8 exemplary community service programs	E,C P/P	Self-reported personal development; reported developmental opportunities; civic responsibility, including school, nonschool responsibility, social competence, political efficacy, anticipated community involvement, political activity	School	Participants cited social relationships and personal development as most important outcomes of service. Reported more developmental opportunities in community service than other contexts. Experimental and control students increased in school responsibility and in anticipated social involvement and political activity. Experimental students had greater gains in social competence. Individual school mediated community service outcomes.
Krug (1991)	H.S.	4 service programs: at-risk students, tutoring, student assistant, nature guide	E,C P/P	Self-esteem; attitudes toward school and community	Characteristics of experience as indicated by Characteristics of Experience Checklist and journals	Significant effects for programs involving at-risk and minority students on self-esteem and attitudes toward school and community. Program impacts -- mediated by opportunities for reflection and program planning and supervision.
Procter (1992)	H.S.	4 community service programs in different locations and types of schools (public/private)	E,C P/P	Alienation (social isolation, political efficacy, powerlessness); evaluations of students and teachers	Context and type of community service program	Mixed results. Effects of community service were mediated by context and type of service, e.g., students in all-female, parochial school declined in social isolation; suburban students in urban service program significantly increased in powerlessness. Interviews showed support for community service programs.

Study	Level	Program	Design	Outcomes measured	Independent variables	Results
Middleton (1993)	H.S.	Community service	E,C P/P	Social and psychological outcomes, including social-emotional adjustment, self-esteem, social skills, social interest, helping disposition; self-reported impacts assessed through open-ended questions	Students' ratings on whether they felt needed, felt important, or were allowed to help; number of hours	Quantitative data showed gains from treatment group on self-disclosure. Felt need, felt importance, and number of hours predicted gains in self-disclosure. Participants reported gains in self-esteem, caring, sense of importance, relationship development, and attitudes toward self and others.
Williams (1993)	H.S.	Required community service program	E,C P/P	Social and personal responsibility; satisfaction with experience	Duration of experience; type of service experience (community project, personal, political); Characteristics of Experience Checklist	No significant effects for community service experience of 10 hours on SPRS. More than 10 hours predicted gains in social and personal responsibility regardless of type of service. Four items on Characteristics of Experience measure correlated with satisfaction.
Dewsbury-White (1993)	Mid.S.	Food drive project	E,C P/P	Subject-matter achievement, involvement in service-learning project, extracurricular activities, students' ratings of the meaningfulness of different aspects of the service project	Experiential component (yes or no); instructional model (content integrated vs. isolated)	Students who visited site "better informed" about social problem than those who didn't visit. Content-integrated model of instruction led to significantly higher subject-matter scores. Students considered creation of valued product most meaningful aspect of project.

Author (Year)	Grade level	Program	Design	Measures	Moderators	Findings
Fertman, Buchen & Long (1993)	K-12	44 PennServe school- and community-based programs	E P	Student comments		Students indicated many benefits of service-learning, e.g., ability to influence community and adults' perceptions, ability to relate academic learning to real world. Student concerns related to lack of respect from adults and staff.
Kraft, Goldwasser, Swadener & Timmons (1993)	K-12	28 Colorado ServeAmerica programs	E P/P	Attitudes toward social responsibility, efficacy, school; self-assessment as helpful person; ethnographic data on projects, journals, comments of students and staff	Grade level (middle vs. high school); gender	Ethnographic data and comments highly positive, but pre-posttest showed few differences in attitudes toward social responsibility, efficacy, school. Students increased on one self-concept item: "People feel good ... around me." Males scored lower in attitude and self-concept than females. H.S. students scored higher on a few attitude items.
Silcox (1993)	H.S. (Russian & American students)	Cooperative international environmental project	E P/P	Scientific knowledge; social responsibility; self-confidence; intrinsic motivation; concern for environment; acceptance of others	Nationality (American, Russian)	Significant gains for both groups in scientific knowledge, social responsibility, concern for environment.
Waterman (1993)	H.S.	Literacy Corps project	E,C P/P	Self-esteem, social responsibility, intrinsic/extrinsic academic motivation, reading achievement		Significant increases in self-esteem, social responsibility. Scores on academic motivation remained constant while comparison students showed decrease.

Shumer (1994)	H.S.	Community-Based Learning Program, a drop-out prevention program including community service, civic education, career exploration, academic learning	E,C	Student attendance, grades	Characteristics of programs and students' experiences assessed through participant observation, surveys, case studies	CBL Program -- significant effects on attendance and grades. Surveys, case studies indicated field experience and tutoring most important aspects of CBL Program.
Brill (1994)	Mid.S. & H.S. (with disabilities)	Service-learning projects; most inclusion experiences	E P	Teacher reports of changes in student behavior; academic performance; attitudes; functional skills, socialization, and relationships with nonhandicapped students	Degree of disability	All or nearly all teachers reported improved socialization and attitudes. Several reported improved behavior, academic performance, and attendance. Adolescents with mild disabilities improved in academic skills and attendance. Moderately to profoundly disabled gained in socialization and relationships with nonhandicapped students.
Marks (1994)	H.S.	Service programs in independent schools	E	Community participation, citizen efficacy, social conscience	Gender, ability, religiosity, political orientation; school press (cooperative or individualistic and competitive); degree of integration of service and learning	Service involvement predicted significant gains in citizen efficacy. Gender, ability, religiosity, political orientation were related to participation. Cooperative school press related to higher participation, efficacy, and social conscience than individualistic press. High integration of service with academics positively related to gains in social conscience. Low integration negatively related to efficacy and social conscience.

Author	Grade level	Program	Design	Variables	Moderators	Results
Melchior & Orr (1995)	Mid.S. & H.S.	12 ServeAmerica programs	E, C P/P	Personal and social responsibility, communication skills, work orientation, acceptance of cultural diversity; formal and informal service behaviors, intent to serve; sense of competence and control, attitude toward school and engagement, attendance, GPA, alcohol and drug use	Grade level, gender, race and ethnicity, at-risk status; program type, hours, quality	H.S. participants -- significant gains in personal and social responsibility, communication skills, work orientation. H.S. and Mid.S. students reported increased service behaviors. H.S. and Mid.S. students -- increased attendance; Mid.S. students -- increased hours homework. Few systematic effects for any mediating variable except program quality. Higher-quality programs (more challenge, reflection, etc.) related to greater increases in service involvement, personal and social responsibility, communication skills, work orientation, attendance.
Ridgell (1995)	H.S.	State-mandated 9th grade service-learning program at 3 high schools	E P/P	Personal and social responsibility; locus of control, intent to serve	H.S. program (college prep or standard); gender; involvement in school and community activities outside of service; school	Students in college-prep program had higher personal and social responsibility scores and locus of control. Females scored higher on personal and social responsibility and intent to serve. More-involved students had higher locus of control.

			E			
Yates (1995)	H.S.	Social justice course involving assistance in soup kitchen	P/P	Process of identity development as revealed in transcendent reflections (reflections relating service to personal experience and to social and moral issues) and emotional and relational engagement; plans to volunteer	Prior community service, family service, gender, religious denomination and attendance; initial levels of reflection and engagement	Transcendent reflections increased during service. Service was emotionally engaging for most participants. Service experience and family service predicted level of initial reflection. Level of initial reflection predicted later reflection. Emotional engagement -- prerequisite for increased reflection and plans to volunteer.

Service-Learning and Evaluation:
An Inseparable Process

by Robert Shumer

At a Wingspread conference on service-learning and evaluation, Stephen Hamilton of Cornell University suggested that evaluation was the systematic collection of data to answer specific questions about a program. Michael Patton (1990), national expert on assessment, defines evaluation as "any effort to increase human effectiveness through systematic data-based inquiry" (11). While most people agree on the systematic collection of data, there is much debate over why and how evaluation should be completed. The purpose of this chapter is to explore some of the critical issues in evaluation and to discuss the unique relationship between service-learning and evaluation. What follows is a discussion of the different approaches to evaluation, an examination of the underlying assumptions that separate service-learning from more traditional education, evaluation implications based on those differences, and, finally, concluding examples of how evaluation can be implemented with service-learning programs.

Different Approaches to Evaluation

During the past several decades, discussion in the field of evaluation has centered around different philosophical approaches. Positivistic notions emphasize value-free assessments that usually incorporate mathematical models of prediction and explanation (Scriven 1967; Stufflebeam 1994). Others suggest that evaluation needs to be more responsive and less structured (Guba and Lincoln 1988; Stake 1975), based more on naturalistic methods of inquiry (Fetterman et al. 1996; Patton 1990; Spradley 1980; Van Manen 1990; Whyte 1991). The controversy focuses both on how information is best collected and the role of those being studied in the evaluation process. For the positivists, the goal of evaluation is to measure programs through independent standards that do not actively involve the people and programs being studied in the design of a data-collection process. For the naturalistic group, no meaningful evaluation can be conducted without the active involvement of the program participants throughout information gathering and analysis. The purpose of the evaluation is to understand the world from the perspective of the participants. While there is wide difference between these philosophies (and others, such as participatory research, action research, critical research, and empowerment evaluation), these approaches all have potential for use in assessing service-learning programs.

Some Assumptions About Traditional Education and Service-Learning

To understand the issues of evaluation and service-learning, it is important to examine the fundamental educational principles that separate traditional educational settings from those using service- and community-based programs. In traditional classroom environments, learning occurs primarily through the conveyance of information to students from people (such as teachers and speakers) and symbolic materials, such as books, worksheets, and media (Coleman 1977; Dewey 1938; Freire 1970). The evaluation process assesses what students retain from the information transmitted or requires students to demonstrate solutions to typical problems. Assessments are usually done using some kind of paper-and-pencil process, with all learners in a program evaluated using the same instruments. The learner is frequently described as being outside the evaluation process. Evaluations are done to or on learners to measure outcomes deemed important by sources external to the program (and frequently apart from the faculty member or the administrative unit).

In contrast, exemplary service-learning programs not only include the assessment of information gained but also require the learner and learning system to determine community needs and to assess community outcomes in order to monitor the effectiveness of the service itself. While evaluation is considered an external phenomenon for conventional learning situations, service-learning makes it an integral part of the educational methodology, requiring evaluative processes be applied in order to develop the instructional program. Service-learning integrates evaluation into the very essence of its being at every level, from the individual student to the program to the community served. In service-learning, the student shares control of the evaluation with teachers, community members, and all those impacted by the service activities.

This level of control, among all participants in the service-learning process, illustrates an important distinction between service-learning and traditional education. In traditional programs, power over what is learned usually resides with the teacher and the educational establishment. Students are directed in the learning process, and that direction is dictated by the teacher. Given this normal flow of knowledge, from teacher to student, evaluation systems in traditional settings follow this same pattern, again from teacher to student. Since teachers control the majority of learning, they assess what is learned by focusing on the intended outcomes of the instructional program.

In service-learning, the element of control is diffused — all participants control some aspect of the learning program. The notion of reciprocity of learning is paramount: Each participant learns something from the others. Students learn from and about community members. Teachers learn from students. Community participants learn from students and teachers and, in return, provide instruction about the community and about themselves. Given this scenario of relationships, evaluating service-learning programs is, in fact, multidirectional at all times. No one individual controls all the learning. Responsibility for assessment does not rest just with the teacher; it is shared by all. Embedded in this sharing is the *responsibility* for each and everyone to evaluate the learning process. The fact that the service cannot be separated from the actions of evaluation and learning leads to the conclusion that this is a process of praxis, evaluation praxis. Embedded in all service-learning activities is the unity of service, learning, and evaluation.

Given this understanding, there are many reasons to do evaluation for exemplary service-learning. At minimum, at least eight concerns drive the evaluation:

- Students need to perform community assessments to determine program emphases.
- Students need to evaluate the impact of service activities on the community.
- Students need to evaluate their own learning from the service activities.
- Instructors need to evaluate whether students are learning appropriate information/skills/concepts from the activity.
- Program managers need to determine whether the service-learning method is an effective instructional strategy.
- Community members need to determine the impact of the service on local improvement.
- School district and state standards need to be assessed in terms of student learning.
- Funders and others who financially support service-learning need to determine whether or not to continue their support based on established criteria of success.

Clearly, other questions need to be addressed as one considers the variety of information stakeholders, or people who will use the findings. For K-12 settings, certainly administrators and school boards are interested in evaluating the relative successes of the methodology. In higher education, department chairs, deans, other administrators, and policy formulators need to know whether service-learning is effective in achieving its desired goal.

Roles of Participants in Evaluation

The focus of this essay is on practical issues of how to include and practice evaluation principles and processes as part of the service-learning experience. Emphasis is placed on the role of evaluation for the student, the community, the educational staff, and the educational governance system. Also germane to the topic is the role of teacher preparation systems, including undergraduate and graduate programs and, specifically, programs designed to prepare novice and experienced teachers to implement high-quality service-learning programs.

Students and Teachers as Evaluators

Students are important actors in the service-learning effort. The role of educational institutions is to help prepare learners for all of life's challenges, including employment, family, friendships, civic participation, and the myriad of other tasks required to live a productive, happy, and fulfilling life. Part of this process is not only to help them learn facts but also to instill in them an understanding of the learning process. Dewey (1938) referred to this process as "scientific method" — systematically examining life's challenges with thoughtful approaches that involve asking questions, generating theories or hypotheses to explain how solutions can be achieved, implementing actions to address the problems, *evaluating the results of those actions,* and, finally, determining next steps to address new or sustaining issues related to the initial problems encountered. The goal is to provide learners with the knowledge and skill to do their own assessment.

A scholar who has studied how professionals learn in real-world situations refers to this process as "reflection-on-action" and "reflection-in-action" (Schön 1983, 1990), where evaluation and assessment are key components of the learning process. The major activity in professional practice is determining which issues are to be addressed and then assembling a series of activities to solve the problems. The process of learning about the issues and how they are solved can be called *evaluation.*

Providing learners with the skills and knowledge to perform their own assessment is one way to look at evaluation. Empowerment evaluation (Fetterman et al. 1996) is a concept and practice that connects evaluators with program participants (teachers and other organizational adult practitioners) to engage in a process of continuous program improvement. As with service-learning, the goal of empowerment evaluation is "to help program participants evaluate themselves and their program to improve practice and to foster self-determination. It is necessarily a collaborative group activity, not an individual pursuit" (Fetterman et al. 1996: 5). Fetterman goes on to explain that for empowerment evaluation, the "assessment of program value and worth is not an end point, as it often is with traditional evaluation, but part of the ongoing process of program improvement" (2). The Alliance for Service-Learning in Education Reform (ASLER) Standards of Quality (1995) remind us that exemplary service-learning includes formative and summative evaluation: Programs are always monitored as they develop and assessed at program end for analysis of outcomes [see p. 41]. There is a continuous spiral of action, reflection, and further action that makes both the learner and the community reciprocally "better" for engaging in the process.

What service-learning brings to educational evaluation is the active engagement of students, teachers, and community members. Unlike most evaluation practices (Cousins and Earl 1995), where outside evaluators work with adults in school systems (such as with teachers, administrators, board members), service-learning involves students, teachers, and community members in activities where the curriculum and focus of learning is the evaluation itself. The learning, in this context, is driven by the need to understand what is happening in the program and how it can be continuously improved. Service-learning can engage students as the primary source of evaluation services through their educational programs. Service-learning students are in the perfect position to do much of the work themselves (Campbell, Edgar, and Halstead 1994). The learning of academic subjects is accomplished by participating in collaborative activities with members of the community and the teaching staff. Thus, the need to understand what is learned from the service experience drives the evaluative/reflective processes for all participants.

Teachers, too, engage in evaluation processes. They evaluate what students learn to complete their service activities, how communities respond to the service, and what students actually learn from engaging in the service process. Teachers also study the impact of service on the students themselves, determining how the methodology motivates and enhances learning.

Community Evaluation

Evaluating the impact on community is always required in service-learning programs. It is a shared activity involving students, teachers, and community members, because each has a stake in the outcomes produced. It is important to know and understand the effects of the service on the community. Standards for the field (ASLER 1995) require students to "make meaningful contributions to the community."

Working with communities to be involved in the evaluation process is an important component of service-learning. Sigmon (1979), an early contributor to the field, has suggested several guiding principles for service-learning efforts as they relate to the community, including:

• Principle 1: Those being served control the service(s) provided.

• Principle 2: Those being served become better able to serve and be served by their own actions.

• Principle 3: Those who serve also are learners and have significant control over what is expected to be learned.

Both students and community members participate in the evaluation process by assessing the value of the service delivered and by working to transfer the power of self-evaluation to the community at large. Through a process of using self-help/self-directed materials (Calhoun 1994; Herman et al. 1987; Office for Substance Abuse Prevention 1991; Patton 1987; Shumer and Berkas 1992; Stecher and Davis 1987), one can produce collaborative community evaluators capable of judging what needs are being met and what further needs should be addressed. So service-learning not only means working with school-based program participants on how to do evaluation; it also means helping everyone involved to participate in some evaluation activity.

Undergraduate and Preservice Evaluation

As part of the process of developing school-based evaluation studies, it is possible to use outside individuals and organizations to assist in the overall planning and implementation of evaluation designs. Following models described in various settings (Cousins and Earl 1995; Kraft and Swadener 1994; Neal et al. 1994; Shumer et al. 1995), educational evaluation can be developed and enhanced through participation of local colleges and universities, as well as other organizations with evaluation expertise. Such engagement of faculty, students, and community resources can help program participants develop better designs and more effective reports.

Besides those involved at the school and community levels, preservice teachers, student teachers, and inservice teachers need to know evaluation strategies and techniques. First, all undergraduates, whether in education or not, need to know about theories and practices of evaluation. Such activities need to be included in the undergraduate curriculum, especially as it relates to learning in community settings. These college students should be familiar with both positivistic and naturalistic approaches and should have opportunities to practice these skills in the assessment of their undergraduate experience (Boyer 1987). Whether through service-learning courses, internships, or field studies attached to academic disciplines, undergraduates should have an opportunity to conduct assessments of their own learning and the learning of others. Courses in statistics, ethnographic methods, and other data-collection and assessment approaches need to be part of the preservice experience. Programs such as one that existed in the sociology department at the University of Colorado in the 1970s (Pinto 1994), or in human ecology at Cornell University in the 1980s (Stanton 1990), and in sociology at UCLA in the 1980s and 1990s (Shumer 1990) emphasized undergraduate learning of ethnographic methods as part of their study of social science disciplines. Students had specific coursework in areas related to data collection and analysis, over a period from one to three quarters, as part of their academic program. Students would work in communities, provide forms of service, and apply principles of evaluation to collect information and to write formal ethnographic reports about their investigations. As with all these examples, the integration of service-learning processes into preservice courses provides a context for learning evaluation. Such a context makes the evaluation a meaningful exercise, intimately connected to the development and implementation of educational programs.

Besides the undergraduate experiences, student teachers need to have opportunities to learn and develop their evaluation skills and understandings. It is not enough to just learn about teaching through lecture/methods classes; it is required that student teaching experiences be replete with projects that allow student interns to evaluate student learning and program effectiveness as part of the teacher preparation process.

Service-Learning and Academic Research

While practical evaluation is important for the conduct of service-learning, practitioners can partner with university and professional evaluators to engage in research that tests theories of service-learning. Such studies need to be conducted to challenge the underlying assumptions about service-learning, especially as it affects the development of citizenship skills, academic knowledge, and work-based skills. Examination of the role of service-learning in motivation theory, attribution theory, learning transfer theory, and social learning theory is appropriate to improving our understanding of service as a vehicle for meaningful learning and significant community involvement. Some studies raise important questions about the real impact of service on civic and social development (Newmann and Rutter 1983; Smith 1994). Without strong evaluations that address the theories associated with service-learning, skeptics will continue to question its validity as an educational strategy and its utility as a vehicle for social engagement.

Doing academic research on service-learning is no easy task. Unlike traditional educational programs, where curricula tend to be fixed, the methods of instruction controlled, and the expected outcomes predictable, service-learning is anything but fixed, controllable, and predictable. Often the learning environments are different, the curriculum is developed for specific students at specific sites, and the learning activities vary, depending on the time of day and the person "instructing." Such conditions defy the assumptions of positivistic paradigms and limit the notions of comparability and standardization. Three notable researchers who have conducted many studies of experiential and service-learning, Hedin, Conrad, and Hamilton, conclude that on many occasions the individual student needs to be the unit of analysis and the assessment instruments need to reflect the specific learning that occurs in the field (Conrad and Hedin 1991; Hamilton and Zeldin 1987). To do significant studies that examine the theoretical bases of service requires thoughtful design. It also involves accessibility to well-developed, high-quality service-learning programs and suitable comparisons.

Some Evaluation Models

Although theoretical issues are important, the major focus of evaluation is on program implementation. While theoretical studies will better help to understand the role of service-learning in the education process, evaluation of actual program activities remains the most important application of evaluation practice. The following examples are offered as models to illustrate the kind and scope of evaluation necessary for high-quality service-learning. They are also offered to demonstrate that service-learning, when done properly (Shumer 1987), follows methods of sound educational practice. Learning through service activities should be no different from any other kind of effective learning approach. However, anyone can do service through a variety of community agencies, religious organizations, and individual programs. Schools are not necessary for service to occur; in fact, most service has been done traditionally outside of schools. The primary reason schools and colleges should engage in developing service-learning is because it is assumed that such an instructional method is more effective than traditional programs alone in teaching about academic knowledge and skills, about personal development, and about responsibilities associated with living in a democratic society. Testing this assumption is one of the important reasons to do research and evaluation.

Patton (1990) helps frame the process of evaluation by posing six areas critical to any plan of study. Before creating a design, one should consider the following questions:

1. *Who is the information for and who will use the findings?*
2. *What kinds of information are needed?*
3. *How is the information to be used? For what purposes is evaluation being done?*
4. *When is the information needed?*

5. *What resources are available to conduct the evaluation?*

6. *Given answers to the preceding questions, what methods are appropriate? (12)*

While these questions help structure designs for program evaluations, they are pertinent for any assessment. Questions, in fact, are the driving force for most evaluations (Shumer and Berkas 1992). They frame the intent for students, for teachers, and for all participants in the service-learning process.

In practice, most service-learning evaluations follow prescribed patterns. Just as service-learning programs tend to use preparation, action, and reflection as major activity domains, so too do evaluation cycles go through needs assessment, program development, and evaluation. Usually the initial assessment determines community emphasis: What issues are to be addressed? This is important to guarantee that the program focuses on real concerns, as defined by community members themselves. Next, programs are designed to meet these needs. Students, teachers, and community members work collaboratively to develop the most effective program to deal with the established objectives. Last, students, teachers, and community members all evaluate the effectiveness of the program in meeting stated goals, and each participant evaluates the learning that takes place as the project unfolds.

Melchior and Bailis (1996), two evaluators of national service-learning programs from Brandeis University, recommend some general guidelines for doing evaluation. They suggest there are four critical starting points for teachers who want to evaluate their programs: (1) defining goals, (2) clarifying expectations, (3) looking at information already collected, and (4) documenting what is done. Goals refer to participant, institutional, programmatic, and community focus — determining the purpose or outcomes of the program impact. Clear expectations means describing realistic gains or outcomes. Examining information already collected is a call to not create a whole new set of demands on the program. Determine what kind of data naturally occur and develop a system of evaluation that uses the information already available. Portfolios, student journals, school records, and parent/student/teacher evaluations are good examples of naturally occurring documents. Last, describe the program: What do people do as participants and how are people affected by the student activities? The more explanation, the better the audience understands what is happening and the more likely one can interpret the information collected to show relationships between program and impact.

Program Examples

Two models are presented here to illustrate the evaluation process associated with service-learning in schools and in teacher education programs. The purpose of analyzing these programs is to demonstrate the kind and scope of evaluation practices that can be performed.

A Middle School Initiative

In the first example, we describe an evaluation system for a middle school program. In this case, seventh grade students in a core program are looking to begin a service-learning initiative in their school. The stated purpose is to help meet community needs for youth and to teach students academic and basic skills through the completion of service activities.

As mentioned earlier, the first phase of evaluation for service-learning establishes community needs. Working with the teacher, community leaders, and parents, students construct a written survey to ask what needs there are for youth in a certain age bracket. The survey is distributed to community members, youth (ages 9 to 12, the focus of the study), and parents. To ensure better response rates, students also conduct interviews at a local mall following questions on the survey. Mailed returns and interview responses are analyzed by the class. Students evaluate the data and complete a written report, which is submitted to a parent advisory group and the local Parks and Recreation Department staff for feedback (since the survey identifies recreational activities as the primary need).

The teachers (in a basic core configuration of language arts, math, social studies, and science) continuously perform needs assessments of the tasks required for the project activities. Survey construction, interviewing skills, and statistical and descriptive analysis are taught to help students accomplish their tasks. As the program develops, teachers continue to teach appropriate skills and subject-matter knowledge associated with the project, from speech preparation and delivery to information about the developmental needs of preteens. Written skills as well as math applications are constantly taught in conjunction with the service activities. The teachers evaluate the learning of the first phase's activities by assessing the quality of writing, the math computations, and the oral presentations.

Community members assess the results of the survey by giving feedback to students on their interpretation of the data through the written report. They tell them that they agree with the results of the survey — that there is a real need for more recreation programs through the Parks and Recreation program. This need translates into more sports leagues, with more adult coaches and business sponsors.

During this first phase, each participant group — students, teachers, and community members — performs a needs assessment and evaluative role. Each contributes to the establishment of the next phase of the effort, the actual instructional program.

In a typical second phase of evaluation for service-learning, all members of the initiative, minimally students, teachers, and community members, use the needs assessment data to determine the actual programmatic and instructional activities. In this example, the community need for more recreation programs for children in this age category translates into an active program by the students to recruit new coaches and new business sponsors to assist with the development of the teams. Students decide to develop a speech project to present their case to local business groups, such as the Rotary and Lions Club, to recruit coaches and business sponsors. Working with their teacher, students develop a plan to recruit adult volunteers and business sponsors. Students do some initial research to find out what approaches they should take for each goal. They plan to interview existing coaches and business sponsors to determine why and how they participate. Using this information, coupled with other information provided by their teachers about the art of persuasion, they then develop speeches and presentations to convince adults to join their cause.

Evaluation activities for this second phase involve student assessment of their learning: how and why coaches and business sponsors participate in recreation programs; how to present speeches; how to collect data; and how to arrange to meet with adult service groups. The teacher also evaluates their work, determining how much they learn about oral communication, written communication, and critical thinking. Community members, especially coaches and business sponsors, evaluate the speeches for content and potential effectiveness. Those who hear the speeches also judge the effectiveness of the arguments and the success of the oral presentations. Thus, each participant has an opportunity to evaluate some aspect of the service-learning and potential success of the venture.

As the project moves into the third phase, evaluation of the entire effort, everyone assesses the overall accomplishments of the initiative. This serves as the more summative evaluation, as described in Standard 7 of the ASLER Standards, where major outcomes are reviewed and new goals established. In this example, students count the number of coaches and sponsors recruited and the number of new youth engaged in recreational activities. This report includes percentage of successes, comparing people hearing the speeches with the actual number recruited. Students analyze reasons for their results. They also develop surveys and interview schedules to question Recreation and Parks staff, current coaches and sponsors, and kids in the age group and their parents to determine whether the new coaches, teams, and programs are acceptable and useful in meeting the community needs. Last, they report on future efforts to sustain and expand the current recreational programs in the community.

Teachers evaluate the overall learning achieved by students in the various disciplines supporting the effort: language arts topics in speaking, writing, critical thinking; math topics using statistical presentation of data; social studies topics relating to youth and adult roles in meeting human needs, psychology issues relating to youth development and to persuasion. The service-learning initiative produces many pieces of evidence for these evaluations, including written speeches, survey instruments, oral reports, and written documents. These can be collected in individual student portfolios or through class assignments. Often state discipline frameworks provide guidance in developing the methods of assessment.

Teachers also need to evaluate the effectiveness of the methodology of service-learning in motivating and teaching students the required subjects and skills. Through interviews, students' journals, and parent conferences, information should be available to determine the overall effectiveness of the effort. Input from community members, too, provides valuable feedback about the overall learning produced by the project.

Community members, especially Recreation and Parks staff, coaches, business sponsors, and parents, can assess the overall impact on the targeted youth audience. Through written evaluations and personal testimonials, data can be collected to determine what community members affected by the service initiative thought of the program.

This rather lengthy discussion of the three phases of evaluation illustrates the complexity and continuity of the evaluation process in the development and implementation of service-learning initiatives. Evaluative acts drive the entire agenda, continuously requiring participants to determine what is done, what is learned, and what is taught. The relation between evaluation and the service initiative is inseparable. At each step, the participants, from students to community members, engage in some form of evaluation. It is impossible to proceed with a good educational program without this. Wiggins (1992) sums it up best when he says, "Good assessment is inseparable from good teaching" (32).

A Teacher Education Model

In our second example, we examine the evaluation process for a student teaching program engaged in service-learning. For illustrative purposes, we attach the program to the previous example, focusing on the role of a student teacher assigned to work with the middle school core teaching group. The emphasis of the assignment is on language arts, so we examine that discipline's contribution to the overall effort.

In the first phase of evaluation, the student teacher performs a needs assessment of the community. In this case, that means determining what needs students in the class have in order to perform the learning activities for the project. Using actual project activities, the student teacher assesses student proficiency in doing surveys, conducting oral interviews, and writing reports based on survey and interview data. Based on needs, lessons are constructed that ensure students have the knowledge and skills to perform the necessary tasks.

The formulation of plans, the implementation of instruction, and the analysis of processes and outcomes are continuously shared with the cooperating teacher. Such a partner is consulted for feedback and guidance on development of new approaches. Master teachers are especially important sources of information on both classroom issues and concerns about off-campus instruction. Learning to do service-learning requires expertise in both classroom processes *and* out-of-class methods — tasks more difficult and complicated than regular classroom instruction alone.

In addition to the instructional program assessments, the student teacher maintains a written account of her/his involvement in the entire service-learning initiative. Using personal journals and a case study format (Shulman 1991), the student teacher tracks issues that arise pertaining to actual instruction and to personal concerns related to emotions attached to the teaching process. Frequent opportunities are provided to discuss these personal assessments and comments with both the master teachers and the supervising staff.

During the second phase of the project, the student teacher continues to evaluate the academic and skill needs of the students as they jointly develop the instructional program. Presentation of lessons on formal and informal speeches, as well as formal and informal writing, top the teaching agenda during this portion of the effort. Working with the master teacher, the student teacher pays constant attention to the instructional process, matching lessons and activities with the demonstrated competence of the students. Additionally, the student teacher needs to continuously evaluate the motivational state of students, ensuring that obstacles and issues that arise doing the activities of the project do not deteriorate or become detriments when potentially "bad" experiences occur.

In the last phase, evaluation of the overall effort, the student teacher needs to examine both the instructional lessons and the service activities in promoting good education. Often this process can be framed in district or state requirements for learning outcomes. This is accomplished through review of the oral and written products, as well as through interviews with students themselves. Students in the class provide important information to the novice teacher about the relative impact of the service experience in learning the skills and subjects normally taught in school. In this case, the reciprocal roles are highlighted, with the students "teaching the teacher" about the difference between traditional and service-learning programs.

Thus, the evaluation process for student teachers follows the three phases found in most service-learning programs. In this example, the focus of reflection and evaluation is on the interaction among community needs, student needs, and the instructional program that arises as a result of the continuous interaction. Learning to do service-learning involves constant assessment of the connections among students, instructional activities, and community engagement. New teachers have the arduous responsibility to try to make sense of the whole process as they experiment with and practice teaching in a complex educational system. The challenges are greater than simply learning to teach in a classroom-based program, yet the rewards of mastering the system are exhilarating.

Conclusion

Evaluation is embedded in good service-learning. As one reflects on or measures the value of the service experience, evaluation becomes a significant driving force behind the learning. Evaluation occurs at all levels and among all participants in the service initiative. Students assess the need for service, the effectiveness of the program established to meet the community needs, and the personal learning that takes place as the process unfolds. Teachers assess the effectiveness of the strategy for good teaching, what students learn from the experience, and the quality of learning that takes place in the community. Community members (those receiving service) evaluate the effectiveness of the service program in meeting their needs. Program administrators evaluate whether or not service-learning programs achieve their desired outcomes. Student teachers evaluate the instructional requirements presented by service-learning projects, the effectiveness of the instruction in supporting the knowledge and skill needs of the students, and the overall impact of the learning and products on the attitudes of students toward learning, school, and personal development. The list goes on: Everyone involved in the learning segment of the service is engaged in some form of assessment.

The relationships between service-learning and evaluation go far beyond the expectations outlined in the ASLER Standards. Doing "formative and summative evaluations" is a given in good programs, yet evaluation is much more intimately tied to the learning activities of students, community members, and those developing programs. Formative evaluation is not just a programmatic requirement done by external evaluators; it applies to all who participate in or who are affected by the service-learning program.

Service-learning and evaluation are inseparable. The notion of evaluation praxis, that is, the interconnectedness of evaluation and instruction, perhaps best describes this unique congruence of program and practice.

References

Alliance for Service-Learning in Education Reform. (1995). *Standards of Quality for School-Based and Community-Based Service-Learning.* Chester, VT: SerVermont.

Boyer, E.L. (1987). *College: The Undergraduate Experience in America.* New York, NY: Harper & Row.

Calhoun, E.F. (1994). *How to Use Action Research in the Self-Renewing School.* Alexandria, VA: Association for Supervision and Curriculum Development.

Campbell, P., S. Edgar, and A. Halstead. (1994). "Students as Evaluators." *Phi Delta Kappan* 76(2): 160-165.

Coleman, J.S. (1977). "Differences Between Experiential Education and Classroom Learning." In *Experiential Learning: Rationale, Characteristics, and Assessment,* edited by Morris T. Keeton, pp. 49-51. San Francisco, CA: Jossey-Bass.

Conrad, D., and D. Hedin. (1991). "School-Based Community Service: What We Know From Research and Theory." *Phi Delta Kappan* 72(10): 743-749.

Cousins, J.B., and L. Earl, eds. (1995). *Participatory Evaluation in Education: Studies in Evaluation Use and Organizational Learning.* London, Eng.: Falmer Press.

Dewey, J. (1938). *Experience and Education.* New York, NY: Collier Books.

Fetterman, M., S. Kaftarian, and A. Wandersman, eds. (1996). *Empowerment Evaluation: Knowledge and Tools for Self-Assessment and Accountability.* Thousand Oaks, CA: Sage.

Freire, P. (1970). *Pedagogy of the Oppressed.* Translated by M.B. Ramos. New York, NY: Herder & Herder.

Guba, E., and Y. Lincoln. (1988). *Effective Evaluation: Improving the Usefulness of Evaluation Results Through Responsive and Naturalistic Evaluation Approaches* San Francisco, CA: Jossey-Bass.

Hamilton, S.F., and R.S. Zeldin. (Winter 1987). "Learning Civics in the Community." *Curriculum Inquiry* 17(4): 407-420.

Herman, J., L. Morris, and C.T. Fitz-Gibbon. (1987). *Evaluator's Handbook.* Newbury Park, CA: Sage.

Kraft, R.J., and M. Swadener, eds. (1994). *Building Community: Service-Learning in the Academic Disciplines.* Denver, CO: Colorado Campus Compact.

Melchior, A., and L. Bailis. (Spring 1996). "Evaluating Service-Learning: Practical Tips for Teachers." *CRF Network* 4(4): 1-4.

Neal, M., R. Shumer, and K. Gorak, eds. (1994). *Evaluation: The Key to Improving Service-Learning Programs*. St. Paul, MN: Center for Experiential Education and Service-Learning, University of Minnesota.

Newmann, F.M., and R.A. Rutter. (1983). *The Effects of High School Community Service Programs on Students' Social Development*. Final Report. Madison, WI: Wisconsin Center for Educational Research.

Office for Substance Abuse Prevention. (1991). *Prevention Plus: Assessing Alcohol and Other Drug Prevention Programs at the School and Community Level*. Rockville, MD: U.S. Department of Health and Human Services.

Patton, M.Q. (1987). *How to Use Qualitative Methods in Evaluation*. Newbury Park, CA: Sage.

———. (1990). *Qualitative Evaluation and Research Methods*. 2d ed. Newbury Park, CA: Sage.

Pinto, L. (1994). "Service-Learning Propelled by Action Research: A Quarter of a Century of Glory to Ashes, Ashes to Glory, and More of the Same." In *Building Community: Service-Learning in the Academic Disciplines*, edited by R. Kraft and M. Swadener, pp. 49-58. Denver, CO: Colorado Campus Compact.

Schön, D.A. (1983). *The Reflective Practitioner*. New York, NY: Basic Books.

———. (1990). *Educating the Reflective Practitioner*. San Francisco, CA: Jossey-Bass.

Scriven, M.S. (1967). "The Methodology of Evaluation." In *Curriculum Evaluation*, edited by R.E. Stake. AERA Monograph Series on Curriculum Evaluation, Vol.1. Chicago, IL: Rand McNally.

Shulman, J.M. (November 1991). "Classroom Casebooks." *Educational Leadership* 49(3): 28-31.

Shumer, R. (1987). "Learning and the Workplace — An Ethnographic Study of the Relationship Between Schools and Experiential-Based Educational Programs." Unpublished doctoral dissertation, University of California, Los Angeles.

———. (1990). *Field Studies Guide*. Los Angeles, CA: University of California–Los Angeles, Field Studies Development.

———, and T. Berkas. (1992). *Doing Self-Directed Study for Service-Learning*. St. Paul, MN: University of Minnesota, Department of Vocational and Technical Education.

Shumer, R., J. Maland Cady, et al., eds. (1995). *Youth Works. AmeriCorps Evaluation: First Year Report, 1994-95*. St. Paul, MN: University of Minnesota, Department of Vocational and Technical Education.

Sigmon, R.L. (Spring 1979). "Service-Learning: Three Principles." *Action* 8(1): 9-11.

Smith, M.W. (Fall 1994). "Community Service Learning: Striking the Chord of Citizenship." *Michigan Journal of Community Service Learning* 1(1): 37-43.

Spradley, J.P. (1980). *Participant Observation*. New York, NY: Holt, Rinehart & Winston.

Stake, R.E. (1975). *Evaluating the Arts in Education: A Responsive Approach.* Columbus, OH: Charles E. Merrill.

Stanton, T. (1990). "Service-Learning and Leadership Development." In *Combining Service and Learning: A Resource Book for Community and Public Service,* edited by J. Kendall, pp. 336-353. Raleigh, NC: National Society for Internships and Experiential Education.

Stecher, B., and A. Davis. (1987). *How to Focus an Evaluation.* Newbury Park, CA: Sage.

Stufflebeam, D.L. (1994). "Empowerment Evaluation, Objectivist Evaluation, and Evaluation Standards: Where the Future of Evaluation Should Not Go and Where It Needs to Go." *Evaluation Practice* 15(3): 321-338.

Van Manen, M. (1990). *Researching Lived Experience: Human Science for an Action Sensitive Pedagogy.* Albany, NY: State University of New York Press.

Whyte, W.F., ed. (1991). *Participatory Action Research.* Newbury Park, CA: Sage.

Wiggins, G. (May 1992). "Creating Tests Worth Taking." *Educational Leadership* 49(8): 26-33.

Service-Learning Professional Development for Experienced Teachers

by Don Hill and Denise Clark Pope

The differences between new and experienced teachers suggest creative approaches to professional development. Preservice teachers spend a year (sometimes two years) studying the field of education and working diligently to develop new curricula and to practice pedagogical techniques that are often at the cutting edge of educational reform. Many enter the field with a strong sense of idealism, hoping to make a difference in the lives of the children they will teach; in addition, many show a strong naiveté about working in schools and the frenetic day-to-day existence of busy teachers. Experienced teachers, on the other hand, often do not have the time or energy to keep up with the latest school-reform efforts, and many scoff at what they believe are ever-changing fads being touted by schools of education. We hear from the veteran teachers, "We tried that 20 years ago. Who has time to create completely new curricula? Got any proof that this new stuff works better than what I already use? My kids are doing fine. Let me close my classroom door and get back to doing what I do best. . . ." The idealism is still there, but it has been tempered by the reality of the almost impossible demands the educational system places upon teachers and the coping mechanisms many have developed to survive in the occupation for so many years.

In the following essay, we synthesize some of what we have learned over the years while providing service-learning professional development for experienced teachers at the Service Learning 2000 Center, a project of the Stanford University School of Education. We have organized the chapter into five "key challenges" that seemed particularly relevant for this book. We use concrete examples to explain strategies we have used to overcome (or at least ameliorate) the following five challenges:

1. enticing interest in service-learning as a teaching strategy;

2. helping teachers craft service-learning projects that are integrated into the curriculum;

3. designing workshops to increase the chances that teachers will actually implement the projects they develop;

4. facilitating effective reflection strategies for teachers to use with their students;

5. finding effective ways to help teachers build collegial support at their school sites.

These five challenges are relevant for both inservice teacher professional development and preservice teacher education. In fact, some of the strategies we suggest for meeting such challenges have been used successfully for both new and experienced educators. However, we have based these approaches on our understanding of the different realities inservice and preservice teachers face each day. In addition to a general difference in attitude toward school-reform efforts, experienced teachers often establish relatively set curricula and tend to have little time to consider changing the way they conceptualize and promote learning in their classrooms. The professional development activities described below have been designed to help entice teachers to use service-learning to enhance existing curricula and to encourage them to experiment with pedagogical methods.

Before addressing these five specific challenges, we would like to offer some general principles we use in our work that encourage effective professional development:

- Honor and respect teachers for what they know and do.
- Walk your talk. Collaborate when you talk about collaboration, use students when you discuss student voice, and evaluate your programs the same way you recommend participants evaluate theirs.
- Provide quality work time for teachers to wrestle with their own service-learning challenges, even when that means eliminating valuable content from your workshops.
- Establish and nourish a learning environment that is serious but playful, where people feel encouraged to share honest feelings and risk trying new ideas and skills.
- Plan formal and informal opportunities for constructive feedback from workshop colleagues and staff.
- Culminate workshops by sharing concrete projects and specific plans for action.

We describe below how we have attempted to apply these principles to five important professional development challenges that must be handled well if service-learning is to become a valued and sustainable educational method in K-12 schools.

Challenge 1: Enticing Interest in Service-Learning as a Teaching Strategy

Professional development fails immediately unless it entices teachers to imagine a practical payoff for serious involvement. This poses special difficulties for people seeking to promote service-learning because implementing the reform appears on the surface to be an impossible task. Service-learning, at first glance, looks like a program that asks teachers to add one more element to an already overburdened curriculum, spend hours of out-of-class time making connections with agency representatives, and create a system for overseeing and evaluating student work off campus. Such a formidable program understandably leads to teacher hesitation if not open opposition. Imagine the following faculty meeting scenario, for example:

> The principal and two teachers at Arundel High School have long been advocates of service-learning. For three years, the teachers have integrated service-learning projects in their courses, which have been widely praised. Yet no other staff members at the school have expressed interest in using service-learning. Last year, the two teachers made a short presentation on their programs at a faculty meeting and invited teachers to meet with them at lunch the following week to discuss how service-learning might be incorporated into other school courses. No teachers came to talk. Refusing to give up, the principal arranged a three-hour morning workshop for the entire faculty on service-learning later in the year and invited an outside service-learning facilitator to lead the workshop.

Staff at the Service Learning 2000 Center have walked into this situation many times. In order for teachers at Arundel or similar schools to seriously consider using service-learning, they must first understand what it means, visualize how it might work with their own students, and feel that it could be worth the effort. A three-hour workshop can be a wonderful opportunity to move teachers from a natural stance of ill-informed suspicion and hostility to one of open exploration of ideas for future implementation. Although each school and faculty pose unique opportunities and challenges, there are a number of general strategies that help improve the chances for success:

1. *Begin the workshop by confirming an awareness of the teaching realities the faculty is facing and by offering a low-key approach to service-learning as a possible resource.* Be a person who helps teachers decide whether service-learning could be a good fit for the school rather than a salesperson who thinks she has a nifty solution in her briefcase.

2. *At the outset, ascertain the degree of service-learning knowledge among the faculty.* A simple way to do this is to place a spectrum line numbered 1 to 10 on an overhead or easel pad, with number 1 defined as someone who has never heard of service-learning and number 10 as someone who could be leading the workshop. By asking audience members to select the number that best represents their degree of service-learning knowledge, you can create a visual graph of faculty knowledge by a quick show of hands. This exercise also works well when a spectrum line is placed on the classroom floor and participants are asked to walk to the position that best represents their degree of service-learning knowledge. This modification allows participants to literally see where they "stand" vis-à-vis other workshop colleagues.

This two-minute exercise tends to encourage audience comfort and respect because it gives participants a sense of the group and where they fit in. It is also an effective way to gather quick insight as well as being an instructional idea that can easily be adapted by teachers for classroom use.

3. *Provide a variety of ways for faculty to learn about service-learning.* One good way to get faculty interested in the value of service-learning is to invite students to talk about their experiences. When students talk with excitement and pride about service-learning, faculty listen. They are particularly impressed when students who have been turned off to school explain how and why their attitudes have been transformed. Inviting faculty who teach similar students in similar schools is also very effective, particularly when faculty candidly share what worked well and what was difficult. Videos are another way to entice interest. Even a video of modest quality, awkwardly created by students and teachers, often rings more true and can be more persuasive than a highly polished, professional production. Somehow, when teachers can say to themselves, "This teacher [or video] illustrates something I could do," they tend to look more favorably on service-learning.

4. *Arrange for teachers to participate in a service project as part of the workshop.* Involving teachers directly in service may be the single most effective way to entice interest. This is especially true if time is set aside for teachers to share how they felt about their service experiences and to discuss what they learned. Even relatively simple experiences such as spending an hour interviewing a senior citizen at a retirement home and writing a reflection piece on the visit have profoundly impacted teachers and have helped them to understand how similar experiences could affect their students.

5. *Clearly establish a small number of knowledge goals for the workshop.* These goals provide a framework for teachers to think about service-learning as a possible instructional strategy and can be revisited at the end of the workshop to demonstrate to participants the knowledge they have gained. Furthermore, it is much easier and more productive to advocate an understanding of service-learning than to push for its implementation. We suggest that by the end of an introductory workshop, all participants will know:

- the difference between service-learning and community service;
- five or six key elements of high-quality service-learning.

6. *Structure the majority of time for teachers to work in small groups* applying service-learning concepts to classroom and school situations that are roughly analogous to their school realities. We illustrate this small-group process in the following discussion of Challenge 2, which includes strategies to teach the difference between community service and service-learning and how to reinforce understanding of the key elements of high-quality service-learning.

Challenge 2: Helping Teachers Craft Service-Learning Projects That Are Integrated Into the Curriculum

Service-learning, by common definition, means integrating community service with classroom instruction. Service-learning, by common practice, can simply mean doing community service for classroom or school credit. The crucial difference between these two realities poses complex challenges for professional development. Although explaining the distinction is relatively easy, doing it in a way that does not undercut the accomplishments and feelings of teachers who currently use community service is a more subtle challenge. This is an important subtlety, moreover, because teachers who value community service are normally the best resources for developing service-learning programs.

The Service Learning 2000 Center has often been asked by service-learning coordinators to come to a school that has a strong reputation for its "service-learning" program. Upon closer examination, we find a good community service program that needs to be transformed into a quality service-learning program. We approach this staff development challenge by designing a series of highly interactive small-group experiences that ask teachers to use their knowledge and skills to help shape the meaning of high-quality service-learning. One of the most successful ways to get teachers to conceive of the possibility that they might use service-learning in their classrooms — a necessary first step to actual implementation — is to engage them in simulated situations where they talk and think as if they already were practicing service-learning teachers.

Before they are ready for the simulations, however, teachers need to understand the differences between community service and service-learning. We begin by presenting the Service Learning 2000 Center quadrant diagram (Figure 1). This diagram uses two intersecting spectrum lines to create four quadrants. At the Unrelated Learning point on the left end of the horizontal line, there is no connection between service and what is being taught in the classroom. At the Integrated Learning point on the right end of the horizontal line, service is tightly woven into the goals of the class. At the Low Service point on the bottom of the vertical line, there is either little or no service. At the High Service point at the top of the vertical line, the service is well organized and meets an important community need. The ultimate goal is to develop projects that fit in quadrant II in the top right corner of the diagram because they promote "high service" and are "highly integrated" into the curriculum.

After explaining the quadrant diagram, we pass out a small number of service project descriptions (Figure 2 on p. 96) and ask teachers individually, and then in small groups, to plot each description in one of the four quad-

Figure 1

The Service Learning Quadrant

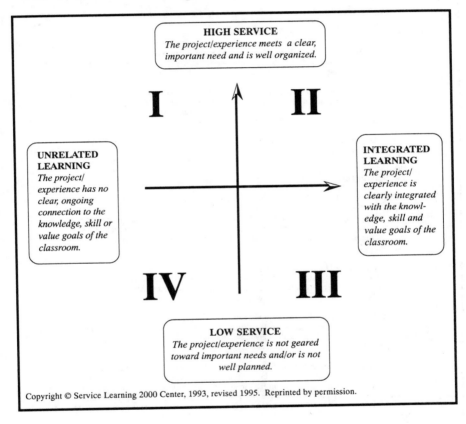

HIGH SERVICE
The project/experience meets a clear, important need and is well organized.

I   II

UNRELATED LEARNING
The project/experience has no clear, ongoing connection to the knowledge, skill or value goals of the classroom.

INTEGRATED LEARNING
The project/experience is clearly integrated with the knowledge, skill and value goals of the classroom.

IV   III

LOW SERVICE
The project/experience is not geared toward important needs and/or is not well planned.

Copyright © Service Learning 2000 Center, 1993, revised 1995. Reprinted by permission.

Figure 2

Quadrant Exercise

Read each case and decide where it belongs on the Service Learning Quadrant.

A. The Oxnard school district votes to require that all students contribute ten hours of voluntary service to their high school every year to deal directly with increasing problems of campus vandalism which have almost brought classroom instruction to a halt. A clerk in the counseling office is assigned to record participation hours so that handling the service requirement does not become an extra burden for classroom teachers.

B. Mrs. Templeton organizes her middle school program to help a neighboring elementary school restore music in its curriculum. Students in her classes go to the elementary school and tutor individual students in how to play instruments. The tutoring program culminates with a joint concert at the end of the year.

C. The teachers at Joaquin Miller Middle School decide that all their students should be doing community service. In order to avoid a logistical nightmare, they contract with their local Volunteer Center to place three hundred of their students in non-profit agencies and to track the number of hours students are working. The students are placed in a wide variety of jobs.

D. The freshman English teachers at Mandalay High School organize their curriculum around the theme of community. In addition to reading literature that focuses on community issues, all students are asked to volunteer during the school year to contribute to either their school or local community. An adult volunteer is the service; she helps place students in a wide variety of projects that run from working on a farm, to volunteering in a blood bank.

E. Mr. Snickers uses homelessness as a central theme for a nine week unit in his English class. In addition to reading a novel about homeless youth, and several poems providing a variety of perspectives on the homeless, his students write and act out a series of skits in class on different problems faced by the homeless.

F. Mrs. Cardoza spends two weeks in her fifth grade class studying how many different cultures have celebrations similar to Thanksgiving in America. Students bring in cans at the end of the unit which she delivers to Second Harvest Food Bank to help give a little bit of Thanksgiving to people in need.

G. Ms. Ramirez organizes her general science class to increase earthquake preparedness in her students' neighborhoods. She begins this project by having speakers from the U.S. Geological Survey and going on field trips organized by grad students in geology at UC Berkeley. The project culminates when students create earthquake preparedness pamphlets in English and Spanish and go in teams of two to distribute the pamphlets to their neighbors.

Service Learning 2000 Center
50 Embarcadero Road Palo Alto CA 94301 415-322-7271 fax 415-328-8024

rants. These descriptions include strong quadrant II projects, community service projects similar to those offered at the school, and projects that illustrate each quadrant section. Invariably, after active discussion, teachers learn to apply the quadrant design effectively and reach consensus on where to plot most, if not all, projects.

It is important, however, to culminate this exercise by asking small groups to take one or more projects that are not in quadrant II and to brainstorm specific ways to move the project in that direction. This activity is particularly powerful if projects are selected that are similar to existing school efforts so that staff can use their own thinking to offer significant improvements. For example, elementary school teachers who organize canned food drives that are totally disconnected to the curriculum typically think of an array of ways to connect the drive to important ideas they teach, such as nutritional health, weights and measures, and food preferences in different cultures.

Case study analysis is another effective way to stimulate teachers to think like service-learning practitioners. We use a case in which a small group of teachers plan an ambitious park cleanup and senior citizen project for their students (Figure 3 on pp. 98-99). The case includes details about the planning process and student experiences at two sites in order to provide a concrete context for talking about implementation. Although both projects include a number of positive goals and illustrate a lot of hard work by the teachers, they also illustrate the consequences of not respecting the key elements of high-quality service-learning. For example, not involving students in the selection of the park for the cleanup day led to a lack of interest and commitment on the part of the students, since the park selected was not in their immediate community.

We normally introduce five or six key elements of high-quality service-learning (see Figure 4 on p. 100) before passing out the case, and we then ask teachers to use these elements to assess the key decisions the teachers made in the case. In the process of reading the case and discussing the issues that emerge, teachers instinctively begin to internalize elements of high-quality service-learning and start to sound like service-learning practitioners.

Understanding the difference between community service and service-learning, however, is only the first step toward development of high-quality service-learning curricula. We recommend selecting a few detailed descriptions of high-quality service-learning curricula that include specific knowledge, skill, and value goals for students as well as several service and learning activities. Discussion of these concrete examples can then be used to help teachers think about the design of their own classroom curriculum. It is particularly important to ask teachers to include in their curriculum

Figure 3

A Service Learning Case Study- Juanita Elementary School

As you read the case study, identify the decisions or actions taken by José and Laurie which you believe contribute to the project's problems. Indicate in the margins the places where the elements of high quality service learning are ignored or violated.

Laurie and José began their third year of teaching at Juanita Elementary School full of excitement and renewed dedication. Encouraged by a friend at a neighboring school, they had applied to become a Pilot Service Learning Project which provided them with permission to work together as a team for their two fifth grade classes as well as granting four days of released time to plan. Their Project called for José to teach writing to both classes and Laurie to teach science to both classes. Most importantly, it called on them to develop a service learning strand that would "make their English and Science curriculums come alive."

This team teaching opportunity could not have come at a better time. Laurie and José had both started to become discouraged with teaching because their students increasingly seemed more interested in being entertained than in trying to learn. In addition, most of the faculty and the principal seemed much more concerned about controlling behavior than developing stimulating teaching strategies to make the curriculum engaging and meaningful.

Now they were certain that this year would be different. Mr. Cardozo, the principal, might not have understood what service learning was all about, but he had signed their Pilot proposal without asking any questions and congratulated them for being selected. He seldom visited their classrooms and certainly would not pay much attention to how they crafted their service activities.

Laurie and José called their Pilot "Connecting Learning with Community Life." The service learning part of the pilot called for combining their two classes to work on large scale community service activities and to set up activities for small groups of students to do service in agencies.

During the summer, José contacted the Happy Palms Senior Home to make arrangements for students in both classes to visit in groups of eight accompanied by an adult supervisor. The Director agreed to assign a nurse to meet the children and make suggestions for what the children could do during their one hour visits. He also agreed to assign someone to help make sure that all students were connected with their driver at the end of the visits. José also met with the Director during a day of released time to review goals for the project, go over details, and explain how he planned to have the students use their experience at the Happy Palms to stimulate a series of personal writing assignments during the school year.

Laurie focused her time in the summer on establishing contacts with the Recreation Department to plan two Saturday morning clean-up days at Central Park during the fall. She also attended a service learning workshop to learn strategies for getting kids "serving and learning together."

Late summer and September enthusiasm began unraveling in October after the first two visits of students to the Happy Palms Home. The second week in October, José walked into his late Thursday afternoon weekly planning session with Laurie and dumped a pile of reflection cards on her desk written by students the morning after their one hour visit to the home.. "I think we might have a tiny speck of trouble here," he said. Laurie felt her face start to twitch and her stomach tighten as she flipped through the student comments:

"Those people were yucky."
"I was so scared."
"Why do old people smell so bad?"
"Please don't make me go back."
"I don't want to ever grow old."
"I didn't know what to do or say. My old man was asleep."
"The lady I talked to seemed so lonely. She didn't want me to leave. I think I made her feel a

little better."

"My mom says it's wrong to send people away to die."

"My lady asked me why I was there and I didn't know what to say."

"I really liked the man I met. He asked me to push him down to a Bingo game but the nurse said we had to go back to his room."

Laurie looked up and said, "You're right. We need to think this over, but not now. We need to talk about next Saturday before that becomes a second crisis." She then went on to explain that she planned to begin the park clean-up day in the school's multiple purpose room with an activity that she had learned at her service learning workshop. Then, a district bus would pick up all the students and take them to Central Park. Recreation Department workers would meet the students and give them bags to collect debris and also some rakes for the bigger kids to use. The day would end with a picnic at noon that a group of parents and supervising adults from her class had agreed to provide.

Saturday was not a winner. Laurie had placed six huge outlines of human bodies on butcher paper in different areas of the multipurpose room floor. When the students arrived, she organized them into six teams of seven and asked each student on the teams to select a key part of the outlined body and print on that part how it could contribute to community service. Laurie looked forward to seeing the kids conceptualize and visually represent ideas like the service learning consultant had demonstrated in the summer. She expected students to circle the heart and write words like love and compassion and circle the head and write words like analyze and solve problems. What happened was a lot of confused, chaotic chatter and expressions like "the heart pumps blood", "the head protects the brain" and "feet let us stand up."

Disappointment with the "great body activity" quickly faded from Laurie and José's memory as soon as the district bus dropped the kids off at Central Park. The Recreation Department gave each student a bright orange bag and directed them in teams of two to specific areas. The kids began working with enthusiasm and amazing dedication. Laurie and José stood together watching their students with relaxed smiles tinged with surprise and pride.

But, with almost two hours left in the morning, most students started to get bored. They began to wander away from their team to pair off with friends or go off by themselves. Everyone stopped working except for four or five kids. To make matters worse, a Youth Authority van pulled up and a group of older youths accompanied by a uniformed officer got out and began doing the same work at a different section of the park. The adult volunteers setting up the picnic started to get nervous about what they called "these juvenile delinquents," while the fifth graders watched with fascination. A parent volunteer turned to Laurie and said, "It seems strange your students are volunteering their Saturday time to do something that convicted young offenders are doing for community service punishment."

A second volunteer, the older brother of one of the fifth graders, asked José why he had chosen this park for clean up when almost none of the kids ever used it themselves. Couldn't the students do something closer to home?

The day ended with a great picnic that all the kids really enjoyed. The food represented favorites from several cultures and there was enough left over to make a major donation to the Father Joseph Food Kitchen on the way home. José and Laurie enjoyed watching the kids eating and playing together but they could not shake off the two troubling questions posed by the adult volunteers.

Monday was a day not to remember. Mr. Cardozo summoned Laurie and José to his office at the beginning of the lunch period.

"I received a call this morning from the mother of a child who was very upset after visiting some kind of a senior home in one of your classes. I didn't know what she was talking about. I calmed her down by saying that there would be no more trips to senior homes this year. I confirmed to her that education at Juanita starts and ends at the school.

"Could you please tell me what is going on around here? I do not want to get any more phone calls about either of your classes."

Figure 4

Elements of High Quality Service Learning

1. *Integrated Learning*

   When integrated learning occurs, the service activity enhances the important knowledge, value, or skill goals of the class or school.

2. *High Service*

   Work that is considered high service meets a real need in the community (as defined by the community), is age appropriate, well-organized, and gets something done.

3. *Student Voice*

   Students should be engaged in as many aspects of project planning as possible.

4. *Reflection*

   Reflection should take place before (to prepare), during (to troubleshoot), and after (to process) service activities.

5. *Collaboration*

   All stakeholders (including administrators, agencies, businesses, community members, parents, students, teachers) are involved in planning, execution and evaluation.

 Service Learning 2000 Center

design a specific description of the connection between student service activities and classroom learning. Helping teachers to find the words to describe this integration of service experiences with learning goals is both difficult and important.

One might think that the war is won when teachers understand what service-learning is and complete a tentative curriculum design for their classroom. Our experience suggests, however, that effective preparation is not the same as actual implementation. Maximizing chances for implementation is the subject of the next challenge.

Challenge 3: Designing Workshops to Increase the Chances That Teachers Will Actually Implement the Projects They Develop

Too often we hear of innovative professional development programs that offer a few days' worth of exciting teaching strategies, engage educators in active learning, and stimulate reflective conversations about school reform. Then, at the end of the program, the educators thank the leaders for running a top-notch program, return to their respective school sites, close their classroom doors, and teach in much the same way they did before the professional development opportunity. We can't really blame these educators. They are busy. They have existing curriculum units with which they have had success. It is much easier to return to old familiar ways than to embark down new paths that demand creative energy, unfamiliar teaching techniques, and often hours of work to set up service opportunities and develop strong curricular ties. Our challenge as experienced teacher educators is to design high-quality professional development programs where the teachers actually implement the service-learning projects they develop in our programs.

Over the years, we have generated specific strategies to approach this challenge. Rather than just talk about service-learning pedagogy and curriculum, we spend much of our professional development time helping teachers develop quality service-learning projects *during* our workshops and institutes. For instance, participants at our two-day curriculum development workshops receive their curriculum assignment on the first day. They have the next two days to work with their teammates to develop the framework for a high-quality service-learning curriculum to implement in the fall. We set up the parameters of the assignment early on: The educators will complete a "service-learning curriculum development portfolio" by the end of the workshop and will present a one-page overview of their project to the large group. Ideally, the completed curricula will model the center's principles for high-quality service-learning. Specifically, the service activities will be integrated into the curriculum and will address real community needs. In addition, the service-learning project will feature strong collaboration with the community and will allow ample time for students to reflect on their learning and for students to voice their opinions throughout the project. Finally, the teachers are asked to include ideas for "authentic assessment" strategies and evaluation techniques as well as a tentative time line for implementation in the fall semester. With a detailed design in hand, teachers are more likely to follow through with implementation plans.

In each case, we encourage teachers to start small and simple. We know from experience that big projects tend to fail: They sap time and energy and leave teachers feeling frustrated and overwhelmed. Small projects that lead to small successes often result in the personal satisfaction and confidence that is needed to build larger projects in the future. This general strategy helps to ensure that the teachers will develop high-quality projects and helps to facilitate a smooth implementation process in September.

After running curriculum development workshops over the years, we have found the following guidelines to be most helpful:

1. *Strike a balance between instruction time and work time for teams of teachers.* We do our best to incorporate teacher work time into most of our professional development workshops, often cutting back on direct instruction to allow ample opportunities for teachers to develop their curriculum projects. Workshop participants usually have up to three hours a day to meet with teammates to brainstorm project ideas and to develop specific service-learning lessons. We usually require teachers to come to the workshops in teams of two or more, comprising any combination of classroom teachers, administrators, community agency staff, parents — anyone who is committed to implementing the service-learning project. We've found that the collegiality and the enthusiasm generated in the teams often helps to counteract frustration and the temptation to abandon the project that may occur when the difficult task of implementation begins.

2. *Break down the curriculum development process into small, doable steps through the use of a portfolio.* In order to help ensure that the teacher work time is productive, we have designed a curriculum development portfolio that breaks the development tasks into small, critical steps. Depending on the specific workshop, the portfolio may include pages on personal motivation for integrating service-learning into classes, a description of the current class into which you hope to integrate service-learning, a project brainstorm, specific learning goals and service goals for students, ways to involve youth in the planning of the curriculum, reflection activities, effective community collaboration, logistical concerns, a tentative evaluation plan, and/or a page on getting started.

For example, team members may work on specific portfolio pages designed to encourage thinking about effective community collaboration. One page (Figure 5 on p. 104) asks teams to list and rank the other partners that will be involved in project planning and implementation, including less active partners such as district administrators and local businesses that nonetheless may play a role in the final project. Another page (Figure 6 on p. 105) asks them to brainstorm a list of community-based organizations in their area that may be useful for their projects.

When the workshop comes to an end, most teams will have done some good thinking about each aspect of service-learning curriculum mentioned in the portfolio, and many will have quality project ideas that they can later fine-tune and implement.

3. *Use professional and peer coaches to provide effective curriculum development consultation.* During the daily teacher work times, center staff members and experienced service-learning practitioners serve as team coaches; they circulate from team to team, listening to the planning process, offering advice, and answering questions about the portfolio assignments. These coaching sessions provide ongoing information on issues that may cause difficulty, and they help to motivate teams to produce quality projects. In addition, each team participates in a peer review process where team members present their curricula to other school teams for further improvement. Both the coaching and the peer review opportunities gently force teams to work through the entire portfolio process and to leave the workshop with better-developed projects.

We often use the service-learning "dipsticks" illustrated in Figure 7 (on p. 106) to help peer review teams focus on specific project areas that need improvement.

4. *Plan several opportunities for future networking and technical assistance.* At the end of the workshop, the center's work is not yet complete. To further encourage teachers to actually implement their projects, center staff work hard to keep in touch with participants and to monitor their progress. We often hold reunion meetings to celebrate implementation progress and to offer collegial support to those who are facing unforeseen obstacles. We also offer staff coaching time and other resources, including some fellowship and minigrant opportunities, to help participants in any way we can.

One key to the success of any service-learning project is the quality of the time set aside to create meaning from the experience. We now turn to ideas to enhance that process.

Figure 5

Connecting Service and Learning to Improve Schools and Communities
Portfolio
Entry Four

STAKEHOLDER PREVIEW

Listed below are potential stakeholders in your service learning project. Once your project is defined, complete this worksheet. STEP ONE: In column A, circle YES or NO to indicate if that group of people is a stakeholder in your project. STEP TWO: For all groups that are stakeholders, in column B, use the categories below to indicate their anticipated level of involvement.

Categories

A = Will be involved in all stages of planning, execution, and assessment.
B = Will be involved in some facets of project planning, execution and assessment.
C = Will be kept up to date on project progress and invited to give input.
D = Will be kept up to date on project progress.
E = Will be involved only in project execution.
F = Not sure about their level of involvement at this time.

POTENTIAL STAKEHOLDER	COLUMN A	COLUMN B
yourself	YES NO	_____
teachers _____	YES NO	_____
teachers _____	YES NO	_____
teachers _____	YES NO	_____
administrators _____	YES NO	_____
administrators _____	YES NO	_____
school staff _____	YES NO	_____
school staff _____	YES NO	_____
your students	YES NO	_____
other students	YES NO	_____
parents	YES NO	_____
student council	YES NO	_____
parent groups/PTA	YES NO	_____
site governing groups/site council	YES NO	_____
school board	YES NO	_____
community-based organization staff	YES NO	_____
community-based organization staff	YES NO	_____
clients of community-based orgn	YES NO	_____
board of community-based orgn	YES NO	_____
local businesses	YES NO	_____
local businesses	YES NO	_____
press/media	YES NO	_____
funders	YES NO	_____
elected officials	YES NO	_____
other: _____	YES NO	_____
other: _____	YES NO	_____

Service Learning 2000 Center

Figure 6

Connecting Service and Learning to Improve Schools and Communities

Portfolio
Entry Seven

Community Resources

Think of the area within a 1-2 mile radius of your school. Use the following list as a starting point for determining which community resources are located within that area. Write their names and location below, and tell how they might be a resource for your project.

- Chambers of Commerce
- Nursing homes
- Senior citizen activity centers
- Non-profit agencies
- Hospitals and clinics
- Businesses
- Professional organizations (AAUW, Bar Ass'n)
- Malls and shopping centers
- Churches synagogues, mosques, temples, etc.
- Youth-serving organizations (YMCA, Big Brothers & Sisters, etc.)
- Civic organizations (Kiwanis, Jaycees, Soroptimists, Scouts, etc.)

- Media outlets
- Community Centers
- Libraries
- Parks & recreation facilities
- Day care centers & pre-schools
- K-12 schools
- Colleges & universities
- Police stations
- Fire stations

Service Learning 2000 Center

Figure 7

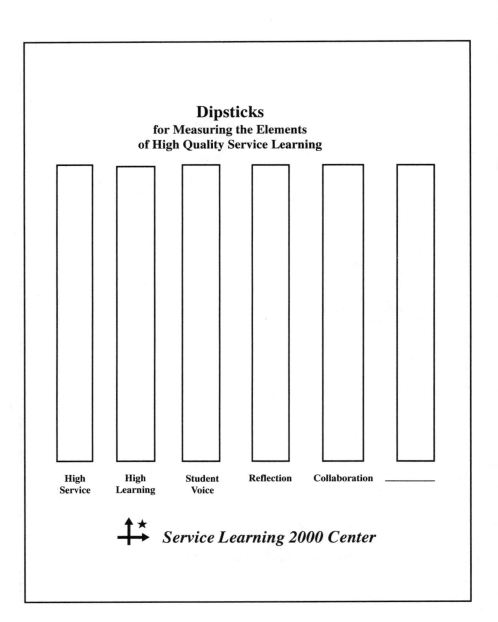

Dipsticks
for Measuring the Elements
of High Quality Service Learning

High
Service

High
Learning

Student
Voice

Reflection

Collaboration

_____

Service Learning 2000 Center

Challenge 4: Facilitating Effective Reflection Strategies for Teachers to Use With Their Students

Imagine the following scenario. A service-learning evaluator asks a student in an eighth grade English class if she remembers "reflecting" on her service experience: "Lisa, did you ever do something called 'reflection' in your English class where you had a chance to reflect on your work with the oral history project? You know, did you ever spend class time thinking about how your work made a difference to the seniors and how it connected to the English curriculum?"

"Oh yeah," replies Lisa. "We spent about 20 minutes discussing the oral histories we wrote about the senior citizens. We talked about what a tough assignment it was and how some of the old people were really friendly, while others were sort of hard to get to know. We also discussed how difficult it was to write a whole essay based on a few answers to some interview questions. And that was pretty much it. Then we just turned in the papers and went on with our normal lessons."

Lisa's situation is a fairly common one. In this case, reflection time has been squeezed into the last few minutes of class after the service experience has taken place. The discussion seems to focus on superficial issues, such as logistical problems the students may have encountered, instead of focusing on powerful connections between the service experience and the literature the students had been reading in class. And even though the teacher assigned an essay (writing the oral history of a senior citizen), it is not clear from Lisa's comments that the written assignment served as an effective reflection tool. We get the sense that it was "just another essay" to turn in for a grade.

We have seen this scenario many times in our work. Service-learning teachers know they are supposed to make time for reflection — that they need to help their students process what they have learned from the service experiences. As good educators, they realize that the experience alone is not enough; students need help making the link between service and learning, and reflection is the key to this link. However, in the busy chaos of school life, reflection time usually takes place only after the service has been completed, and more often than not, the time spent reflecting is merely superficial — a quick discussion or a brief journal entry scribbled before the bell rings.

We know that this type of reflection is not enough for most students. We also know that facilitating effective reflection sessions is no easy task. By using the guidelines below, we help teachers and students learn to design quality reflection activities:

1. *Reflection is most effective when it occurs before, during, and after the service activities.* In the field of English education, this strategy is similar to developing "into, through, and beyond" activities for reading literature. For instance, in the oral history project above, teachers may wish to alleviate some of the students' fears about the service experience and spark their thinking about the differences between adolescence and old age (a theme they have been studying in novels and short stories). Before meeting the senior citizens, the students might be asked to predict how the seniors will act toward them or to reflect on their greatest fears about interacting with people who are 60 to 70 years older than they. Similarly, throughout the project, students might keep a journal depicting any differences or similarities they notice between teenagers and senior citizens. They may want to document any changes in their "senior buddies" over the few weeks that they visit, or note particular stories that they hope to include in their oral histories.

After the service experiences, students may want to discuss connections to the literature or to reflect on stereotypes that may have been uncovered as a result of the project. Along with the written oral histories, a brief writing assignment may also be used to synthesize lessons learned and to foster critical thinking about the barriers that exist between teens and the elderly in their community. When these reflection strategies are combined over time, the students are able to recognize the purpose of the assignment and are more able to make meaning from their visits with the elderly.

2. *Some of the most compelling reflection sessions actively involve people who are receiving the service as well as students who are doing the service.* Both the students and the service recipients should benefit reciprocally from effective service-learning. To help facilitate this reciprocity, reflection sessions can take place at the service site, where all members can reflect on their experiences together. For example, in the oral history project, the seniors may want to participate in a discussion with the students about the stereotypes they may have held of each other before the service experience and how they may have changed over the course of the project.

3. *Utilizing a wide array of reflection strategies is an effective way to engage all students in learning from service.* Howard Gardner's (1983) theory of multiple intelligences is one of the most effective tools we have found to help people design reflection strategies that meet the needs of different learners. Gardner describes seven different intelligences that people use to solve problems and construct meaning: linguistic, logical/mathematical, spatial, musical, bodily/kinesthetic, interpersonal, and intrapersonal. Most of us are stronger in some of these areas and weaker in others; however, commonly used reflection strategies tend to focus on linguistic intelligence in the form of discussions, journal entries, and reflective essays. If we design reflection activities that utilize a variety of these intelligences over time, we can

engage students whose strengths lie in many of the other areas. For example, teachers may ask students to act out what they have learned from a project or create art pieces or musical compositions that capture their experiences without using words. (See our 1993 *A Concise Guide to Reflection* for more examples of reflection strategies that draw upon multiple intelligences.)

4. *When students learn to take responsibility for planning reflection sessions, they are truly making the link between service and learning.* Just as incorporating student opinions and choices into a service-learning curriculum can help build student support and interest in the project, encouraging students to plan reflection activities may foster stronger reflection. Students can take some of the burden off teachers and plan creative and diverse reflection strategies throughout the service experience.

Another way to alleviate the burden on service-learning teachers is by building collegial support at the school site, a topic we explore in the following section.

Challenge 5: Finding Effective Ways to Help Teachers Build Collegial Support at Their School Sites

Many people think that the greatest problem facing service-learning today may be the burnout of current service-learning teachers. At a time when their expertise and enthusiasm are most needed, many teachers feel tired, discouraged, and isolated. They need to find increased collegial support if they are to help expand service-learning or even to continue their current efforts.

In a typical example, Claudia is the only teacher at her high school who has been using service-learning as an instructional strategy. Her program has been going well, but she has had no success getting other teachers involved. Most teachers are either indifferent or openly critical because they think that content is being sacrificed by having students volunteer in the community or in other schools. Claudia often finds it difficult to get teacher approval for her students to miss classes to participate in periodic service activities. What disturbs her most, however, is that more students are not experiencing the power of service-learning at her school. Teachers like Claudia continually ask the Service Learning 2000 Center, "How in the world can I get faculty members who already feel overwhelmed to take a serious look at service-learning as a resource for their teaching? How do I build greater support for service-learning at my school?"

Our experience suggests that bringing teachers in Claudia's situation together for a workshop can provide valuable help when the workshop is designed around five fundamental, if somewhat paradoxical, principles:

1. *Teachers are very good problem solvers when they have time to think togeth-er in a collegial environment.* Specific problems that seem overwhelming to an individual teacher can often be more effectively tackled by a group. Furthermore, ideas that emerge from collective teacher thinking may feel more powerful and tend to be implemented more often than suggestions made by outside presenters.

We use a simple and fun group activity to help dramatize this truth. We set up small groups of five or six teachers and then structure a series of one-minute reflections and sharing of ideas. Initially, each person defines his or her challenge for building support at a school site. Then, each group selects one problem for focus and allocates one minute for writing suggestions and one minute for each person to share written suggestions. The activity ends with the teacher reflecting on the four or five suggestions offered. Experience affirms that four or five teachers giving one minute of advice to a colleague almost always leads to valued, concrete help.

2. *The long-range impact of "building support workshops" may depend as much on the personal relationships that are cultivated as on the quality of the content pre-sented.* Explicitly encouraging both informal connections and formal struc-tures for networking with other participants increases the chances of proj-ect implementation.

This observation has led to a major change in how we conduct institutes and workshops. We used to set aside time for teams to work alone on a spe-cific challenge and then bring the teams back to share what they had done. We now encourage teams to work on their projects in relaxed, common areas in order to allow spontaneous conversations and interteam advice to emerge. We have also learned that matching different kinds of projects for peer coaching strengthens the project designs and fosters personal relation-ships in unexpected ways. For example, we brought together a high school teacher at a juvenile court school with a fourth grade teacher for peer coaching support. The coaching conversation led to a previously unplanned pen pal connection between the court school students working on a garden project and the fourth grade students working with senior citizens at a vet-erans' hospital. This unlikely pen pal connection stimulated surprisingly good writing for both student groups and sparked an additional joint service project: The court school students sent plants they had grown to their fourth grade pen pals across the bay, who, in turn, gave the plants to their service-learning "buddies" at the veterans' hospital.

3. *Teachers need and value specific suggestions on building support that teach-ers in similar schools have used effectively.* The Service Learning 2000 Center has created a booklet containing a collection of strategies used by teachers enti-tled *Building Support for Service Learning* (1996) that we often use in our pro-

fessional development workshops. We have found that many teachers appreciate having a list of teacher-tried ideas to consider adapting to their own school situation, no matter how simple the ideas may seem. Two examples of teacher wisdom included are:

• After identifying teachers who are likely to be open to service-learning, select and share with them examples of existing service-learning projects in their subject areas that have worked well at other schools.

• Begin by offering to do something for a teacher rather than asking a teacher to do something extra for service-learning. For instance, offer to involve two or three students who are not doing well in another teacher's class in a service-learning project that your class is doing; then have the students report back to that teacher for extra credit.

4. *Teachers should have a chance to observe and practice skills that will help them in their service-learning efforts.* For example, teachers are often able to request 5 or 10 minutes to make a faculty presentation. Designing and actually practicing such a presentation in front of friendly critics is a valued opportunity. Role playing a luncheon conversation to persuade three colleagues to consider using service-learning as an instructional strategy is another effective example.

5. *Teachers should leave the workshop with a specific plan to expand service-learning at their school site.* This plan should be written, should include at least one or two concrete actions in the next week or two, and should be shared with at least one workshop colleague. Teachers can also be encouraged to schedule time for a phone call progress report with a colleague.

Conclusions

We have in our possession many written descriptions of innovative service-learning projects that will never see the light of the classroom. We meet plenty of workshop alums who give us a list of reasons for failing to implement their projects or to gain support from school faculty: Teaching assignments change, the projects demand extra funds that never materialize from the district or community sources, or the projects seem too daunting to complete, even with the support system of a school team and a local service-learning center to help with the logistics.

Despite these obstacles to successful professional development for service-learning, we have found that the strategies outlined in this chapter do entice interest, stimulate the design of integrated curriculum, encourage implementation, increase the variety of reflection activities, and help teachers build support at their sites. Service-learning may be difficult to implement, but it is a reform that is making education come alive for youth and teachers across America. Effective professional development helps make service-learning possible. We hope that this chapter helps others work with educators to break down more classroom walls and turn more communities into meaningful places of learning and service.

References

Gardner, Howard. (1983). *Frames of Mind: The Theory of Multiple Intelligences.* New York, NY: Basic Books.

Service Learning 2000 Center. (1993). *A Concise Guide to Reflection.* Palo Alto, CA: Service Learning 2000 Center.

————. (1996). *Building Support for Service Learning.* Palo Alto, CA: Service Learning 2000 Center.

Teacher Education and Service-Learning: A Critical Perspective

by Robert Shumer

The service-learning movement has seen significant growth in the past decade. Bolstered by federal legislation such as the National and Community Service Act of 1990 and the National Service Trust Act of 1993, and promoted by states and local school districts that are requiring service for graduation, service-learning is moving from the fringes into the mainstream. With a recent pronouncement by Jeremy Rifkin (1996), noted economist, on the status of work in America that "service-learning may be the antidote for society" (44) well into the next century, many people in the fields of education, economics, and the social sciences are viewing the development and expansion of service-learning as a serious agenda item. Given this need and desire for expansion and development, the preparation of teachers to deliver this educational philosophy and methodology is more important than ever.

Preparing teachers for service-learning, however, is easier said than done. While previous sections of this book have highlighted successes and advancements in the field, there are eight critical issues that must be addressed if we are to move effectively into the next century armed with the programs and policies necessary to expand learning into the community. The purpose of this essay is to identify and discuss these important concerns.

Issue 1: Community Service or Service-Learning

The first issue is clarifying the difference between service-learning and community service. Many school-based programs being implemented around the country promote the engagement of young people in service activities in their community. And an increasing number of teacher education programs introduce new teachers to personal involvement in service [see Part 3 of this volume for descriptions of 14 of these programs]. Some programs, such as those for middle schools, recommend preparation in service activities:

> Standard 11.0 in the National Association of State Directors of Teacher Education and Certification (NASDTEC) "outcomes based" standards specifically mentions "youth service," stating the expectation that the beginning teacher "organizes, operates, and continuously improves a youth service program." NASDTEC also states that "college students in their preparation programs should be involved in community activities themselves in order to serve as a role model." (Scales and Koppelman 1997: 119)

While the intent of this standard is to prepare beginning teachers for involvement in service programs, it is not clear what kind of programs are being developed. The recommendations for new teachers to "model" involvement in service activities themselves in no way guarantee that the experience will be that of service-learning, where there is intentional connection between the service and the learning activities. Rather, the suggestion is that teachers simply become familiar with youth service programs.

We need to be clear about the distinctions between community service and service-learning. Research on community service (U.S. Department of Education 1997) suggests that almost half the 6th through 12th grade students already volunteer. These volunteers tend to be 11th and 12th grade white females who receive high grades. Parents with college degrees especially tend to raise children who participate in community service. So home and community have a strong influence on developing a pattern of service.

This same report (U.S. Department of Education 1997) indicates that schools can promote service, and even service-learning. When schools offered service opportunities, students were more likely to participate in community service. More than half the students who regularly engaged in school-related community service reported that their service was incorporated into the school curriculum. This sounds a lot more like service-learning.

The point is that preservice and teacher preparation programs that encourage development of youth service programs are not necessarily promoting the understanding and practice of service-learning. Clearly, voluntarism and community service are important practices to be developed by schools, but they are not the same as service-learning. Helping people to understand the differences will make preparation of teachers who know and understand the principles and practices of service-learning an easier task.

Issue 2: Defining Service-Learning

Once we get past the distinctions between community service and service-learning, we are still left with a second issue of defining the nature of service-learning. Some people use the term as though it means the same thing to all people. We know that is not so. In a delphi study of practitioners and academics on the subject, we found that there were many "forms" and content areas for service-learning (Shumer et al. 1993). Eleven school-based and 15 community-based forms were identified, ranging from a short classroom-based project to an entire curriculum delivered through team-taught, interdisciplinary, community-based initiatives. Others have noted a continuum of program formats (Conrad and Hedin 1987), a variety of definitions (Giles et al. 1991), and a complexity of purpose (Stanton 1987). As we begin to prepare teachers for service-learning, we must acknowledge the diversity of settings and forms, preparing them for all the possibilities. There is no single service-learning program; teachers must know how to conduct programs across the continuum and adapt models to fit local settings.

Issue 3: Professional Development

The need to know the range, scope of program possibilities, and distinguishing characteristics of service-learning focuses attention on a third issue, professional preparation of teachers. This applies not only to service-learning professionals but also to the field of education itself. For years, experts in teacher education, from John Goodlad (1991) to Arthur Wise (1991), have lamented about the low status of teachers in the professions and about the lack of control over who enters and who practices the craft. Until we can assure other teachers, parents, and community members that those who practice service-learning are professionals, properly trained and knowledgeable about the philosophies and practices of high-quality education, service-learning is destined to remain on the fringes of educational reform. Service-learning teachers must understand both the theory and practice of the profession. They should know the history of the movement and the underlying principles that connect it with other educational reforms. Clearly, we expect that service-learning professionals know more than just how to do it. This means those who engage in developing and implementing service-learning programs must work with state and local credentialing bodies to determine minimum standards for entry and practice, as well as collaborate with staff developers in school districts and college-based teacher preparation programs, to establish curricula that ensure educated practitioners in the field. While I am not suggesting this process will be easy to achieve nor recommending one form of credential or certification over another, failure to deal with the issue of professional standards will block the expansion of service-learning into the mainstream of educational practice.

Issue 4: Training and Modeling

The concern with professionalization of the field leads naturally to a fourth issue of how we educate our new and experienced teachers to implement service-learning in its highest forms. A brief status report on what we are doing now may lead to a better understanding of where we need to go with preparation. Notwithstanding some of the fine examples found in this book, where organizations and institutions are delivering good education, most of the service-learning preparation in the country is being accomplished through short-term workshops sponsored by community-based organizations or colleges, rarely lasting beyond a few hours or a few days. This observation seems consistent with teacher reform in general — that much of teacher education reform is addressed through workshops by a "mini-industry of consultants" (Sykes 1996: 465). While trainers have experience doing some forms of service-learning, fewer have personal experience in the range of service-learning models available.

Given this scenario for the current state of teacher preparation programs, what do we know about teacher education that suggests these practices be modified? First, we know that changing teaching takes more than a one-shot workshop. In an article by the same name, Goldenberg and Gallimore (1991) summarize their research by saying:

> (1) The "new kinds of teaching" required to implement the reforms are described in terms too general for teachers to use, and (2) even if these new kinds of teaching were clearly defined, current staff development practices are inadequate to effect meaningful change.
>
> One solution is to say good-bye to quick-fix workshops. We must, instead, create contexts in teachers' work lives that assist and sustain meaningful changes. These contexts should consist, preeminently, of engaging teachers in rigorous examination of teaching: the concrete challenges and problems they face, the range of possible solutions, and most important, close examination of whether, over time, there is progress in addressing these challenges.
>
> Staff development, in other words, must be grounded in the mundane but very real details of teachers' daily lives and in the form that provides the intellectual stimulation of a graduate seminar. (69-70)

The authors recommend staff development that revolves around "instructional conversations," where faculty meet to discuss issues that move their teaching practice along the lines of the new reforms. Their message is teachers need to discuss instructional change, over a long period of time, in the context of their work, and in the spirit of continuous improvement. This same concept is reinforced in more recent work on "cognitive coaching" (Costa and Garmston 1994).

The findings of Goldenberg and Gallimore support the work of Donald Schön (1983, 1990) and his study of the development of professional practice. According to Schön, developing professional practice is not about brief informational sessions; it is about the creation of a reflective mind-set, where problems in the workplace become the substance of discussion and solutions. Problems for professionals do not come prepackaged in little boxes, to be analyzed in neat classroom settings. Rather, one of the dilemmas in professional practice (and most life settings) is figuring out what the issues are in the first place, before one develops solutions and programs that address the problems. Therefore, professionals need to learn how to identify problems in the context of their work and need to understand how to develop programs that seek to solve the dilemmas identified. This prescription applies to all teaching.

Besides knowing how to function as a reflective practitioner, those who have studied the evolution of teacher behavior (Berliner 1988; Huberman 1989) have noted specific cycles in the lives of new teachers. Often the first year is spent "muddling through" and "following." New teachers model what was modeled for them during student teaching. Next, they become "follower/independents," making some changes in their methods. After that they become independent, taking more control over what they do (Bullough and Baughman 1993). Then they move to mastery or experimentation. In this phase, they develop a style of their own, creating their own approach and engaging their own philosophy and method. After many years, they finally arrive at a professional stage where they totally control their own work. Thus, we know teachers refine their skill and confidence over several years. They also rely heavily on the models exposed to them during student teaching to shape their first formal experiences in the teaching world.

Research also tells us that reform of teacher education is best accomplished through long-term capacity building. Such initiatives involve collaborations between teachers and colleges and universities that focus on enhancing real-world practice of instruction (Floden et al. 1995). Creating networks between a critical mass of teachers and teacher educators (many of whom come from the ranks of teachers) builds capacity to sustain change in the way teachers practice their craft. State education agencies, teacher unions, and others concerned with the professional development of educators are all part of the capacity-building network required for long-term, sustainable change.

Thus, the research cited from the studies of teaching and educational reform suggests that modifications need to be made in teacher preparation to sustain the service-learning movement. Long-term commitments need to be established between teachers and teacher education units, both in colleges and in school districts. Programs need to focus on using "instructional conversations" and "cognitive coaching" where teachers and teacher educators talk to one another about the daily work of teaching in new settings and new structures. Focus on using the real-world, contextual nature of service experiences allows for emphasis on reflective practice, enhancing the overall development of the newer teacher. Short-term awareness sessions need to be replaced by long-term, interconnected efforts that focus on learning by doing and constant analysis of the teaching process. A critical mass of teachers, college faculty, district-level staff, state education agencies, and community experts needs to support the effort.

Issue 5: Teacher Education Programs — Theoretical or Practical?

While this joint collaborative process seems to be headed in the right direction, a fifth set of critical issues emerges that, if not addressed, could undermine the whole effort. In a study done at a college of education (Shumer 1992), I attempted to determine what a teacher preparation program would look like if service-learning were to be included. Results of that study indicate there are a few areas of concern. First, community members believe that the process of learning to do service-learning is experiential in nature. It has to be done through engagement of individuals in the service-learning process. Yet community members did not trust university faculty to allow for sufficient hands-on learning, believing that university faculty were more interested in theory than practice. Faculty, on the other hand, thought service-learning could not be included in existing courses, suggesting that the teacher education programs are already too full of "stuff" that needs to be taught, that introducing it as a separate program undermines the general program and marginalizes the effort. One faculty member simply said, "What would you take out of the existing curriculum to allow service-learning in?"

While a small study in size, two important concerns are raised for developing effective implementation of service-learning in colleges and universities, especially in large, public, research institutions. First, how do we establish trust and respect between the educator and the students? Community members clearly felt that trust and respect came from people who had done service-learning themselves and who understood the experiential nature of the learning. Second, how do we ensure that the preparation is broad enough so students do not become experts solely in service-learning methodology without having sufficient breadth of knowledge and exposure to be good teachers? Faculty were concerned that preparation would be too narrow, focusing only on service activities. These concerns focus attention on the dual issues of practical, experiential methods of preparation that also need to include theory and generalizable instruction.

Issue 6: Preparing Community Members to Be Responsible Partners

The issues raised in the last several pages direct us back to the driving question of how we should change current preparation for preservice and experienced teachers in the practice of service-learning. We now know there are several exemplary programs around the country. In addition to the programs sponsored by the Council of Chief State School Officers (1995), some of which are highlighted in this volume, college- and district-led programs from coast to coast are beginning to incorporate service-learning into teacher education. Few models, however, address a sixth critical issue in preparation for service-learning: How do we prepare the community members who work with youth to collaborate effectively to ensure academic learning is occurring through the community experiences? Several people have confronted this issue in relationship to experiential and service-learning (Conrad and Hedin 1982; Hamilton 1990; Minnesota Office on Volunteer Services 1993; Shumer 1987b). Most agree that some form of preparation is necessary for people who are charged with assisting teachers in the community component of learning to ensure that good learning is taking place. In my study of a community-based learning program in a secondary education setting (Shumer 1987a), I found that curriculum was more likely to be followed at community learning sites when staff at the site were involved in actually developing the learning objectives and activities. If this is so, we must consider how to educate community members who deliver instruction in the field. They must learn how academic agendas are presented and dealt with in the context of service activities.

Issue 7: Finding Enough People and Programs to Mount a National Education Effort

Preparation of community members to support service-learning perhaps brings us to a seventh issue in developing exemplary programs in teacher education. If good service-learning programs incorporate knowledgeable teachers, supportive administrators, collaborative and informed community members, and students engaged in real service and real learning, how do we develop enough good models from which novices can learn and practice their craft? Clearly, if new teachers initially learn to teach by imitating models (Berliner 1988; Huberman 1989), then we must have strong examples of service-learning in our communities that serve as effective preparation arenas. Efforts by the National Youth Leadership Council to develop a series of "generator schools" (supported by a grant from the W.K. Kellogg Foundation) and initiatives by the Close Up and Constitutional Rights Foundations to develop Active Citizenship Today (ACT) schools (supported by the DeWitt-Wallace Foundation) are a good start at creating service-learning models in a few communities. But they are not enough. Every community that wishes to engage in the preparation of teachers for service-learning needs to have excellent models in place, with individuals who can serve as master teachers and mentors to the new initiates. This may take more foundation assistance, as well as staff development and teacher education units to invest in this development while the actual teacher preparation programs are being produced. Without a strong network of model programs, which present the range of service-learning initiatives, there will be little sustainable infrastructure to prepare new teachers. Yet many service-learning programs are relatively new and do not have the length or breadth of experience to serve as model sites (Shumer and Belbas 1996). The service-learning movement may have to team up with other programs that have been doing community-based learning for decades, such as cooperative education, career and school-to-work programs, and civic education programs. Together, there should be many more "experienced" models on which to build strong preparation programs.

Issue 8: Breaking With Past Patterns of Classroom-Only Instruction

A challenge, and perhaps the most difficult to overcome, is the tradition of education in America. Teacher-directed, classroom-based instruction has been the dominant model of teaching for at least the past century. Research on teaching tells us that "often, despite their intentions to do otherwise, new teachers teach as they were taught" (Kennedy 1991: 16). So no matter what we try to change, teachers will carry forth the classroom traditions they were exposed to as children. In order to seriously change the way new teachers teach, we must recast our thinking about teacher education. Based on this information, teacher education really begins in kindergarten and progresses through graduate school. While we need to alter the way we prepare teachers in our undergraduate and graduate programs, we also need to realize that the simultaneous transformation of K-12 education is just as vital [see Myers and Pickeral, beginning on p. 13, for a discussion of issues in reforming education K-16+]. Long-term change requires that we attend to reforming the basic educational system to include service activities at all levels of instruction. Seymour Sarason, in his books on educational reform (1991, 1993), requires the entire system be altered to ensure that pieces of the reform are not lost. So it seems with service-learning: No systemic change will be sustained unless the whole system is transformed in the process. While this is no small task, failure to understand the implications of this message may minimize the reform and undermine the effort in the long run.

Conclusion

These eight critical issues raise concerns about our ability to produce sustainable high-quality teacher preparation programs for service-learning. Although there are admittedly some obstacles, the task is not insurmountable. American youth and society are beginning to develop service-learning initiatives and models to engage and connect our educational system with the communities that house them. Schools need not continue to be social islands, and communities can be more involved in the total learning of young people.

The most current literature on professional development of teachers suggests we need to modify our approach to teacher education reform (Sykes 1996; Wilson et al. 1996). Rather than emphasizing short-term workshops and training, we need to concentrate more on long-term efforts to engage teachers in the context of their work, involve community members in the development of curriculum and program designs, create the capacity of systems to support teacher learning and growth, and connect all involved in the process of problem-based learning. In so doing, successful models of teacher education for service-learning will be developed and sustained. With thoughtful action, we can deal with these issues and develop the kind of programs that move service-learning strongly into the 21st century.

References

Berliner, D.C. (1988). "Implications of Studies of Expertise in Pedagogy for Teacher Education and Evaluation." In *New Directions for Teacher Assessment: Proceedings of the 1988 ETS Invitational Conference*, pp. 39-67. Princeton, NJ: Educational Testing Service.

Bullough, R., Jr., and K. Baughman. (March/April 1993). "Continuity and Change in Teacher Development: First Year Teacher After Five Years." *Journal of Teacher Education* 44(2): 86-95.

Conrad, D., and D. Hedin. (1987). *Youth Service: A Guidebook for Developing and Operating Effective Programs*. Washington, DC: Independent Sector.

———. (1982). "The Impact of Experiential Education on Adolescent Development." In *Youth Participation and Experiential Education*, edited by D. Conrad and D. Hedin. New York: Haworth Press.

Costa, A., and R. Garmston. (1994). *Cognitive Coaching.* Norwood, MA: Christopher-Gordon Publishers.

Council of Chief State School Officers. (1995). *Integrating Service Learning Into Teacher Education: Why and How?* Washington, DC: CCSSO.

Floden, R., M. Goertz, and J. O'Day. (September 1995). "Capacity Building in Systemic Reform." *Phi Delta Kappan* 77(1): 19-21.

Giles, D., Jr., E. Honnet, and S. Migliore, eds. (1991). *Research Agenda for Combining Service and Learning in the 1990s.* Raleigh, NC: National Society for Internships and Experiential Education.

Goldenberg, C., and R. Gallimore. (November 1991). "Changing Teaching Takes More Than a One-Shot Workshop." *Educational Leadership* 49(3): 69-72.

Goodlad, J.I. (November 1991). "Why We Need a Complete Redesign of Teacher Education." *Educational Leadership* 49(3): 4-10.

Hamilton, S.F. (1990). *Apprenticeship for Adulthood.* New York, NY: Free Press.

Huberman, M. (1989). "The Professional Life Cycle of Teachers." *Teachers College Record* 91(1): 31-57.

Kennedy, M. (November 1991). "Some Surprising Findings on How Teachers Learn to Teach." *Educational Leadership* 49(3): 14-17.

Minnesota Office on Volunteer Services. (1993). *The Power and Potential of Youth in Service to Communities.* St. Paul, MN: Department of Administration, Minnesota Office on Volunteer Services.

Rifkin, J. (January 31, 1996). "Rethinking the Mission of American Education." *Education Week* 25(19): 44,33.

Sarason, S. (1991). *The Predictable Failure of Educational Reform.* San Francisco, CA: Jossey-Bass.

————. (1993). *The Case for Change: Rethinking the Preparation of Educators.* San Francisco, CA: Jossey-Bass.

Scales, P., and D. Koppelman. (1997). "Service Learning in Teacher Preparation." In *Service Learning,* edited by J. Shine. Chicago: National Society for the Study of Education.

Schön, D. (1983). *The Reflective Practitioner.* New York, NY: Basic Books.

————. (1990). *Educating the Reflective Practitioner.* San Francisco, CA: Jossey-Bass.

Shumer, R. (1987a). "Learning in the Workplace: An Ethnographic Study of the Relationship Between Schools and Experience-Based Learning Programs." Unpublished doctoral dissertation. University of California–Los Angeles, Graduate School of Education.

————. (1987b). "Taking Community Service Seriously." *Journal of Community Education* 15(1): 15-17.

————. (1992). "Teacher Education and Service-Learning." Unpublished manuscript. St. Paul, MN: University of Minnesota, Department of Vocational and Technical Education.

————, and B. Belbas. (February 1996). "What We Know About Service-Learning." *Urban Education* 28(2): 208-223.

Shumer, R., N. Murphy, and T. Berkas. (1993). "Describing Service Learning: A Delphi Study." St. Paul, MN: University of Minnesota, Department of Vocational and Technical Education.

Stanton, T. (January/February 1987). "Service-Learning: Groping Toward a Definition." *Experiential Education* 12(1): 2,4.

Sykes, G. (March 1996). "Reform of and as Professional Development." *Phi Delta Kappan* 77(7): 465-467.

U.S. Department of Education, National Center for Education Statistics. (1997). *Student Participation in Community Service Activity*. NCES 97-331, by Mary Jo Nolin, Bradford Chaney, and Chris Chapman. Project Officer, Kathryn Chandler. Washington, DC: U.S. Department of Education, NCES.

Wilson, S., P. Peterson, D. Ball, and D. Cohen. (March 1996). "Learning by All." *Phi Delta Kappan* 77(7): 468-476.

Wise, A. (November 1991). "We Need More Than a Redesign." *Educational Leadership* 49(3): 4.

Diverse Perspectives of Service-Learning and Teacher Education

by Joseph A. Erickson

When it is done right, service-learning involves many parts of the community and touches the lives of people from different backgrounds. Each person and community has an important story to tell. This section is an attempt to communicate some of these messages.

In this section, we hope to give people from diverse backgrounds an opportunity to give voice to their concerns, tributes, and advice as to how we might employ service-learning in our programs of teacher preparation. Some of these voices come from professionals in the field of education — teachers, administrators, and the like. Their perspectives help us to understand the different professional and institutional needs that must be satisfied in order for service-learning to be successful. Other voices come from the wider community — parents, students, and diverse cultural communities. These messages remind us of the multiple ways service-learning can impact peoples' lives.

Working With Preservice Teachers to Improve Service-Learning: A Master Teacher's Perspective

by Christine Hunstiger Keithahn

Imagine fifth grade students begging to be taught how to write business letters, eagerly standing for hours in a small back room bagging rice and oatmeal, giving up valuable recess time to tutor kindergartners, or enthusiastically publishing poetry books to share with elderly clients at a restorative care center. What makes these students so eager to give of themselves, to care for others, to be selfless in this selfish world? They have been bitten by the service-learning bug and experienced the joys of learning while serving. They have discovered that using their hearts, heads, and hands to help others can be a more interesting way to learn the basics of reading, writing, and arithmetic.

Even for an educator who is wholeheartedly committed to the ideals of service-learning, planning and implementing service-learning projects can be a time-consuming, logistical challenge. Working with preservice teachers who are knowledgeable in the ways of service-learning has made it possible for me to include service-learning in my curriculum. From a classroom teacher's perspective, there is no greater gift than the added support and energy provided by preservice teachers. Because of the teacher education students from Seattle University I have been fortunate enough to work with over the last four years in my intermediate classroom at Hawthorne Elementary in Seattle, Washington, my students participate in service-learning projects regularly.

Since service-learning projects enable everyone involved to give in his or her own way, the preservice teachers' assistance has varied, depending on their interests, expertise, experience, and the needs of the project. The largest, most complicated project my students and I have participated in involved the making, marketing, and selling of ceramic artwork dinner plates. The $1,500 profit was presented to a local food bank, where we also donated our time to help bag and distribute food. This complex, labor-intensive project was spearheaded by two highly capable preservice teachers. The children were divided into two committees. One was responsible for the marketing and distribution of the plates, and the other selected the food bank and organized the work parties. The committees were facilitated by the preservice teachers, thus allowing me to concentrate on curriculum integration.

In the case of this project, having two extra teachers on hand allowed for better small-group discussion, provided drivers for transportation to the food bank, and permitted us to divide the numerous tasks associated with such a project. Additional adults also enabled greater adult-student interaction that is often difficult in a regular crowded classroom.

From bell to bell, the classroom teacher is tied to the classroom and the students. Using the phone or visiting an agency during the normal workday is often nearly impossible. This is an avenue where preservice teachers can assist. As college students, their schedules are far more flexible. Those who worked on our intergenerational project with a nearby restorative care center were able to make most of the necessary preliminary phone calls and visitations needed to link our classroom with the agency.

One of the easiest, most common, and yet most valuable service-learning experiences is the cross-age tutoring project. Like thousands of classes across the country, my fifth grade class meets weekly to tutor, read to, and enjoy the company of kindergarten buddies. Preservice teachers have been used in a number of ways to enhance this experience. They have been in charge of the initial meeting, planned reflection lessons, and developed experiences to build rapport between the kindergartners and their fifth grade partners. Lessons on how to interact with younger students can take on a new meaning when delivered by someone other than your teacher.

It is not necessary for the university students to be with the project from the start for a valuable experience to occur. For example, my fifth grade class was joined by two prospective teachers midyear while in the midst of a well-established tutoring cycle. We decided that the reflection process needed to be enhanced with this ongoing project. The preservice teachers were particularly interested in the students' thoughts on tutoring without my input. Therefore, I was not allowed to attend their reflection sessions. A final book and video project facilitated by the interns displayed the students' learning.

In working with the elementary students, particularly without the teacher present, the preservice teachers are provided with a real-life classroom experience. They quickly learn that students do not always behave as the textbook portrays. Valuable first-hand experience in dealing with discipline often results. They learn to teach and manage a classroom by doing it. In providing this opportunity, the education profession benefits in having better-prepared teachers while adhering to one of the basic tenets of service-learning: Learn by doing.

The ideals of service-learning are further disseminated in sending preservice teachers into the school. They are generally energized, optimistic, and full of fresh ideas. The classroom teacher becomes the learner as the interns share their vitality and knowledge of the service-learning process. Furthermore, the collaborative effort enables more extensive brainstorming and helps alleviate some of the isolation a classroom teacher can experience. The reflection process is deepened when the teacher has additional adults with whom to reflect.

Even in the best situations, problems do arise. Working with preservice teachers is no exception. It is a time-consuming process that often requires numerous after-school meetings to coordinate the activities with the additional adults. The classroom teacher needs to serve as the liaison of information. I have found that having a central notebook or folder helps keep all the adults on the same page. Frequent communication is required to ensure the quality of the experience for all involved. Reflection is essential.

Trying to mesh the university and the elementary schedule has proven to be quite challenging. Class schedules are not always compatible. In recognition of this hurdle, Seattle University cleared five days in the preservice teachers' calendar to be used solely for time in the classroom working on service-learning projects.

A good project takes time. Building relationships takes time. One academic quarter is not very much time. Quite often the children and I felt we had just gotten to know the preservice teachers, and, before we knew it, the quarter was over. A possible solution to this problem, if a good match among intern, teacher, and students has been made, would be for the preservice teacher to stay on in the classroom to do his or her student teaching.

In a carefully planned service-learning project, all those involved are affected, learn, and change for the better. Each participant grows intellectually, emotionally, and spiritually while using his or her heart, head, and hands to better our community. With the additional support, energy, and resources brought to the experience by preservice teachers from Seattle University, I have been able to include service-learning as a key part of my academic program. My students, the preservice teachers, our community, and I all have reaped the rewards of this union.

A Recent Teacher Education Graduate's View of Service-Learning

by Theresa J.H. Magelssen

As a very recent graduate of my college's teacher education program, I still feel much more like a student than a teacher. My experiences as a student *participating* in service-learning far outnumber my experiences as a teacher *implementing* service-learning, so my following reflections on the topic will be more from a student's and student teacher's perspective than that of a professional teacher. As a student, however, I found learning through service to be very rewarding in my own education, and as a teacher I look forward to giving my students the chance not only to learn by doing but also to learn by doing for others.

Service-learning was not a component of my education in my elementary, junior high, and high school years. Oh, I rang bells for the Salvation Army one year for a high school honors society and made the annual church youth group caroling trip to one of my hometown's many nursing homes, but I never really participated in what I would consider to be service-*learning*. Not that I'm dismissing my early service activities as merely trite and token gestures of service (although that argument could be made), or that I'm suggesting that neither activity could have been a learning experience. The way in which my high school volunteering was structured, however, kept it from becoming true service-learning. The difference that I have found between those early service experiences and later service-learning experiences is the lack of any kind of formal reflection following the events. Never in high school did I process a service experience, either formally in writing or informally through discussion. To tell the truth, the only thing that ever followed my ringing and singing was a couple of cups of scalding cocoa and too many holiday cookies.

I didn't really encounter what I consider to be true service-learning until I got to college. Throughout high school I had always considered myself a fairly socially minded person, but I knew (ringing and singing aside) that I really did not have a whole lot of action to back up my beliefs. So when I reached college, one of the first courses I took was entitled Exploring Human Services, which had a very large service component. It was an interim course, meaning it was the only class I took for the month of January. I spent 20 hours a week for four weeks volunteering at the Multiple Sclerosis Achievement Center in St. Paul, Minnesota. My duties for the first two weeks were in the physical therapy room, helping clients do stretching exercises to loosen up the muscles in their legs and arms and assisting them in exercises to maintain the strength of those limbs. My second two weeks at the MS Achievement Center were spent in the occupational therapy room, helping clients perform fine motor activities, such as painting, to maintain the flexibility and strength in their hands and wrists. In both areas I also performed many non-therapy-related tasks, such as changing catheter bags, painting finger nails, and helping an older client who had little use of his hands to smoke his daily cigarette. It was an intense month, as one might imagine, working closely with and becoming attached to the clients, knowing that all of their hard work was not going to help them climb back up the steep slope to recovery but was, at best, going to help them to maintain their tenuous position and not slide down into some further debilitated state.

The intensity of my experience alone, however, was not what made my time at the MS Achievement Center into a service-learning experience. Granted, the discomfort I encountered while bell ringing at minus five degrees doesn't hold a candle to the range of emotions I went through when working with struggling MS clients, but as I alluded to earlier, I think that both activities *could* have been service-learning experiences. It was not the nature of the experience that made the difference between my high school and college volunteering but, instead, the additional class requirement of keeping a journal and having regular in-class discussions that allowed the class's participants to reflect, rethink, and process experiences. One of the goals of Exploring Human Services was, of course, for us to understand the actual challenges (both practical and emotional) of having a human-services occupation, and the journals and discussions helped us to do that. Keeping a journal allowed my classmates and myself to record what we had encountered throughout the day, helping us to reexamine our day's activities and remember our reactions and the practical/factual information we learned each day. It's amazing how much one can forget — even on the ride home — and writing in our journals helped us prevent meaningful parts of each day from being lost. I believe that it is extremely important to retain the thoughts, information, and concepts acquired when volunteering, for it is those parts of the service experience that will later be applied by the student to future situations.

Unlike some other service-learning experiences I would later have, Exploring Human Services did not have specific instructions for what was to be recorded in our journals, so I was fairly free to make discoveries about my service and those whom I served without being guided to any particular conclusion or area of concentration. One very important conclusion that I and others in the class drew about serving is that it involves a lot more than simply sweeping down and helping the so-called unfortunate. As a save-the-world first-year student, I learned about some of the technical difficulties involved in human services, but, more important, I learned (through both my experience and written reflections) that *compassion* is a far kinder and more useful feeling than *pity* in one who is providing a service to another.

That need for compassion between equals was dramatically (or sometimes I believe melodramatically) reinforced in my life when, following an unexpected spinal cord surgery, I found myself in a similar position to the clients I had worked with at the MS Achievement Center. The rehabilitation I underwent to recover from nerve damage involved the same physical therapy exercises to regain the use of my arms and legs and the same occupational therapy to regain the fine motor skills of my hands and fingers. During that time, I really noticed and appreciated the doctors, nurses, and therapists who treated me as an equal, and I was struck by the importance of realizing that when providing service, we are often not that far away from being the people whom we are aiding.

My reason for recounting this story (other than to put in a plug for compassion) is to point out that, although the lessons I learned and observations I made while in the hospital were important, they were essentially a fluke and not everyone (thank goodness) needs to experience both sides of every service experience he or she participates in to make it a learning experience. What I learned in the hospital certainly reinforced what I had already discovered through observing and writing in my journal during my service-learning experience at the MS Achievement Center, but because I had already thought about the need to treat clients as equals in my past reflections, the lesson was a review. Designing service experiences for students that involve reflection, whether through journals, class discussion, or another form of reflection, is what I believe truly creates service-learning.

I encountered a beautifully simple example of this integration of service and reflection during my first student teaching placement. I was in a kindergarten classroom, and the theme unit was "Bears." Consequently, my cooperating teacher had set up a ranger station, and each day during choice time some students were sent outside as rangers with an adult to pick up trash from the playground with trash sticks (long dowels with nails attached to their ends). At the class's meeting time, the outside rangers would then show the trash they had picked up, and the class would talk about the effects of litter, discuss why things like candy wrappers were so common, and talk about the need for a garbage can on the school playground. These 5- and 6-year-olds were providing a service to the school, a service that, because of its simplicity, could have simply become one of the day's assigned jobs but, because of the added element of reflection, became a series of ecology and environmental lessons.

Looking back on my first service experiences, I have tried to think how I as a coordinator or teacher could have made the bell ringing and carol singing (or like events) into learning experiences. One way I have considered is giving participants specific things for which they journal. Since neither experience was a multiple-day service experience, the participants would have to be asked to observe just one or two things — for example, a person ringing a bell for the Salvation Army could be asked to observe people's body language when they were either donating money or walking by. During the following hot-chocolate-and-cookies get-together, one could ask the participants about the reactions they had encountered and observed, and these reactions could then lead the group as a whole into a discussion of their experience and what they learned from it. In the same way, volunteer carolers at a nursing home could be asked to observe the environment and people they are serving and discuss their reactions to the nursing home environment during an ensuing group discussion. I don't believe that service-learning always has to involve structured means of reflection, but it always has to involve some form of reflection.

I think that what I will always try to remember and act on as a future teacher is the fact that service-learning does not have to be complicated or intense to be meaningful. Although my experience as an MS Achievement Center volunteer was much more challenging and emotionally draining than the evening I spent singing Christmas carols at the nursing home, the real difference between the two lies in the fact that one involved reflection and the other didn't. I feel that, as teachers, it is our responsibility to try to organize unique service experiences for students to participate in, and to work hard to look for the everyday service experiences that merely need to be highlighted and used for learning by both students and teacher.

A K-12 Administrator's Perspective

by Mary J. Syfax Noble

School Administrators Wear Many Hats

A school administrator's job is crowded with many competing — and time-consuming — activities. Today's school administrator is expected to be a change agent, a visionary, a collaborator, a community advocate, an instructional leader, and a researcher and still remain flexible to respond to special projects assigned by the superintendent. It is sometimes a stretch to fit all these roles into a workable package. Service-learning can serve as a vehicle to incorporate the many roles the K-12 administrator is called to play.

Service-learning is an educational process that not only provides academic content matter but also involves students in making positive community contributions, providing a context for the development of social and citizenship skills. By promoting service-learning in his or her school, an administrator can synthesize these two goals into one.

Service-learning is also an important mechanism for developing a positive learning community. It assists schools in making important connections to the broader community. Schools have long functioned as if they were separate rather than an integral part of their communities (Hendrickson 1985) and thus have failed to draw upon many available resources in the community. In this decade, many administrators find themselves short on resources of all types for their schools. Through the use of service-learning, parents, students, staff, businesses, community agencies, and community leaders are invited into the activities of the school. If done well, this will lead to productive involvement of the community in the learning environment of the school. This sets the stage for community-involved shared decision-making activities, such as site-based leadership teams encouraged by so many public school–reform advocates.

Connections to School Reform and Revitalization

Service-learning is a critical part of the entire school-reform picture. It is not the only answer, but it is a process that does several things at the same time, all of which are crucial to school reform. Educators often ask, "Do I have to add this on to everything else I'm doing?" The answer is a simple "no!" because service-learning does not compete with the standard curriculum. It supports and deepens the curriculum for all students. No group of students gets singled out. All students can benefit from service-learning. Service provides a tailor-made point of convergence for school and community partnerships, which are among the most productive strategies for school renewal.

. For example, at Webster Open School, in Minneapolis, Minnesota, the new school year was celebrated by engaging in a service-learning project. The project turned out to involve not only students and staff but also many community members from the neighborhood in which the school was located. A team of teachers created a curriculum outline that was cross-discipline, multicultural, and multi-aged. This one activity increased the amount of participation in service-learning from 0 to 88 staff participants! It is important to note that the school administrator in this case started working with just a few staff members who were interested in service-learning. The plan was not only to increase participation in service-learning but also to encourage staff to see students, families, and the outside community as valuable resources.

Service-learning could promote school reform in other ways:

• Service-learning revitalizes learning for students and staff. Students develop problem-solving strategies and leadership skills. This causes staff members to rethink the validity of what is being taught and gives both groups a common language and focus.

• Service-learning is deeply rooted in a sound understanding of the way people think and learn. As teachers struggle with the lack of time for teaching important content, service-learning provokes them to look deeper into what is being taught by length, volume, and depth, forcing teachers to confront the question, "What is the most efficient and effective way to deliver the curriculum?"

• Service-learning helps students understand that they don't just live in neighborhoods and communities but are connected to them. For example, a middle school discovered that creating a school/community public art space eased tensions between residents and students of the school. The educational objectives of the project included having the school become a civic partner with the community, extending the classroom into the community, creating an interdisciplinary educational service-learning experience, and fostering students' life skills.

• Service-learning can affect the entire school culture because it changes the belief system of the people in a school as students, faculty, parents, guardians, and community partners work together toward a common goal, building a sense of cooperation and bringing an integrated approach to learning.

Barriers to Success

In some schools, implementing service-learning is relatively easy because of the type of school and philosophy. But other areas may be a struggle, for the process of service-learning does have obstacles. For instance, the number of families that do not speak English as a first language may be a barrier. The location of the school and the large area from which its students are drawn may not facilitate efficient mobility within the community. But these are small obstacles. Perhaps more important is the belief (in some respects true, at least in the beginning) that community-based education requires more preparation by teachers and students than other educational approaches. Greater time demands make it difficult to integrate community-based activities into an already busy school day.

Another roadblock is the belief by teachers that building administrators will not support students' leaving the school grounds for community projects. Liability concerns are often at the top of the list for school and district administrators. Also, administrators need to manage the amount of time expended by staff to successfully implement new programs, and service-learning is no exception.

What Can Administrators Do to Help?

There are a number of ways school administrators can support service-learning. An important first step is to make sure service-learning is tied into the school's mission or vision. This should lead to discussions among staff, parents, administrators, and others regarding appropriate and inappropriate procedures. This could lessen the chance liability will become a barrier, because the school will have developed regular expectations, policies, and procedures with regard to service-learning activity.

Gathering school and community support is also important. The administrator can take the lead in initiating community partnerships and support; then the participants continue the process from that point.

Another suggestion is to start out small. Work with a focused group of teachers and students performing specific and visible work in the community. This raises the chances for early success — which may set the stage for greater involvement in the future. It may take just a small group of people with a spirit of commitment to make a project a success. In any case, every program needs at least one "zealous champion" for it to get off the ground and succeed. "Zealous champion" is how the author of a Ford Foundation–sponsored study described the leaders who had successful service-learning projects (National Crime Prevention Council 1988). Administrators can become those champions of service-learning by just being supportive, persistent in their efforts to make sure the school structure supports the service program, committed to educational excellence, action oriented, constantly watchful for barriers, and last, but most important, comfortable taking risks as long as well-being and safety of the students are not compromised.

References

Hendrickson, L. (1985). "Community Study." ERIC Digest 28. ED 268 065.

National Crime Prevention Council. (1988). Reaching Out: School Based Community Service Programs. Washington, DC: National Crime Prevention Council.

A Service Recipient's Perspective

by Janet Salo, with Susan O'Connor

The service-learning project in which I participated had some unexpected benefits for my family. The goal of this service-learning project was to match my family with a pair of preservice teachers so they could better understand the educational needs of students who have disabilities. My son has Down's syndrome and is in the fourth grade. I started the project with the notion that I would be able to give regular education students something valuable. My preconceived notions included the idea that my family, and particularly my son, would give the preservice teachers information on the impact of developmental disabilities on a family. I thought I could be a resource for the preservice teachers and that this would be their chance to really see the everyday struggles and joys of being a parent of a child with a developmental disability. I felt I could be their guide for demystifying disabilities.

Service-learning is something with which I became acquainted as soon as my son, Evan, was born. I became involved in a nursing student service-learning project, but to tell you the truth, they gave me more than I possibly could have given them. They taught me skills for taking care of my child. When I started in this service-learning project, I felt that this time I really had something to give rather than just take. I had weathered the questions of well-intentioned strangers asking questions such as "Doesn't he have good muscle tone for having Down's syndrome?" Now he was just another fourth grade student in an inclusive classroom.

This service-learning project seemed to fill a need I had sensed through Evan's inclusive education. The regular education teachers appeared to have had limited or no contact with individuals who had developmental disabilities. I gave his regular education teachers literature on classroom modifications and information on Down's syndrome. I seemed to gravitate toward teachers with at least some experience in the area of developmental disabilities. Service-learning seemed to make the most sense for preservice teachers to understand the needs of my son. I felt confident that I could offer hands-on training and information to the preservice teachers.

The preservice teachers came to visit us at our house. My son became very excited to have people come to visit and talk with him. When the preservice teachers, Amy and Angela, arrived, I wasn't sure where to begin talking about education. I just started talking about Evan and his daily activities. He is included full time in a regular fourth grade classroom in Minneapolis. He gets along well with his peers. His teacher is always trying new ways to involve Evan in the classroom activities. Most of his social skills are on a fourth grade level, but his academic skills are at a first grade level. The challenge in the regular classroom is to keep his self-esteem at a high level. He can become frustrated when he compares himself with other students. Amy and Angela observed and talked with Evan about his school experiences. Evan started to get out his favorite books, papers, and assignments from school. He became quite animated and started talking with the students. And he then decided to bring out a bowl of tortilla chips to entertain his "guests." When Amy and Angela left, I felt as if I hadn't given them enough information.

Amy and Angela met us again at an educational meeting. I still wasn't confident that they were getting all the information I had hoped to convey to them, such as the ongoing stress my son feels on a daily basis struggling to compete with "regular" students, the amount of time my son puts into his education outside of the classroom, his impressive ability to totally ignore inappropriate behavior in other students, his sometimes wavering self-confidence, and his sense of intense accomplishment when he achieves a goal.

The next time we saw Amy and Angela, they had completed a mock MAPS (futures planning) project. Amy and Angela completed the large project with great accuracy and had detailed Evan's accomplishments, hopes, dreams, and fears. He beamed when he saw that paper. He seemed so surprised that Amy and Angela had taken the time to literally draw out his life and that they had recognized the importance of his accomplishments. He was most impressed by the image of a tree he had climbed, and he proudly said a full sentence: "Look, Mom, I climbed up the tree." Amy and Angela had seen my child as an individual. They had no trouble seeing him as a person, which is sometimes difficult for me when all I hear about is my son's problems. His learning style didn't put off the preservice teachers; they saw Evan as a person with strengths as well as needs.

After I completed the project, I realized I had some very different notions about regular education teachers. I had thought they had to be initiated into the world of developmental disabilities slowly and carefully. This was not true. By talking with us for a relatively short amount of time, they were able to distill important information about Evan. I had had my own preconceived ideas that regular education teachers were uncomfortable with people who have developmental disabilities. I found out that this also wasn't true. I had assumed that this would be time-consuming and the results might be less than impressive. It turned out that Amy and Angela had given a gift to my son — the gift of seeing him as an individual, not as someone who needed to be fixed. They took him at face value and came up with some solid ideas for teaching Evan the skills he would need in the future. I appreciated their honesty and their ability to observe the entire situation. The best thing that happened was that I now could see the regular education teacher as an individual, just as the preservice teachers saw my son as an individual.

Service-learning is important to me because it opens doors to real hands-on experiences. As you can see, both the preservice teachers and I gained through these experiences. My greatest fear had been regarding the amount of time I would need to commit to the work. But I found that the time involved was fairly short (five hours) and that the payoffs for both the volunteer family and the preservice students were well worth the effort involved. Service-learning promoted greater understanding between my family and the preservice teachers.

The greatest benefit of this program was the exposure it provided to both my family and the preservice teachers to "the other side" of education. When we can better understand each other, we can greatly enhance the inclusion of individuals with disabilities in the general education classroom.

Collaborating With the Community:
A Campus-Based Teacher Educator's Story

by Rahima C. Wade

Collaboration is an essential aspect of service-learning programs in teacher education. While much has been written about the process of involving community members in the design and conduct of service-learning projects, collaboration in the real world can be filled with many small victories and challenges that are difficult to portray in a list of stages or "how-to's." The following story of the collaboration between one teacher education program and two community agencies will serve to illustrate how a collaboration may evolve, with trials and successes along the way.

In the fall of 1993, I decided that I wanted to build a community service-learning component into my elementary social studies methods course. Given the mission of social studies education as informed and active citizenship, a community-based component seemed like an important addition to the course. After talking with community members at United Way and a variety of social service agencies about the needs in Johnson County, Iowa, I decided to focus on two populations, the elderly and children from single-parent families. Individuals from both of these groups had needs that were not currently being met by local agencies. Also, intergenerational service-learning had some promise for connection with the social studies, for example through conducting oral histories.

With much enthusiasm, I began talking to our local Retired and Senior Volunteer Program (RSVP) coordinator and the director of the local Big Brothers/Big Sisters program (BB/BS). Both of these people were enthusiastic about the collaboration. We decided that groups of four individuals (two teacher education students, one senior citizen, and one elementary-age child from a single-parent family) would meet weekly throughout the semester for shared activities that would evolve from their varied needs and interests. Everyone would benefit, and everyone would serve; it seemed perfect.

The first task was recruitment. While the teacher education students were required to complete the project as part of the methods course, we needed to find volunteer seniors and children who wanted to participate. There were many children on the BB/BS waiting list and a high percentage of elderly living in this community that the RSVP coordinator thought would be interested. We anticipated that recruitment would take just a few weeks.

However, recruitment did not proceed as we anticipated. The seniors did not respond to our flyers, and it took many hours of visits to nursing homes and care centers on the part of both the RSVP coordinator and myself before we reached the required 40 participants. On the children's side, I was dismayed to learn, after the 40 children had been recruited, that many of those invited by the agency were not the children on the waiting list but rather those who already had matches. The BB/BS caseworkers felt that it was more important to choose children who would be successful in an intergenerational setting. While I was upset about this decision initially, over time I have come to see that their approach has enabled the program to be more successful than it might have been if we had limited ourselves to the waiting-list children.

The first few semesters of the Youth and Elderly in Service (YES) program saw many successes but many difficulties as well. While some groups got along well and enjoyed a variety of activities, others did not. Seniors dropped out because they thought they were going to be tutoring rather than playing games or going out for ice cream. We had children whose parents had signed them up decide they really weren't interested. Teacher education students complained about long commutes in their cars to pick up and meet with their matches. Participants from all groups became ill or moved. Each time we had to replace a senior or a child, it was back to the recruitment drawing board, with sometimes many phone calls before finding a replacement.

In retrospect, I realize that we simply rushed into the program too quickly. Rather than begin with 160 participants, we should have piloted YES with fewer participants. We also should have spent more time on orientation and training, particularly for the senior citizens who participated.

Honestly, if I could have ditched the program in that first year, I probably would have. However, shortly after we started YES, we received a Fund for the Improvement of Postsecondary Education (FIPSE) grant to support the program for two years, and I felt an obligation to continue. Collaboration with many others was essential in our program's getting beyond the "growing pains." Throughout the challenges described above, I worked with individuals from the two agencies involved, and I hired a graduate assistant with some of the grant funds to help with recruitment and scheduling. Gradually, the program improved as we provided better orientation for participants, had children and seniors who participated in the program over a number of semesters, and worked out issues such as transportation and scheduling to the mutual satisfaction of all those involved.

I look back on that first year now, just three short years later, and am amazed at the differences in the program and the collaborative efforts that support it. A particularly important turning point in our collaboration came when the FIPSE grant funds ended. The two agency members and I met over lunch and considered, first, if we wanted to continue YES and, second, how we would do so. We decided that it was definitely worth it, given the benefits to the participants. Our plans included scaling back the number of participants, dividing up the funding and staffing needs, and, most important from my perspective, the two agency members' taking on more responsibility for recruitment, orientation, and scheduling.

The fact that each agency now regularly refers to YES as one of its agency programs is testimony to the shared ownership that has evolved over the three years we have worked together. Our collaboration continues to provide mutual benefits for all involved. Teacher education students continue to learn about intergenerational sharing, and they receive insurance coverage from BB/BS when they participate in YES. The two agencies also benefit as services are provided to their clients, and they can report increased numbers of volunteers in their agency programs. We have developed better scheduling procedures, orientation sessions, and backup plans for health problems such that we rarely deal with the types of problems we encountered during the first year. Each semester, many seniors and children return to volunteer in the YES program because it brings joy and fulfillment to their lives that they wouldn't have otherwise.

This collaboration story illustrates how programs can evolve from a teacher educator's asking community agencies for assistance to a program that is mutually shared and owned. From this experience, I learned that it is important to listen to and honor the needs of all collaborators. I also learned that starting slow, piloting a project with a few participants in order to work out the inevitable problems and challenges, makes it easier on program coordinators. Finally, I have come to recognize how enjoyable, efficient, and successful service-learning programs can be when co-collaborators share the work and the fun of creating service experiences for teacher education students and community members.

Turtle Island Project:
Service-Learning in Native Communities

by John Guffey

Indigenous communities and children have been subjected to an imposed educational system since the beginning of the formal American schooling process more than 200 years ago. It began with the mission schools that were established among indigenous people to "Christianize" the children. When the U.S. government assumed responsibility for Indian education during the early part of the 20th century, federal boarding schools were established. These schools have a long history of abuse and neglect of Indian children. In the beginning, they were generally converted military bases and had a strict and regimented style of administration. Young children were not allowed to speak their own language or practice their traditional ways. Children were brought to boarding schools over distances that at times took them hundreds of miles away from family and community. Once there, they were given haircuts and punished if caught speaking the language of their home, all in the name of civilizing the Native American child.

There is little doubt that the treatment of indigenous people by the dominant society is a dark chapter in American history. Even so, real changes in the education of Native American children did not occur until relatively recently. Native American parents had little input into their children's education until the passage of the Indian Education Act of 1972. This legislation was passed in response to a national study commissioned by the U.S. Senate proclaiming education for Native American youth a national tragedy.

Education for the majority of native youth still lacks success. Currently, Native American students face a range of educational and societal problems that result in school drop-out rates exceeding 50 percent nationwide, high rates of absenteeism, and lower overall academic achievement levels than their nonnative peers.

In the context of American schooling, Native American students have been denied the opportunity to fully engage or develop for themselves the wisdom or knowledge of their home community. The pattern of the school has been to take the native child, among others, out of his or her cultural context and place her or him in a classroom where instruction in a new language and way of life begins to occur. The child is thus distanced from his or her indigenous context: the structures and processes associated with the linguistic, cultural, and biological survival of a particular group of people living within a specific ecological system. Cultural identity and diversity have been constantly challenged by this historical pattern of the common school. Such schooling is an agent of annihilation turned against indigenous people. It is no wonder that of all groups in the country, the highest rates of absenteeism and dropout are found among Native American students.

To help reverse this trend, the National Indian Youth Leadership Project (NIYLP) is developing a network of demonstration sites linking native communities, K-12 schools, community colleges, and universities committed to meeting the needs of indigenous people through education rooted in the values of generosity and service. Essential to this network is a teaching/ learning approach called "service-learning" that encourages young people to address community needs in the context of the academic curriculum and helps teachers build academic outcomes into meaningful community-based projects.

In its work with native communities, NIYLP has observed four things that relate directly to this method:

1. Traditional knowledge and cultural values related to education still exist and may form the basis for significant curriculum development. In the Northwest, communities are once again practicing the art of canoe building. Young people are called upon to help in this work and to learn why and how this is important to their way of life. In the Southwest, agricultural communities along the Rio Grande turn to the land for sustenance. Community gardens and fields are once again being nurtured by young and old members of the Pueblos. In these same communities, bread ovens dot the landscape, offering children the opportunity to share in the meaning and significance of a way of life through their maintenance, construction, and frequent use. In the upper Great Plains, giving back to *maka ina,* "Mother Earth," is recognized as a function of the relationship between humans and the Creator. Connections to nature are recognized in all aspects of the human experience and are celebrated in the ceremonies, language, and daily life of the people. Taking care of the Earth is a complex activity that takes many forms that young people must practice and participate in to learn.

In these examples, we see rich and meaningful content for learning in the context of native communities. Developing curriculum that links service to lifelong education could begin with these and other community-based activities.

2. Learning rooted in the context of community is an organic part of native life. Children's developmental needs are nurtured and met through community-based educational activities. The child experiences the positive reciprocal effects of giving and receiving when learning is accompanied by serving the larger community. In this sense, schooling is not a separate institution but exists as a truly integral part of the community.

3. Native people have concepts and customs, still understood and prac-

ticed in many communities, that precede what is now being called "service-learning." In the Cherokee language, *gadugi* refers to the practice of people helping each other. In Keres, one of several Pueblo languages spoken in the Southwest, *siyudze* is understood to mean "everybody's work," and in Navajo, the phrase *laanaa nisin* glosses as "that which we all desire together." The traditional work of service-learning includes, but is not limited to, the annual clearing of irrigation ditches, for which songs and ceremonies are also performed, erecting dwellings, preparing for, conducting, and cleaning up after feast days, and other social-learning activities involving the whole community.

4. Native American children, like all people, need positive, meaningful learning experiences. If school is irrelevant to one's life, this need is most likely to go unmet. Learning in the context of community, where value is added in the process of giving and receiving, children experience meaning as they come to understand their role as participants and providers in the daily life of their people and environment.

In this project, we propose to implement an approach to learning that recognizes the richness of native culture and encourages its inclusion in education by placing community at the center of the learning environment. This approach is based upon a two-part theory:

1. *People learn best when meeting physical, mental, emotional, and spiritual needs within the context of community experiences.*

The elements and conditions that lead to basic differences in individual and cultural patterns are critical to education both for their specificity and for their variability across time and space. Learning occurs according to diverse interactions and relationships within specific ecological contexts or communities.

The indigenous community, when placed at the center of learning, guides the educational system into a better understanding of the particular needs and strengths of individual learners. An individual's orientation and contribution to place, history, and human values become respected parts of the curriculum and are recognized for their role in further learning.

2. *Learning in the context of community is primarily about understanding and living in harmony with others.*

Everything exists in relation to something else. Community, placed at the center of learning, provides a meaningful context for orienting individuals and society in their relationship to nature, history, and human values.

In the spring of 1995, the National Indian Youth Leadership Project was awarded a four-year grant by the W.K. Kellogg Foundation to demonstrate the effectiveness of service-learning practices on increasing the cultural relevance of K-12 education for Native American students. This initiative, known as the "Turtle Island Project," is designed to meet real educational needs through the practice of service-learning in schools serving Native American students and communities.

The Turtle Island Project began taking shape in September 1995 with six K-12 schools and seven universities joining together from four regions of the country. K-12 sites are located in Brimley, Michigan (Upper Great Lakes); Minneapolis and Red Lake, Minnesota (Upper Midwest); Mission, South Dakota (Northern Great Plains); and Lukachukai, Arizona, and Laguna, New Mexico (Southwest Plateau).

In October 1995, a Learn and Serve America grant from the Corporation for National Service added eight K-12 schools to the list of participating Turtle Island sites. All eight of these sites are in the Southwest: Sunnyside School District in Tucson, Arizona (Sonoran Desert); Hopi High School in Keams Canyon and Pine Springs Community School in Pine Springs, Arizona; and Central High School and Jefferson Elementary School in Gallup and Sky City Community School in Acoma, New Mexico (Southwest Plateau); and Ohkay Owingeh Community School in San Juan Pueblo and Taos Day School in Taos Pueblo, New Mexico (Rio Grande Valley).

The inclusion of schools of education in this project makes an important connection in the cycle of learning that includes students, teachers, and community members. University faculty and student teachers experienced in service-learning will connect more readily with community-based school sites and will contribute to an increasing awareness and application of service-learning methods at the local and the national levels.

The schools of education involved in this project are Bemidji State University in Minnesota; Bay Mills Community College, Lake Superior State University, and Michigan State University in Michigan; Sinte Gleska University on the Rosebud Reservation in South Dakota; and the University of New Mexico at Albuquerque and Gallup.

These institutions have made a commitment to pursue service-learning as an educational philosophy and methodology for teacher preparation. They are involved in a variety of efforts to integrate service into the educational system. Some preservice teacher education students are engaged in planning community involvement and curriculum-based service activities at the K-12 school level. As community members and future educators, these students are able to begin bridging the gap between the school and community as part of their teacher preparation. Some programs are emphasizing native culture and language integration into teacher preparation as a connection to service-learning and community involvement. Other university education students are working under faculty guidance to integrate service-learning into educational policy.

These examples should be seen as parts of a holistic effort in which the different approaches support one another and where models and stories of what works and what needs more study are being shared for the benefit of all.

Not every school or community is expected to incorporate all the approaches to service-learning being explored. The uniqueness of each site is a critical factor that we recognize and support. It is our hope that each site's efforts will inspire and encourage others to reach into their hearts and their communities for the available resources needed to bring schools and education back into a relationship of service to community, of giving and receiving the best we have to offer.

Questions or comments regarding the Turtle Island Project and service-learning in Native American communities may be addressed to National Indian Youth Leadership Project, PO Box 2140, Gallup, NM 87305, ph 505/722-9176, fax 505/722-9794.

Models for the Integration of Service-Learning and Teacher Education

by Jeffrey B. Anderson

This section of the monograph presents 14 models of teacher education courses and programs that integrate service-learning. These models represent a diversity of types of institutions (public, private, large research, liberal arts, historically black colleges and universities) located in various geographic regions of the United States. Graduate and undergraduate courses are included, as are preservice and inservice offerings.

The models show considerable variation in the degree to which service-learning is integrated into course and/or program objectives. They are arranged beginning with individual courses that employ service-learning as a method to achieve course goals. These are followed by courses that share this focus but also endeavor to provide students with knowledge of service-learning as a teaching method and philosophy of learning. Finally, programs are presented that employ service-learning in an integrated fashion throughout a sequence of different courses in order to prepare teachers who have experienced service-learning themselves and are able to employ it as an instructional approach with their K-12 students. Some of these programs also provide their preservice teachers with service-learning experiences in which they work with K-12 teachers and students in a field setting to design and implement service-learning projects.

These models were chosen to provide readers with a sense of the wide variety of different ways service-learning can be linked with teacher education in order to prepare more effective teachers and assist in the reform of K-12 and higher education. An effort was made to allow readers to see that different institutions approach the integration of service-learning and teacher education from distinct perspectives and that in some cases this integration is a process that moves over time from peripheral service-learning in one course to a systemic redesign of teacher preparation with service-learning at the core.

James Madison University

I. Course/Program Title
The James Madison University community service experience is required as part of a six-semester-hour course, Teaching the Young Child, in the fourth semester of a four-semester early childhood licensure program.

II. Category
The course for which service-learning is a part is a comprehensive methods course in early childhood education. It is required for all students in the early childhood program at James Madison University and is the last course that they take before student teaching. James Madison University is a liberal arts state university of 12,000 students. It is located in a city of approximately 35,000 in the rural Shenandoah Valley of Virginia.

III. Conceptual Framework/Objectives
The course Teaching the Young Child addresses issues in physical environment, centers, schedule, thematic planning, assessment, classroom management, working with parents, and working with diverse populations. Through the service-learning component, students experience diversity and reflect on their role in meeting the needs of children and families from diverse backgrounds and with diverse needs.

The majority of the student body of James Madison University is white upper-middle and middle class, many of whom are from the suburbs near Washington, DC. Early childhood students are even more homogeneous, being 96 percent female. The region in which the university is located is also fairly homogeneous, although there is a growing population of Hispanic and Ukrainian immigrants.

The required service-learning experience is meant to expose students to a population with which they have had little or no contact. Through the community service experience, it is hoped that students will get to know people in this population in a personal way. Through this relationship, we want our students to realize that our society is truly diverse, to value diversity as positive, to feel more comfortable with people who are not like themselves, and to reflect on some of the unique needs of others and how they as teachers might begin to meet these needs.

IV. Integration of Service-Learning Theory
To maximize the impact of the service-learning experience, students keep journals of the experience and participate in reflection sessions. Journal

entries are read by the professor, and each student is given feedback on the comments and concerns expressed. Journal entries also serve as the basis for reflection during class time.

Reflection may be formal or informal and take the form of whole-group or small-group discussion, a "people search," or an activity that involves students in writing poetry about their experience. Students share their perceptions of their setting and what they are learning. They begin to make connections between their involvement in the community and their roles as teachers. In-class reflection takes place several times during the semester.

V. Service-Learning Assignments and Activities

The courses required for early childhood licensure involve students in a variety of practica experiences in varying locations and with different age children. For this reason, students are asked to select a nonschool setting for their community service experience. We want our students to get out into the community to see the broader context from which their students will come.

Students may identify their own sites or use the services of the Community Service–Learning (CS-L) Office on campus. This office offers students a variety of placements from among more than 100 agencies in the surrounding community. Agencies are categorized into several areas, including housing and hunger, adult services, programs for the differently challenged, and so on. The center provides orientation sessions at the beginning of each semester during which students can get an overview of the areas and agencies served and sign up for a service-learning slot. Staff members from the CS-L Office will also come to a class meeting to explain programs and register students for placements. Undergraduate students employed as program assistants then make contact with the agency in which a student was placed and arrange for an initial meeting between the student and an agency representative. If a student uses the services of the Community Service–Learning Office, the agency documents hours served, and this documentation is forwarded to the professor through the CS-L Office. Each student is required to complete 15 hours of community service during the course of the semester.

Students are also allowed to arrange for their service-learning site. Students who arrange their own placements are asked to clear the placement with their professor prior to beginning their service.

The most successful placements are those in which students have direct contact with people. These placements may involve students in driving AIDS patients, becoming a "big brother" or "big sister," playing games for an evening session with children at a shelter for abused women, or planning craft activities for the children at the local homeless shelter. These situations are satisfying and rewarding. Students who perform office- or clerical-type jobs are less satisfied, because they do not get to know people and cannot see the results of their efforts. These settings lessen the possibility of achieving program goals for the service-learning component.

VI. Assessment

Students get credit for their community service if they complete the number of hours required in an appropriate setting. Learning from the experience is informally assessed through student responses in journals and comments and contributions made during class reflection. Finally, at the end of the semester, students are asked to let us know how valuable they felt the experience was and how they feel the experience will impact them as classroom teachers.

Informal qualitative analysis of student responses indicates that the experience is an overwhelmingly positive one. Students who initially dread doing their service say that after a couple of weeks they look forward to it. Some students learn that they can successfully undertake and complete tasks that they didn't think they could. One student, for example, worked at the Wildlife Center of Virginia, which cares for injured and sick wild animals. As part of her duties, she was asked to cut up rats to feed to the birds of prey. She didn't think that she could do it, but she did! Although this placement offered no direct interaction with children, the successes experienced showed the student that she could accomplish unpleasant duties such as those faced by an early childhood teacher. Another student worked with a 5-year-old infected by the AIDS virus. She was hit full force with the many challenges that face children and the challenges that she will face as she teaches and meets the needs of children who do not fit the profile of childhood with which she was raised. Other students worked at mental hospitals, nursing homes, and soup kitchens. There they made friends, people with whom they talked and shared stories. These encounters began to break down stereotypes as the mentally ill, elderly, and working poor took on names and faces.

The biggest challenge to the required community service component for early childhood students is time. There is pressure from the state and the university to reduce hours. Requirements for the bachelor's degree have gone from 128 semester hours to 120 hours to guarantee graduation in four years. All programs, majors, and liberal studies alike have been asked to cut. As hours are cut, content must be condensed and in some cases even dropped from the program. Professors must be cognizant of student time and not demand too many outside-of-classroom hours for fewer credits.

VII. Assessment of Service-Learning Placements

Success is measured in the insights that students gain — insights about people and families, about the community, and about the issues that children bring to the classroom. The biggest challenge is placement. Working through the CS-L Office on campus sometimes delays the start of the service experience, and students tend to procrastinate, leaving the service requirement to late in the semester. A second challenge is setting aside class time for reflection. Sharing is essential, yet as the semester progresses, other class content tends to take priority over reflection.

VIII. Gaining Institutional Support

The early childhood program at James Madison University enrolls more than 200 full-time undergraduate students. It is valued and supported by the administration. There is considerable autonomy in program planning, and including a service-learning component was a decision made by the six early childhood faculty. The community service requirement addresses program goals and begins to address National Council for Accreditation of Teacher Education criteria regarding diversity.

IX. Special Characteristics/Financial Support

None

X. Future Plans

With mandates for restructuring of programs and reduction of hours, service-learning has been placed in the first semester of the program rather than in the third. During this semester, students are looking at the role of the teacher, personal characteristics, and issues of bias and multicultural education. The service requirement seems to fit with these issues. This initial experience will then be used as a basis for discussing practice and issues through the entire program. We feel it will give our students a good introduction to diversity.

XI. Contact

Diane Fuqua, School of Education, James Madison University, Harrisonburg, VA 22807, ph 540/568-6783, *FUQUAJD@jmu.edu*

Kentucky State University

I. Course/Program Title

Introduction to Teaching, one of three courses with service-learning components in the Kentucky State University teacher education program.
(Descriptions of the other two follow.)

II. Category

First required course in the teacher education program.

III. Conceptual Framework/Objectives

A lecture and experiential activity course for scholars seeking program
admission into elementary and secondary education fields, this course
explores the realities of American public education and the nature of the
teaching profession, including role, function, benefits, and expectations.
These realities, combined with practical experiences — 20 hours of service-
learning and five clinical hours in a classroom setting — serve as the central
focus of the course.

IV. Integration of Service-Learning Theory

Embedded in this course is the belief that service-learning is a philosophy of
education that brings learning to life, a concept embedded in the domain of
pedagogical knowledge that allows us to effectively blend the cognitive,
affective, and psychomotor domains.

Specific objectives that link service-learning to the course are:

1. to raise the awareness of students about social problems by citing
examples of how schools contribute to social improvement;

2. to provide students with the knowledge and skills to improve society
and the quality of life by fostering care beyond the classroom; and

3. to help students see that they are not only autonomous individuals
but also members of a larger community to which they have some
responsibility.

Two chapters in the text specifically address components of service-
learning. In "Schools and Society," we discuss schools as social institutions;
the role that schools play in promoting students' personal, academic, and
social growth; and examples of how schools contribute to the improvement
of society by promoting a sense of community. In "Students: The Focus of
Your Teaching," we discuss how students differ in their stages of development, with an emphasis on character development. We further explore

opportunities that promote personal, social, and intellectual growth, as well as civic responsibility.

V. Service-Learning Assignments and Activities
Students serve as tutors, mentors, and coaches at preschool and elementary sites; assist the staff at ACCESS Soup Kitchen; and "adopted" a resident of Franklin Manor Nursing Home. Along with spending 20 hours of service-learning at their placements, students are required to construct a concrete representation of a concept that is relevant to their activity/project. This product is to be left with the teachers for their future use.

Placements are coordinated by the university service-learning director with the assistance of the Student Advisory Council.

The text itself is based on relating theory to practice. Students are responsible not only for reading and critiquing articles that deal with various teaching situations, strategies, and techniques related to or that embrace service-learning principles but also for completing service-learning activities assigned to them through the Service-Learning Office.

VI. Assessment
Assessment methods include working professional portfolio development, field observation reports, a microteaching presentation, article critiques, opportunities for peer and self-assessment, reflective journals, and an analytical paper summarizing the service-learning project. Student outcomes include increased self-confidence (both participant and recipient), building personal relationships, earning respect of younger students, and seeing academic and social growth of students. Other results include overcoming shyness, taking a leadership role, developing increased patience, building trust with reluctant students, and saying good-bye at the end of project hours.

VII. Assessment of Service-Learning Placements
Students evaluate their placements by completing a quantitative and qualitative survey; agencies evaluate the student participant/recipient relations and personal growth; the service-learning director along with faculty members involved in service-learning assess and analyze both responses.

VIII. Gaining Institutional Support
EDU 409, Fundamentals and Administration of Secondary Schools has built into its course structure a service-learning Student Advisory Council (SAC). This body of students plans the activities/projects that address the need areas — human, educational, public safety, and environment — as identified by the community. We discuss a procedure for contacting various community agencies, handling necessary paperwork and data entry, dividing the

responsibilities among the members, and holding each group accountable for completion of assigned tasks. The SAC members make the initial contacts with the agencies to identify their needs, explain the program and projects to the classes that are involved, and then match student participants' interest with the appropriate sites. The SAC also compiles the data collected from the survey given at the end of the project. Work-study students are assigned to our Service-Learning Office to assist with the clerical duties and data entry. As the professor who teaches EDU 409, I have been given half-time release as director of service-learning by the university to ensure consistency of purpose.

A campus-wide effort is under way to get vice presidents of student affairs, instruction, and administration to reallocate resources in order to support faculty, staff, and students in daily ongoing routines, to provide faculty training, and to establish business/industry partnerships. One of the goals in *Kentucky State's 1996-2000 Strategic Plan* is to increase/improve relationships between the community and the university. We are in the process of drafting a proposal to the president to demonstrate how service-learning can help accomplish this goal. In this proposal, we will ask for the Service-Learning Office to be renamed KSU's Service-Learning Institute.

IX. Special Characteristics/Financial Support

No special financial support was required to start or maintain this course because it is required for all education majors. Since extensive fieldwork is stated in the university catalogue's course description, we simply used those hours for service-learning as a vehicle for merging theory and practice. We discuss Kentucky State University's teacher education model, which reflects the Kentucky Education Reform Act and Kentucky's Learning Goals. Goal 4 states, "Students shall develop their abilities to become responsible members of a family, work group, or community, including demonstrating effectiveness in community service." Goal 5 states, "Students shall develop their abilities to think and solve problems in school situations and in a variety of situations they will encounter in life." We view service-learning as one means by which we can help our students realize these goals.

X. Future Plans

We intend to publicize the various activities/projects and results of student surveys, survey faculty to see who is already doing some form of service-learning, invite other interested faculty to attend a service-learning inservice, integrate service-learning into our freshman orientation program, and get the service-learning concept written into the university catalogue's description of our teacher education program.

I. Course/Program Title

Methods of Teaching Social Studies/K-12

II. Category

Methods course taken the semester before student teaching.

III. Conceptual Framework/Objectives

This is a course for education scholars whose major is social science. It involves the study of content, instructional methods and materials, and evaluation and assessment for teaching social studies in K-12. In hopes of fostering a foundation for successful classroom teaching, it integrates lecture, interactive participation, technology, and a required 20 hours of service-learning field experience designed to provide students with a theoretical and practical basis for teaching. Emphasis is placed on global/multicultural education. The main goal of the social studies curriculum is to help students attain the knowledge and develop the ability to make reflective decisions and to take successful action toward solving personal and public problems.

IV. Integration of Service-Learning Theory

Also embedded in this course is the belief that service-learning is a philosophy of education that brings learning to life, a concept embedded in the domain of pedagogical knowledge.

Specific objectives that link service-learning to the course are:

1. to raise the awareness of students about social problems by citing examples of how schools contribute to social improvement;

2. to provide students with the knowledge, skills, attitudes, and values essential in becoming responsible adult citizens by fostering care beyond the classroom;

3. to provide all students with opportunities for effective interaction with and appreciation of people from other cultural and intellectual perspectives; and

4. to assess and evaluate current research findings in the curriculum, methods, and materials of social studies instruction that address social issues and human relations.

V. Service-Learning Assignments and Activities

Students work as tutors with ABE and GED students on a one-to-one basis at the Thorn Hill Adult Education Center. Placements are coordinated by the university service-learning director with the assistance of the Student Advisory Council. The text itself is based on relating theory to practice, linking knowledge gained through service with classroom learning/assignments. Students must create a two-week unit that is multiculturally designed and includes a service-learning component.

Items **VI.-X.** are the same as described under Introduction to Teaching.

* * *

I. Course/Program Title
Methods of Teaching English/HS

II. Category
Methods course taken the semester before student teaching.

III. Conceptual Framework/Objectives
This is a course for education scholars involving the study of content, instructional methods and materials, and evaluation and assessment for teaching high school English. In hopes of fostering a foundation for successful classroom teaching, it emphasizes the supportive relationship of all areas of language arts — listening, speaking, reading, and writing — to one another and to other subjects for the purpose of effective communication. It also integrates lecture, interactive participation, technology, and a required 20 hours of service-learning field experience designed to connect theory to practice. Emphasis is placed on global/multicultural education.

IV. Integration of Service-Learning Theory
Embedded in this course is the belief that service-learning is a philosophy of education that brings learning to life, a concept embedded in the domain of pedagogical knowledge.

Specific objectives that link service-learning to the course are:
1. to identify causes of communication barriers;
2. to provide students with the knowledge and skills to improve society and the quality of life by fostering care beyond the classroom;
3. to identify the congruencies between various methods and practical instructional situations; and
4. to assess and evaluate current research findings in the curriculum, methods, and materials of English instruction that address interpersonal communication, empathic listening, and conflict mediation skills.

Item **V.** is the same as described under Methods of Teaching Social Studies/K-12.

Items **VI.-X.** are the same as described under Introduction to Teaching.

XI. Contact
Carole A. Cobb, Director of Service-Learning, Kentucky State University, Hathaway Hall, Room 213, Frankfort, KY 40601, ph 502/227-5918, fax 502/227-6909

Clark Atlanta University

I. Course/Program Title
EDA 610, Community Educational Leadership

II. Category
Required course in the graduate educational leadership sequence.

III. Conceptual Framework/Objectives
The purpose of this course is to facilitate the professional growth of persons who will serve in positions of community educational leadership. Within this audience, the larger group will be school-based practitioners, including community school administrators, school principals, classroom teachers, and community relations specialists. The course also meets the needs of adult and community educators working in community colleges, nonschool settings, and other institutions offering community-based education.

Community education has been defined as a program, as a process, and as a movement. While all these interpretations are portrayed in this course, emphasis is given to the *process* dimensions of the field, i.e., community education as a strategy for community building, development, and empowerment. While the broadening of educational opportunities serves to enlarge the capacity for both individual and social choice, participation in defining the *what, why, when, how,* and *where* we learn is believed to be inherently empowering. The *process* dimensions of community education, thus, are interpreted as educational experiences for community residents of all ages that will empower them to take charge of their lives and their communities in order to make them better places to live.

The objectives of the course are designed to assist participants to: (1) understand the historical, sociological, and organizational contexts for community educational leadership; (2) develop skills in conceptualizing and initiating community educational systems; (3) understand and apply different modes for planned community change; (4) develop skills in community action, research, and analysis; and (5) enlarge their understandings and appreciations for the civic roles of professional educators.

IV. Integration of Service-Learning Theory
The theory and practice of service-learning is integral to the design of this course. Since its inception, it has sought to model community-based education through experiential teaching and learning. An action research mode governs the instructional model.

In addition to assigned readings and class discussion, students partici-pate in a case study of an urban, distressed community. They work as a research team to identify a problem or issue of significance to the local com-munity and, in so doing, establish a collaborative context for research and practice. Following entry into the context, an action research design is devel-oped and implemented. After data are acquired, students develop a com-prehensive plan for problem resolution and report their findings and the results of their study to community collaborators.

Throughout the course, reflective activity is pursued in a variety of modes, including individual, group, and whole class. Emphasis among these modes varies from class to class, depending on the nature of the assign-ment. Students maintain individual journals and complete field reports. Class time is provided for team discussion, planning, and reflection, and field experiences are related to course content and objectives through whole-class discussion and reflection.

At the conclusion of the course, the class meets with community col-laborators at an appropriate off-campus site, and results of the study are presented. The reflective mode is continued, and community feedback is uti-lized to correct any possible misperceptions. Copies of the research report are left with appropriate community contacts. While this course has always been experiential in nature, as noted above, the introduction of service objectives and methodology has broadened the scope of community collab-oration and involvement in the project, expanded the role of reflection, and ensured that new solutions are left behind for community benefit.

V. Service-Learning Assignments and Activities

Clark Atlanta University is located in an urban, distressed community where 24,000 residents experience high rates of poverty and welfare dependency. Census reports and other surveys tell us that approximately half of neigh-borhood adults are school dropouts. Most lack fundamental literacy or job skills. Fewer than half are even counted as in the labor market. An intergen-erational cycle of poverty is creating an underclass within the environs of the university.

Service projects are community-based, not site-specific, and are devel-oped through consultation with local community representatives. The exact nature of the project has varied from course to course, but all are oriented toward action research. As noted above, the projects are integrally related to course objectives. The class works as a research team under direction of the instructor. The text is *Reforming Public Schools Through Community Education* by Minzey and LeTarte (Kendall-Hunt, 1994). Text and lecture provide general background on community educational leadership. Supplemental materials, articles, and documents relating to the particular project are provided.

VI. Assessment

Learning outcomes are assessed through reflective discussion and written reports, including working products such as surveys, interview schedules, observation protocols, and the like (depending on the nature of the particular project). Students' field experiences are reviewed weekly and form the basis for reflection and discussion around the topic of the day.

Individual evaluation and grading is based on comprehension of key concepts and skills, and mastery of course objectives. Individual journals are not graded, but the field reports are. They constitute 25 percent of the final grade. Team reports are rated at 50 percent of the grade, and work received from teams receives a common evaluation. In a final paper, students assess the applicability of the community education leadership to their current or future roles. This constitutes 25 percent of the grade and is essentially a reflective piece.

VII. Assessment of Service-Learning Placements

In this course, the success of the project as a whole is evaluated by the instructor. Assessment data are gathered from students through reflective discussion and through informal discussions with community contacts. The interaction among students, instructor, and context is very close. The instructor functions as research director and is constantly aware of student progress.

The first service-learning project was a comprehensive development plan prepared for the steering committee of the neighborhood council. Teams of students were assigned to work with community task forces. Members attended meetings, supported the leadership, and conducted field research. Results were shared with the task force and the steering committee. A second project narrowed the scope of research to the community school program at the local high school. A market survey was developed and administered. Primary data collection was supported through interviews with key informants and documentary research. The final report was shared with local school officials. Still another project focused on parent centers in local schools. Students developed an intensive, structured interview schedule supported by observation and document analysis. A report with recommendations on strengthening parent programming was shared in a group meeting with correspondents.

One of the consistent challenges of action research is securing access to key informants. This happens in spite of legitimation by appropriate representatives. Student researchers are given an introductory letter signed by the instructor and noting the community contact person. Still, scheduling informants is difficult, and, when scheduled, informants may be reluctant to share sensitive information. Of course, these difficulties are subjects for reflective discussion and underscore the necessity of utilizing multiple sources of information.

In some instances, students' perception of the community and concern for personal safety is a challenge. Here we discuss the utility of teaming with local residents before venturing into what may be unsafe areas for visitors. Local residents know the territory, and know where to go and not to go. They legitimize the presence of strangers in the neighborhood.

VIII. Gaining Institutional Support

The adaptation of this course as a vehicle for service-learning was a response to a larger effort to institutionalize service-learning in the teacher education curriculum. In preparing to introduce service-learning, education faculty adopted a policy that said, in part, "Service-learning is integrated into the teacher education curriculum at all levels and provides opportunities for experiential learning, individual reflection, and organized group discussion." Unanimous support for this principle eased the way for utilizing service-learning as a pedagogy in a sequence of classes in the graduate and under-graduate curriculum.

An explicit objective of the policy was to prepare education personnel to integrate service-learning into K-12 schools and classrooms. This objective has not been accomplished nearly so well. Utilizing service-learning as a pedagogy is easily done by education faculty, most of whom are familiar with experiential education. Instruction designed to prepare teachers requires greater familiarity with the developing field of theory and practice, however. Faculty development workshops and written information are pro-vided to heighten awareness and command of the field.

IX. Special Characteristics/Financial Support

No special financial support was required to initiate or maintain this course. The course was revised in 1992 as a response to an institutional initiative to develop academically based service opportunities. The institutional initia-tive was supported by a grant from the Commission (now Corporation) on National and Community Service.

X. Future Plans

While the service objectives of this course appear to be fully realized through the action research design, it is likely to evolve toward an increas-ingly *participatory* format with community involvement not only in setting directions for research but also in planning and implementing the research design as well as reviewing the findings. This evolution would enable stu-dents to develop increasingly refined skills for community collaboration, especially in the critical area of needs assessments.

XI. Contact

William H. Denton, Professor of Educational Leadership, Clark Atlanta University, James P. Brawley Drive at Fair Street, SW, Atlanta, GA 30314, ph 404/880-8493, fax 404/880-6081

Valparaiso University

I. Course/Program Title

Problems and Possibilities of Children and Youth in Contemporary Society: A Personal and Professional Inquiry

II. Category

This is an integrated studies required course that offers students of social work, sports management, secondary physical education, teaching athletic training, and elementary education the opportunity to explore their personal and professional relationships and ethical practice implications. Through examination of contemporary learning of children and literature studies of cross-cultural relations, students will compare philosophies, practices, and potentials affecting the arena of professionalism.

III. Conceptual Framework/Objectives

These are the objectives guiding all Arts and Services integrative studies courses:

1. to develop factual understanding of a contemporary problem or issue requiring disciplinary knowledge at an advanced level and involving more than one discipline;

2. to examine the range of alternatives involved in human choice by exploring conflicting viewpoints and values concerning the problem or issue;

3. to consider appropriate responses to the problem or issue as a responsible citizen, based in part on a personal assessment of ethical values;

4. to engage in this inquiry both orally and in writing at an advanced level.

The course focuses on the problems and possibilities of children and youth growing up in contemporary society. Students will explore these areas:

1. the problems and possibilities as they are defined in the three disciplines: social work, physical education, and elementary education;

2. visions, values, and voices of African Americans, Hispanics, Native Americans, and Asians;

3. problems such as homelessness, poverty, substance abuse, teen pregnancy, unemployment, etc. that make it difficult to realize visions, values, and voices;

4. connections between the problems and the possibilities.

IV. Integration of Service-Learning Theory

Integrating service into academic study holds great promise for enhancing student learning and fostering civic responsibilities among a next generation of college graduates. This course requires that students experience a multicultural type of service-learning experience. This will help students see relationships between courses of study and the society that lies beyond the walls of the institution.

V. Service-Learning Assignments and Activities

Each student must fulfill 25 hours of community service. We require the assessment be a multicultural/cross-cultural type of experience. Their attendance must be documented and certified by a letter with a signature of the supervisor in charge of the assignment. A list of community service assignments or activities for the course is developed by the professor with input from the students. The various types may include mentoring programs with students from various school districts. Other students will participate in projects in juvenile centers or nursing homes with senior citizens.

Placements are administered by the lead professor in class. In this class, there is also a professor from each discipline (elementary education, social work, and physical education) who contributes to teaching the class.

The required text for this course is *Savage Inequalities* by Jonathan Kozol (1991). This particular text gives the students a good picture of our many social problems in urban America as well as their impact on families and children. Students are also required to turn in a reflection paper on a journal article that deals with problems facing families and children in our society. It should primarily state how the problems affect families and children from the various minority groups.

Students are required to document their thoughts and experiences in the community, reflecting critically on seminar presentations, readings, and discussions. They make connections between their experiences in the community and their experiences in class as well as their thinking about themselves as citizens in the multicultural society. They also think about their roles as social workers, athletic trainers, sports management professionals, or teachers.

VI. Assessment

The following criteria are used to assess and evaluate students' work:
- attendance and participation (10%);
- field service component. This includes 25 hours of service-learning plus a 10-page reflection paper on the student's experience and how it relates to what we are doing in class (30%);
- a review of an article from a professional journal in the student's field

of study that deals with one of the major problems to be discussed in class concerning families and children (10%);

• oral group presentation. Students are divided into groups to make oral and written presentations on a major topic discussed in class, such as drug abuse among teens, drop-out rates, gender, or teenage violence (20%);

• final paper. Reflective paper on how a student personally and professionally sees himself or herself in relationship to American children and youth today. A student will use examples from his or her experiences, from class presentations and discussions, and from assigned readings to explain his or her statements (15%);

• final examination (15%).

The service-learning portion of the class is the best indicator of genuine learning success. Student reflection papers document these successes. The greatest challenge to teaching this course is the vast amount of time and effort it takes to keep the course exciting, dynamic, and interesting.

VII. Assessment of Service-Learning Placements

Service-learning placement sites are evaluated by the lead professor in the class. The mentoring program with students from the city of East Chicago, Indiana, a tutoring program with students from a local middle school, and programs connected to projects with juvenile detention centers were the most notable placement successes in the course.

VIII. Gaining Institutional Support

We have no critical issues to overcome concerning institutional support for this course.

IX. Special Characteristics/Financial Support

The course is now in its third semester, and the enrollment has increased by 50 percent. Other students from other disciplines are now also enrolled in it.

X. Future Plans

At present, we are developing a collaborative project between Valparaiso University and two local school districts that will probably be the first of its kind in the country. It includes the social work department, nursing, education, music, business, law, etc. working to provide a full-service school to two local schools with large minority populations. Service-learning will be a very important part of this project.

XI. Contact

Jose Arredondo, Department of Education, Miller Hall, Valparaiso University, Valparaiso, IN 46383, ph 219/464-5478, JArredon@Orion.Valpo.Edu

Alverno College

I. Course/Program Title
Assessing Learning Project

II. Category
Interprofessional collaboration.

III. Conceptual Framework/Objectives
The Assessing Learning Project was begun in 1993 for the purpose of supporting the reform efforts of the Milwaukee Public School (MPS) District through a focus on integrating performance assessment into the teaching/learning process at MPS middle and high schools. In the first two and one-half years, the project has provided three summer institutes for teams of teachers from 26 schools, with follow-up support to the teams in each of the years following the institutes. This number represents more than half of the K-8, middle, and high schools in the district, and the project will allow teams of teachers from all such schools eventually to engage in the summer institute experience and subsequent follow-up. The institutes and follow-up have been guided by Alverno College faculty experienced in reform and performance assessment. "Student assessment as learning" is a process in operation at Alverno College. Integral to learning, the process involves observation and judgment of each student's performance on the basis of explicit criteria, with resulting feedback to the student. It serves to confirm student achievement and provide feedback to the student for the improvement of learning and to the instructor for the improvement of teaching. Alverno faculty involved in the Assessing Learning Project have been able to engage their teacher candidates in the process and to learn more about the realities of today's urban educational settings by working beside teachers in their classrooms on a regular basis.

The project advances the process of implementing more rigorous and appropriate assessment in MPS, building specific links to content standards being developed as part of the implementation of the district's K-12 curriculum reform. It focuses on performance assessment across the curriculum.

The project seeks to (1) provide the district with a more rigorous and appropriate measure of student success by involving middle and high school teachers in developing and piloting a variety of performance assessments; (2) develop a team of teachers at each middle and high school knowledgeable about performance assessment and capable of working with students and other members of the staff; (3) guide and support administrators to promote a climate of trust and collaboration through their role as encouragers of positive change in teachers, teaching, and learning; (4) strengthen the district's emphasis on the development of academic and performance skills in the diverse student population in the district; and (5) document models of exemplary curriculum, instruction, and assessment in middle schools and high schools useful in the training of teachers at Alverno College, whose faculty facilitate the project.

The Assessing Learning Project focuses on communication areas as one of the models that faculty can utilize as a strong example of performance assessment applicable throughout the curriculum. As more teachers become familiar with the reading and writing performance assessments being developed and adopted by MPS, they share a common base for extending their understanding of performance assessment.

The project is tied to developing performance assessment related to the five *core* subject areas (mathematics, science, reading/language arts, social studies, and the arts) and the district's 10 teaching/learning goals. Teachers who participate in the project are taking critical roles in the development of those assessments. The college faculty serve as facilitators in the process. Moving a district as large as MPS through the reform process requires ongoing, concerted work at many levels. Because of the function of assessment as a lever for change, the Assessing Learning Project is important in building the capacity in each school to address needed changes in teaching and assessment, and to create a school culture that supports improvement in the opportunities provided for students and, through those opportunities, student achievement.

IV. Integration of Service-Learning Theory

One of the overriding goals of the project is to guide participants in building a learning community of teachers knowledgeable about performance assessment and capable of working with colleagues in their schools to implement an organizational plan to sustain improved teaching and learning. The service-learning aspect of the Assessing Learning Project is accomplished in three ways. First, Alverno faculty, through the summer institutes, train MPS teachers to meet that goal. Second, Alverno students, training to become middle and secondary teachers — and who are also knowledgeable about performance assessment through their experience with the Alverno curriculum — are placed in schools participating in the project for their fieldwork and student teaching. And third, Alverno faculty call upon the teacher and administrator participants from previous summer institutes to assist the college, its students, and other MPS teachers and administrators new to the process by participating in panel discussions on reform, serving as cooperating teachers, and facilitating the work of teacher/administrator teams in the work of the summer institutes.

V. Service-Learning Assignments and Activities

Alverno project co-coordinators visit the school teams on site throughout the academic year following the summer institute to provide support and resources and to formulate, with the team members, realistic and broad solutions to issues of concern that relate to both the diverse students in the system and teaching/learning processes in the classroom.

The project enables exemplary middle and high school teachers from previous Assessing Learning Project teams to become part of the facilitating team. Teachers who develop experience and expertise with performance assessment in their own classrooms work with new teams of teachers in the summer institute. Teacher participants appreciate the practical advice, authentic applications, and enthusiasm shared by their colleagues for this *change* in the district.

Alverno College teacher education students receive the benefit of working with teams of teachers trained in the summer institutes as their cooperating teachers in field placements and student teaching. Alverno faculty involved in the summer institute supervise these students and maintain ongoing follow-up contact with the teachers and students or hold weekly seminars in the participating schools for the students and their cooperating teachers.

VI. Assessment

To determine the impact of the project and closely related efforts, two areas are examined: the impact of the project on student learning and its impact on a given school. Sources of data regarding the impact on student learning include student reflections and student performance. The reflections are in the form of directed reflective journals in the summer institute, questionnaires, attitude inventories, and self-assessment in general or related to specific performances. Student performance — both public school and college — is observed through writing performance, teacher observations, student participation, and products. The impact on a given school is measured through teacher reports, measures of alternative assessment in schools, administrator reports, and archival data in the form of videotapes, posters, and materials created by teachers for their classrooms.

The project's impact can also be seen in the work of Alverno faculty in their classrooms. Their experiences have led them to adapt their own teaching and classroom practice. They have learned to assist teacher initiates to understand characteristics of school/college partnerships and how to foster such collaboration in the schools in which they practice.

VII. Assessment of Service-Learning Placements

Schools participating in the Assessing Learning Project are part of a system whose goal is to institute assessment-as-learning practices targeting success for all students. The partnership acknowledges the need to relate the effectiveness of teaching and the assurance of learning by all students. Successful schools have a vision that includes student outcomes, system structure, and underlying beliefs, with an emphasis on continual refinement of the vision and expanded involvement of teachers. They focus on meeting the diverse needs of students by creating assessments that are developmental in nature, encourage continuous improvement, and incorporate the district's teaching/learning goals. Their administrators encourage innovation, rethinking, and improvement and view teachers as responsible for instructional decisions and deserving of resources to support student learning and ongoing staff development.

The most sustaining aspect of the project is the school visits that Alverno faculty make regularly following a team's participation in the summer institute. The teams share the work they have done since returning to school and project ways that Alverno faculty might help to sustain the changes that individuals have begun. The Alverno faculty encourage teams to present their work at teachers' meetings and to involve other colleagues in the team's focus. Staff development focus provides an ongoing emphasis on developing teacher-initiated goals and activities that result in sustainable teacher change.

Alverno student participation in teacher project participants' classrooms maintains the teacher's focus on assessment as learning and provides a supportive environment for the teacher initiate to try out performance assessments with students in the context of a *real* classroom where the teacher is knowledgeable about assessment processes and trying out new behaviors as well.

VIII. Gaining Institutional Support

There are five critical issues to gain support for the Assessing Learning Project that participants in the project have developed for creating and maintaining successful change: (1) collaboration among all levels of leadership and power in the endeavor; (2) negotiation of time and resources; (3) tolerance for ambiguity among all constituents; (4) investment in the belief that all students can learn, an investment that is both individual and group-based; and (5) development to high standards of accomplishment. By embracing these critical success factors, participants in the project acquire a sense of moral purpose and a renewed and refined commitment to guiding student learning. The result is that the locus of leadership shifts to the classroom teacher as the primary influence on the success of students. It is this classroom-based leadership, not mandates from above, that provides the basis for successful and ongoing change. Teachers develop a confidence that their newly found skills and abilities around the assessment-as-learning focus actually are helping them to meet the diverse needs of their students.

IX. Special Characteristics/Financial Support

Everyone — MPS administrators, college faculty and students, and teachers — must *together* adopt a set of common goals toward which they are striving and on which they can judge their progress. The Joyce Foundation provided initial funding for the project. The project will be sustained as long as all constituents continue to work as trustworthy colleagues. To continue change in a positive way, administrators have moved away from judging teachers in traditional ways as they struggle with change, instead focusing on the positive processes and outcomes toward changes they are attempting to achieve. Ultimately, the project will be a success if students develop and express the understanding and abilities they need in order to respond to and shape their world.

X. Future Plans

Above all, the project must maintain frequent and open communication. Support for change comes not only in the classroom but also in the hallways where students, teachers, and administrators interact and through school policies that determine consequences for student behavior, both social and antisocial. Support must also come through college programs preparing teachers to teach in that atmosphere. The project will be a success as long as it endures as an active partnership between the college and schools and enjoys enthusiastic support from both communities.

XI. Contact

Julie A. Stoffels, Associate Professor, Alverno College, 3401 South 39 Street, Milwaukee, WI 53234-3922, ph 414/382-6414, fax 414/259-1843, 6219stoffels@vms.csd.mu.edu

Gustavus Adolphus College

I. Course/Program Title
Social Foundations of Education

II. Category
Foundations course.

III. Conceptual Framework/Objectives
The demographics in Minnesota are changing rapidly to include a growing number of Latinos (primarily Mexican Americans) who are choosing to settle here rather than work seasonally. This demographic shift is leading to economic and social pressures on small, rural communities and an increase in tension between Anglos who have lived here for generations and previously settled as well as new Latino residents. This practical service experience offers preservice education students the opportunity to gain insight into another cultural milieu as well as practical experience for teaching in a diverse classroom. The service offers the Latino community the opportunity to design needed social and educational programs with the assistance of student servers. Within the academic context of the course, education in the United States is examined in part through the lens of the Latino experience of education in this country, including racism toward immigrants, language issues, cultural differences and similarities between Latinos and Anglos, and the tension within education between assimilation and affirmation of cultural diversity. Specific course goals include the following:
- to begin to understand contemporary U.S. education through the exploration of important ideas and challenges current in schools today;
- to identify historical influences on current educational practice;
- to examine the role and purpose of education in a multicultural society;
- to examine cultural differences between Latinos and European Americans, particularly as they are manifest in schools in south central Minnesota;
- to explore service-learning as a practical and pedagogical tool for learning.

The mission of our teacher education program is to develop reflective practitioners who are well acquainted not only with the knowledge of their specific discipline but also with the larger social and cultural milieu in which education in the United States is conducted. The Social Foundations class is a required course, typically the first or second students take. The service component of the course helps students begin to integrate theory with practice, a skill they will continue to develop throughout their work in our program.

IV. Integration of Service-Learning Theory

Students engage in a service project during the entirety of the course. Class discussions include knowledge and experiences students have gleaned from their placements as well as using service-learning as a practical tool for learning in their own future classrooms. Students explore the ethics of requiring service, issues to be faced by students once they go out into the field, developing collaborative relationships with community agencies, enhancing awareness of diversity and antiracism through service-learning, and other aspects of service-learning. The service component offers the opportunity to critically reflect on the role of school in a multicultural society, a central theme of this course.

V. Service-Learning Assignments and Activities

Students are placed in the following types of community sites:
- ESL classrooms in the local area (tutoring children and adults);
- regional public libraries (bilingual and/or multicultural reading/story/literacy hours for children);
- local youth center (sports and social activities with Anglo and Latino youth);
- local adult education center (tutoring);
- on-campus writing and mathematics enhancement projects with Latino students (tutoring, mentoring, social activities).

The on-campus service-learning director administers placements.

Readings vary from semester to semester and include journal and newspaper articles and books.

Other assignments used in conjunction with the service-learning placement include:
- a journal on the service project;
- response papers — these are 1- to 3-page reflective responses to specific readings;
- final paper analyzing the inclusion of service-learning in classrooms;
- occasional papers responding to specific prompts, either concerning readings or class discussion;
- a "taking action" assignment, in which students must choose an issue related to Latinos that they want to know more about. After doing some research, including talking with Latinos themselves about the issue, they must take some action (write a letter to a newspaper, speak to a group of students, etc.).

VI. Assessment

Specific assessment techniques include journals, response papers, class discussion, and reports from agency supervisors.

The most notable learning successes in the course are that students develop a greater awareness of their own social identities. In my college, students are mostly white, middle class, rural, Christian, heterosexual, and from the upper Midwest. Just identifying what it means to be white is profoundly transformative for these students. As they think about how their social identities influence what happens in their classrooms and as they examine cultural differences among themselves and between themselves and other racial groups, they begin to develop a deepened understanding of the importance of culture and identity. In addition, students not only learn *about* another culture (in this case Latinos) through readings, films, etc. but also learn something about the life experience of real Latinos by engaging in service in the community. These learnings are documented through student writings and class discussion.

Because these predominantly white students have never been asked to think about what it means to be white, they tend to see their world view as "normal." They come to class with many conscious and unconscious prejudices toward Latinos (some of them come from Minnesota communities where there have been conflicts between Anglos and Latinos) and with very little knowledge about Mexican-American history or culture or the historical relationship between Mexico and the United States.

VII. Assessment of Service-Learning Placements

Service-learning placement sites are evaluated by the on-campus service-learning director, the course instructor, and a work-study student assigned to this project.

The most notable placement success in the course is a partnership between this college and a nearby school district that has led to a Saturday morning enrichment program for Latino students. The preservice teachers in my course who work with these students often seem to learn the most, perhaps because they are with the children for several hours at a time. Other successful placements have been in a local youth center and in an ESL program at an elementary school.

The most notable placement challenges in the course include:

• placements that do not include agencies or programs in which Latinos are fundamentally involved both in leadership positions and as group members; and

• placements in which teachers or program leaders do not see the value of making cross-cultural connections between Anglos and Latinos.

VIII. Gaining Institutional Support

Strategies to gain institutional support and commitment include:

- cofacilitating an on-campus workshop for faculty on service-learning in academic courses;
- advocating with the president of the college and others for the continuation of a service-learning office on campus with a full-time, well-paid service-learning director;
- developing service components as an integral part of several courses in the education department;
- supporting the development of a special-interest residence house for college students called "Service House." Residents engage in a variety of community-service activities and offer meetings and presentations on service for the entire campus.

Other recommendations and suggestions regarding institutional support include these:

- Engaging in service-learning is possible for any faculty member but is made significantly more viable if the institution funds a service-learning director who can coordinate much of the placement and evaluation.
- Including a commitment to service as part of the institution's mission statement provides a basis on which service-learning programs can be built on campus.

IX. Special Characteristics/Financial Support

The service-learning component in this course is unusual in that it specifically links service-learning and multicultural education as complementary philosophies and methodologies. In fact, I believe strongly that a service project without a commitment to multicultural efforts simply reproduces a colonialist mentality among students, the attitude that "we must help these poor people." If service-learning is to be done, it must be approached with a great deal of humility and respect for the community with which one is interacting.

To plan the changes in this course so as to include a service-learning component, I was released from one course section for one semester through a grant funded by the Minnesota Youth Works Higher Education Program. The grant proposal was written by the service-learning director, with assistance from myself and the chair of the Education Department. I used the time made available in this way to meet with Latino and Anglo community members, agency directors, teachers, etc.

X. Future Plans

Future plans include:

- to continue to fine-tune the service-learning component of this course;

- to continue to research the ways in which service-learning and multicultural education intersect;
- to continue to advocate for the inclusion of service-learning in courses across campus;
- to continue to present nationally on service-learning and multicultural education.

XI. Contact

Carolyn O'Grady, Education Department, Gustavus Adolphus College, St. Peter, MN 56082, ph 507/933-6148, fax 507/933-7041, *cogrady@gac.edu*

Washington State University

I. Course/Program Title

Teaching and Learning 450, Content Literacy for Middle and Secondary Schools

II. Category

Required methods course for all preservice teachers in WSU's middle and secondary school teacher certification program. The catalogue description of the course says, "reading and writing in content areas, grades 4-12; integration of service-learning and community-of-learners approaches in teaching literacy skill."

III. Conceptual Framework/Objectives

Diagrammatically, the course can be explained as shown on page 180.

The course is "taught" in keeping with an emphasis upon *contextualized reflective inquiry,* since this emphasis is part of the conceptual framework of the Department of Teaching and Learning's teacher preparation program. Key words related to our conceptual framework are "self-directing," "analyzing," "goal setting," "planning," "monitoring," "evaluating," "reflecting," and "sharing ideas." Congruent with this overall departmental context, the approach of the course subscribes to cognitive, psycholinguistic, and sociolinguistic theories of learning. The various course assignments enable the students to experience, and not just discuss, constructivist theories of learning and to create a literate environment and learning community for and of themselves. During course sessions and while completing out-of-class assignments, students explore and inquire as they read, talk, and listen to one another and then author or coauthor in writing teams various documents for authentic purposes and genuine audiences. The structure of course assignments and experiences is designed to reflect the psycholinguistic perspectives of Kenneth and Yetta Goodman and of Frank Smith ("prediction"), the cognitive learning theories of Piaget and Bruner ("assimilation . . . accommodation . . . equilibration . . . disequilibrium" and "schema"), and the sociolinguistic theories of Lev Vygotsky ("scaffolding" and "zones of proximal development").

Course goals. In this course,

students work cooperatively and individually to draft and revise a number of major [writing] assignments: (1) integrated units, (2) traditional units, (3) journal reviews, (4) professional literacy text reviews, (5) reflective

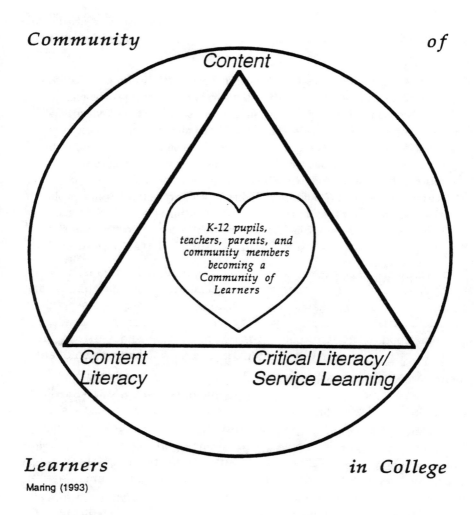

Community   *of*

Content

K-12 pupils,
teachers, parents, and
community members
becoming a
Community of
Learners

Content
Literacy

Critical Literacy/
Service Learning

Learners   *in College*

Maring (1993)

service-learning essays, (6) collaborative research projects, and (7) portfolio cover-sheet assignments. *The creation of content literacy strategies is a major emphasis of the course. Content literacy strategies are embedded within the units students write. Likewise, service-learning dimensions of the units are also integrated into the content of the units or embedded within the content literacy strategies the units contain.*

Units (with their embedded content literacy and service-learning dimensions) and the reflective service-learning essays are, with students' permission, desktop published in a course handbook, *Content Literacy and Service-Learning*. As of fall 1995, students in sections of the course had completed 11 of these coauthored, spiral-bound handbooks. The handbooks are shared with future students in the course for the sake of models and encouragement and with teachers around the state in order to receive feedback and to initiate dialogue and partnerships.

The purpose of the course is to enable participants to learn how to create and implement a learning-community approach that encourages subject-matter learning, reading and writing across the curriculum, critical literacy, and service-learning.

Course objectives. The course has several objectives:

1. to experience and learn about a community-of-learners approach to teaching content-area literacy;

2. to learn how to implement whole-language perspectives (e.g., integrated curriculum, meaningful learning, student centeredness, teacher role as facilitator and guide);

3. by the creation and implementation of content-area literacy strategies and units, to help pupils become more literate;

4. to help course participants develop a broader perspective (for content pedagogy) that emphasizes connections among subject matter, literacy, service, and citizenship.

To achieve these objectives, *inquiry* and *application* processes and assignments are emphasized in the course. Service-learning concepts, information, applications, and practicum experiences in the course are seen as tools to make learning in content and content literacy more significant, more relevant, and more interesting — both for preservice teachers and for their pupils in the future.

IV. Integration of Service-Learning Theory

Learning-community members learn and apply service-learning theories at two levels. First, during the first three weeks of the course, they add the concept of service-learning to their personal knowledge base by completing structured reader-response journal entries related to required readings about service-learning and by watching two videos ("Hearts and Minds

Engaged" and "Today's Heroes"). They also build their knowledge base by writing a *service-learning contract* related to volunteer activities they will complete during the course. On the second level of application and reflection, they complete, by the end of the course, a service-learning reflective essay and units of instruction for pupils that integrate content, content-area literacy strategies, and service-learning dimensions down to nuts-and-bolts aspects. Learning-community members place these units and essays on the World Wide Web. Some students further integrate service-learning theory into their knowledge base and applied levels of comprehension by electing to complete collaborative research projects on the topic of service-learning itself. In short, the integration of service-learning is not professor-centered but is performance-based in terms of learning-community members' outcomes.

V. Service-Learning Assignments and Activities

In the course's service-learning practicum, students select from volunteering opportunities in classroom or community sites. Placements are selected by the students themselves or with the help of the University Community Service Learning Center, chamber of commerce, or other agencies. Students' academic learning related to service-learning is animated by assignments and guidelines in the required course packet ("What Is Service-Learning?" "The Service-Learning Reflection Essay," "Nuts and Bolts of Service-Learning," "Integrating Service-Learning With Content and Content Literacy"), guest speakers, two structured reader-response journal assignments related to the service-learning curriculum and resources, and two videos ("Today's Heroes" and "Hearts and Minds Engaged"). Because of coordination challenges, the students' service-learning practicum is not connected with the service-learning dimensions of the units and literacy strategies they coauthor in class. A few students do not enjoy or approve of the service-learning practicum requirement, but the professor of the course and most students feel it is truly necessary for students to get a feel for whether they will integrate service-learning with content and content literacy in their early years of teaching. In addition, a few students feel that content literacy should be studied in and of itself and apart from the major potentials service-learning offers (e.g., personal growth, character formation, civic responsibility, motivation, relevance, significance).

VI. Assessment

Each assignment, including those related to service-learning, has attached to it a grading/evaluation checklist related to content and to literacy. For example, the guidelines for writing the service-learning reflection essay conclude with the following:

Content and Writing Evaluation

A. CONTENT -- Each of the major parts and their subparts are written about.
      Grade: Circle --   A   B   C   D   F
      Note: Make sure that your essay has two major subheads, i.e., Part One and Part Two. Respond to each required part/subhead in order.

B. WRITING -- Grade for each of the following:
      Critical Reading   _____
      Focus   _____
      Organization   _____
      Support   _____
      Proof   _____

OVERALL GRADE FOR ASSIGNMENT   _____
QUALITATIVE COMMENTS:

One of the major challenges of the course is related to the quality of student work, including the quality of some of the content-area literacy strategies some students create. The writing of lower-quality content-area literacy strategies may be due to the fact that some students are unused to the challenges of the constructivist paradigm and of functioning within the literate-environment/community-of-learners approach. Some of these students may feel more comfortable in courses with lecture/demonstration/regurgitation formats. Finally, a smaller number of students seem to take issue with inclusion of service-learning with content or content-area literacy. Because of the interest service-learning generates and its novelty to some students, a few students, in the past, have observed that the course had too much of an emphasis on service-learning.

VII. Assessment of Service-Learning Placements

The teacher of the course approves the service-learning placements the students propose and channel through the Community Service Learning Center. The instructor carefully reads the service-learning reflective essays each semester so that problematic placements can be avoided in the future.

Too many students seem to favor service-learning placements in traditional cross-age tutoring programs in classroom contexts. Although these experiences provide service-learning opportunities, the teacher of the course encourages students to work in nursing homes, humane societies, Habitat for Humanity projects, environmental agencies, etc. so that they can begin to view teaching, curriculum, and content literacy development in the context of community partnerships. This view of educational reform is more talked about in the university classroom than experienced or committed to by future teachers. The ever-growing number of students who spend excessive hours working during their college years also makes it difficult for many to squeeze in service-learning as part of their course of study.

VIII. Gaining Institutional Support

There seems to be strong institutional encouragement and support for our efforts to integrate service-learning into the required content literacy course and, thereby, into the required "core." Service-learning is also included, but to lesser degrees, in other courses that focus on at-risk pupils, social studies, health education, physical education, and science. A major challenge in our program is finding and training cooperating teachers in Washington state who will accept our student teachers who are interested in using service-learning.

IX. Special Characteristics/Financial Support

Extramural financial support from the Washington Higher Education Coordinating Board and the Corporation for National and Community Service was needed to initiate and sustain the program for the first three years. During this time, the course syllabus was revised, with the help of action research methods, and a 200-page course syllabus/packet was produced to enable preservice teachers to integrate content, content literacy, and service-learning and to carry out the service-learning practicum and reflection required in the course. By the completion of the fall 1995 semester, eleven 150- to 300-page spiral-bound handbooks had been produced and distributed to students, who proudly shared them with teachers and administrators around the state, with parents and relatives, and with other professors on campus.

During spring 1996, the interactive infrastructure was completed so that student coauthors placed their units, content literacy strategies, service-learning integrations, and reflective essays on the World Wide Web. Teachers from around the state and beyond were invited, by postings sent out from the Office of the Superintendent of Public Instruction, to read, comment on, critique (via email or WWW postings), and use and adapt the student-created work. Educators and preservice teachers in Washington and beyond can access these materials at www.*educ.wsu.edu/tl/450*.

X. Future Plans

This innovative, WWW approach for getting feedback from the field from inservice teachers was begun after the period of extramural funding and will continue in increasingly expansive ways with the facilitation of WWW technologies.

Project service leadership director Kate McPherson is working with interested "early-years" teachers in the Vancouver, Washington, area. Gerald Maring is working with the department and is seeking funding to connect volunteering cooperating teachers with interested student teachers who want to integrate content, content literacy, and service-learning dimensions into the student teaching experience.

XI. Contact
Gerald H. Maring, Department of Teaching and Learning, Washington State University, Pullman, WA 99164, ph 509/335-5651, fax 509/335-5046, *maring@mail.wsu.edu*

California State University–San Marcos

I. Course/Program Title
Secondary teacher training program

II. Category
Comprehensive program that integrates service-learning into both a required first-semester course called High Schools of the 21st Century (EDSS 530) and field experiences. Service-learning project has an outcome potential for implementation with the student teachers' own classes during beginning or advanced student teaching.

III. Conceptual Framework/Objectives
The course is part of the newly developed single-subject credential program at California State University–San Marcos (1995-96 was the first year of implementation). The overall purpose of the course is for the preservice candidates to become familiar with the theoretical framework for secondary (high school) reform through a number of assigned readings, observations, and practices. One of the critical assigned readings is *Second to None: A Vision of the New California High School,* which was recently released by a California task force as a framework for high school reform. Many ideas contained in this document were used to assist in designing the goals and curriculum for the program. In addition, some course themes evolved from these concepts, including one called "The Teacher and the Community Interacting," which incorporates the philosophy and underpinnings of utilizing service-learning with high school students.

IV. Integration of Service-Learning Theory
All the themes in the course involve major tenets and concepts that are modeled by the instructor and connected to assignments whose concepts may be implemented either in the beginning field experience during the last five weeks of the first semester or in the advanced field experience during the last 10 weeks during the end of the second semester.

In the theme that focuses on service-learning, "The Teacher and the Community Interacting," preservice teachers are asked to explore both the informal and the formal community that interfaces with the school to which they are assigned. As one outcome of that exploration, it is hoped that they will perceive the value of this organization to the school and the community at large and seek potential ways to utilize this strategy in their own teaching. The local community should be considered a vital component in any school curriculum, as both the individuals and the organizations to which they belong are valuable assets for student and teacher to explore and become knowledgeable about. To this end, they are to design appropriate curricula that would utilize this community resource.

There is much support for school/student interaction in the community. Ernest Boyer, in a Carnegie report, suggested community service be a part of all high school graduation requirements and added that a "service component for all students will do much to help build a sense of community and common purpose within a school . . . and to be fully human one must serve." John Dewey wrote that "the radical reason that the present school cannot organize itself as a natural social unit is because just this element of common and productive activity is missing" (40). In *Second to None*, the California Task Force suggests schools "fully integrate the community into the curriculum by exposing students to real-world problems."

Our secondary faculty at CSU–San Marcos believe strongly that this theme (the teacher and the community interacting) and the resultant service-learning project are very important course and field components that assist in achieving the objective of getting the preservice teacher to understand the role and purpose of community service and resources. If they understand the dynamics, it is more likely they will incorporate service-learning into their own teaching.

V. Service-Learning Assignments and Activities

The specific types of community sites that preservice teachers identify as ones they will use for their project depend somewhat on their own interests and discipline areas as well as the geographical location of their field placement. To assist them in this process, CSU–San Marcos has a service-learning center and coordinator. Early in the course, this coordinator shares information about service-learning through readings and handouts as well as information about specific organizations. The students can use this as a starting point to assist in initiating their projects. Subsequently, they are then given a handout that contains a series of prompts that will assist in this information gathering (see the figure on p. 188). They are asked to identify, contact, and interact with this community organization that in some way impacts students in the high school to which they are assigned. They must also design curricular lesson plan(s) that would utilize this organization within the context of their field placements. More specifically, objectives for this lesson plan must consider the following perspectives in their design:

1. What services does this organization provide to students (schools) and how are they accessed?

2. How could this organization provide career or mentorship opportunities for students within the context of a (my) discipline?

Service-Learning Practicum Prompts for
Secondary Preservice Teachers in
EDSS 530, High Schools of the 21st Century

1. Name of organization:

2. Contact person (name, title, telephone no.):

3. Address:

4. Overview of organization's mission or purpose:

5. Narrative of experiences, including any observations, interviews, and participatory activities (use back or attach a sheet if necessary):

6. Highlights:
     A. In what ways is this organization supportive of schools?
     B. In what ways did this organization demonstrate limitations to working with students (schools)? If so, what recommendations would you suggest to improve in this regard?
     C. How could this organization be used for service-learning, career exploration, or connections to your discipline in conjunction with your high school students? (This will be expanded on during Number 7.)
     D. In reflection, what is the most important impression you are left with concerning this experience?
     E. Could the service-learning experience practicum (or your specific one) be improved? If so, in what ways?

7. Using all the knowledge you gleaned from the practicum, design a lesson plan for your discipline that incorporates the organization you studied as the main focus of the lesson. Into this lesson plan, try to integrate as many of the aspects of learning as discussed in Number 6C (service, content connections, careers).

3. How could this organization incorporate (my) students as part of a service project that would provide them with a real opportunity to benefit the community?

4. In what ways does this organization correspond to the content or topics that are taught to (my) students?

Prior to starting their project, the preservice student teachers schedule a miniconference with the instructor regarding their proposed placements and activities. This is a valuable part of the process in that it offers both the student and instructor time to clarify goals of the individual project.

The prompts of this assignment encourage preservice high school teachers not only to seek information and interact with local service organizations but also to think about ways in which they could apply this within the context of their own classroom (or discipline) as part of an experiential approach toward teaching.

Expectations are that a minimum of a 15-hour practicum will be devoted to completing the service component of the assignment. After they have completed the assignment, they present their findings to the whole cohort in the context of an oral and written presentation during a reflections class, which is held at the completion of each semester. In addition, a vital part of this reflective process would include perspectives on any implementation accomplished during student teaching.

VI. Assessment and VII. Assessment of Service-Learning Placements

Since the service-learning placement and its application (lesson plan) are closely intertwined, both are assessed together. Students often call during the project period seeking advice and additional information on the assignment. As discussed earlier, at the completion of the semester a special reflections class allows time for presentations of the projects, discussion, and both peer and instructor evaluations. This evaluation process includes a student self-evaluation of the experience, an informal peer evaluation, as well as the instructor's critique of its overall effectiveness. The instructor's critique includes these major elements that focus on both the oral presentation and written report:

1. Does the student's interaction with the organization contain real insight and analysis of the effectiveness of this organization as it relates to the school site?

2. How effectively did (could) the proposed lesson plan utilize this organization with the high school students with regard to service, careers, and content-specific knowledge?

One example of a notable success from the first-year projects was one chosen by a foreign language (Spanish) preservice teacher who selected a migrant tutoring organization established for non-English-speaking parents of students at her assigned school site. She learned in her interaction with this organization that some of the grandparents of students at the school actually had the day-to-day responsibility for their grandchildren yet knew little English and consequently could not communicate much with the school. Based on this and in conjunction with this organization, she established a weekly English language seminar for these grandparents to assist them in learning basic English conversational skills. In her small group, which met in the homes of these grandparents, she would have them practice their conversations and then actually call the school to assess their understanding. She extended this concept to her own lesson plans by assigning her Spanish 3 class (which she was student teaching) to assist in this tutoring process. In exchange, some of the people being tutored spoke to her class (in Spanish) on their migrant experiences in Southern California. To assess her students' experience, she assigned an essay that asked them to write on what it would be like to migrate to Mexico from the United States if the economic tables were reversed.

In summary, she created a multidimensional lesson plan in which her students provided a valuable community service that directly connected to their own curriculum (Spanish language and culture) and also allowed them to experience the role of a particular career (teaching). Other examples of student choices were very diverse, including a health-care clinic, a drug and alcohol treatment center, boys' and girls' clubs, and a youth halfway house.

One of the challenges of the project is for the preservice teachers to be able to implement the service-learning lesson plan in their field experience placements. Some of the master teachers already have established curricula, and the student teachers are in their classrooms as short-term teachers (5 weeks and 10 weeks only). In the 1996-97 year, in order to encourage more implementation during the field experience:

1. The preservice teachers will continue to have both options of implementing service-learning with their students during either the beginning or advanced field placement (i.e., first or second semester).

2. Prior to the beginning of the semester, master teachers will be informed regarding the purpose and prompts of the assignment and encouraged to assist the preservice teachers in this endeavor.

3. Students will be encouraged to include a study on the effectiveness of service-learning in the classroom as part of their action research project assignment.

By communicating information to master teachers prior to the school year and increasing the time frame and context of the assignment, it is hoped that opportunities for real implementation will enhance this service-learning experience.

VIII. Gaining Institutional Support

We are fortunate at CSU–San Marcos to have a service-learning center. The coordinator and staff are available for formal presentations and student assistance as well as keeping the faculty abreast of new information and conferences on service-learning. More than 20 faculty and numerous courses (graduate and undergraduate) already incorporate service-learning at CSU–San Marcos. This faculty expertise is a good source of information and support for others seeking information about service-learning.

Each year, there is also a small grants competition to assist in service-learning-related projects and research. The secondary faculty applied for and received one for this past year (1996-97) that assisted in enhancing the service-learning component of the secondary credential program (since we added an additional cohort with five new schools serving as field sites for placements). In addition, this grant is providing support for creating longitudinal research studies that track our graduates and their utilization of service-learning in their own classrooms as they enter the teaching field.

IX. Special Characteristics/Financial Support

The small grants program discussed above will provide some supplementary support for our faculty as well as other faculty and students at our university engaged in service-learning activities. These funds may be used for a variety of purposes, including, for example, curriculum development, attendance at conferences, and staff support. No other special financial assistance is required to support or maintain the role of service-learning in the CSU–San Marcos secondary credential program.

X. Future Plans

In spring 1996, three of the secondary preservice teachers and I presented at a regional service-learning conference held at CSU–San Marcos to share experiences from both a student and an instructor perspective. We hope in the future to have other opportunities for students and faculty to attend and present at appropriate conferences.

A database is being created by one of the students to document all the information gained from each student's experience, including an overview of the organization, contact person, and the manner it was implemented. This database will be made available for each new cohort of students as a source of information they can use in designing their own projects.

The secondary faculty will continue to seek ways of improving the use of service-learning within the credential program as well as studying potential impact of service-learning on local schools as they monitor CSU–San Marcos graduates as they enter the teaching field.

XI. Contact

Joseph F. Keating, Assistant Professor and Program Coordinator, Secondary Credential Program, College of Education, CSU–San Marcos, San Marcos, CA 92096, ph 619/750-4321, fax 619/750-4323, *jkeating@mailhost1.csusm.edu*

References

California Task Force. (1992). *Second to None: A Vision of the New California High School.* Sacramento, CA: Department of Education.

Dewey, J. (1938). *Experience and Education.* New York: Collier Books.

Mankato State University

I. Course/Program Title
Integrating Service-Learning Into the Preservice Teacher Education Program

II. Category
Courses include two in foundations with service-learning components, proposed methods course(s) in curriculum and instruction, and one elective course (foundations) in service-learning for undergraduates and graduates.

III. Conceptual Framework/Objectives
The university, as part of the state university system, is in transition from quarters to semesters; thus, the process of integrating service-learning into the curriculum reflects this transition.

Currently, all preservice teachers have two service-learning experiences in foundations: (1) service-learning as a learning method to achieve academic objectives (practice); and (2) studying about service-learning (theory). Generally, students will experience service-learning as a method first and then study the theory. After semester conversion, it is proposed that the Curriculum and Instruction Department integrate service-learning into specific methods courses. Along with the two foundations courses and the proposed integration into methods, an elective course in service-learning is offered for undergraduates and graduates.

• *Service-learning to achieve academic objectives (practice)*: All preservice teachers are required to complete Human Relations and Interaction, which includes a 12-hour service-learning component designed to meet the following objectives: (1) identify a communication strength and a weakness, (2) identify and practice a full value, (3) demonstrate use of personal power (energy), (4) identify tendencies of being an oppressor, (5) identify negative self-messages that were replaced with positive messages (self-esteem), and (6) identify unexpected learning experiences.

• *Study of service-learning (theory)*: One class session in the present School and Society (which will become Learning in the Social Context taken during student teaching) is devoted to the study of service-learning: (1) planning, (2) implementation, (3) evaluation, and (4) celebration (theory).

• *Application of service-learning in disciplines (methods)*: Service-learning is proposed for implementation in the Curriculum and Instruction Department after semester conversion. The objective is to determine how service-learning can be utilized to achieve academic objectives.

• *Elective course for undergraduates and graduates*: A course devoted solely to service-learning: service-learning as (a) program, (b) activity, (c) course, and (d) integration into curriculum; and service-learning (a) planning, (b) implementation, (c) evaluation, and (d) celebration.

IV. Integration of Service-Learning Theory

Human Relations and Interaction: A major component of this course is devoted to cultural diversity defined in a broad sense, i.e., race, ethnicity, religion, class, gender, sexual orientation, ability, age. In the first class session, each student is asked to rank his or her comfort level with the eight groups experiencing oppression in American culture. The student is asked to complete 12 hours of service-learning that will place the student in direct contact with one of the three groups she or he ranked as lowest in comfort level. In course evaluations, students consistently report that the service-learning experience is one of the most, if not the most, valuable components of the course. In the reflective write-ups, students have indicated that the experience has changed their attitude (disposition), thinking (knowledge), and/or behavior (skills) more effectively than books, teachers, classroom experiences, and tests would achieve.

School and Society: One class session is devoted to a study of service-learning theory to support preservice teachers in knowing about service-learning.

Application in methods courses: The focus will be on practice in identifying means to achieve academic objectives through service and use of reflection.

Elective: (1) study of theory, (2) visit to service-learning sites to see application, and (3) designing plans for service-learning implementation.

V. Service-Learning Assignments and Activities

Human Relations and Interaction: Community placement sites include agencies serving societal groups that experience oppression — food shelves (class, race, ethnicity), shelters (gender, race, ethnicity, class), religious groups (religion), hospitals, nursing homes, physical and mental support services, treatment centers, counseling centers, ABE/GED and alternative education programs (ability, age, class, gender), gay/lesbian/bisexual support (sexual orientation).

Placement administration is currently done by faculty and a university coordinator (AmeriCorps employee). A placement fair is held at the beginning of the course where cooperating agencies set up displays and visit with students who bring their resumes or short narratives. Some students place themselves with agencies beyond those at the fair. Ongoing administration, however, is a weak aspect of the present program. Plans are being developed to institutionalize service-learning by having a university faculty member coordinate all service-learning experiences.

The text for the course includes sections on the eight societal groups experiencing oppression in American culture. Each student also purchases a guide, *Clinical Experience Through Service-Learning*. The guide includes basic information on service-learning for the student and a one-page summary of information for the cooperating agency along with learning contracts, supervisor evaluation, and reflection write-up directions with criteria.

Other assignments are used in conjunction with the service-learning placement. Student "home groups" (average of four students) teach sessions devoted to the eight societal groups. Home groups are required to bring primary resources to the class session, i.e., member(s) of the societal group that is the focus of their session. An additional home group teaches a session on how schools and communities are addressing issues of oppression related to these eight groups.

As service-learning expands, it appears to be crucial that there be university-wide coordination to avoid agencies' receiving multiple phone calls from students seeking placements, to support agencies, to share ideas among faculty, to share ideas among agencies, and to provide ongoing staff development for faculty and agencies.

School and Society: One class session is devoted to service-learning and is taught by a home group of students. The session focuses on basic information on service-learning, including application in disciplines.

VI. Assessment

Human Relations and Interaction: Students complete a write-up in which they reflect on their experiences within the framework of the selected course objectives that are addressed through service-learning. In the sessions taught by students, all students write a reaction paper on each session in which they identify (1) feelings, (2) thinking, and (3) application relating to the theme of the session. Peer evaluation is included.

Students report that being required to implement their service-learning with one of the groups they ranked as "least comfortable" results in positive changes in feeling, thinking, and behaviors that, they contend, would not have happened without direct contact through service.

A learning challenge has been that some students have difficulty in scheduling their hours due to conflicts in schedules.

A recommendation: The requirement to have the student provide service to a group with which the student is "least comfortable" has been highly successful in supporting the student to change attitudes, knowledge, and dispositions.

VII. Assessment of Service-Learning Placements

No formal assessment of placement sites has been established; this is a next step in the process of having a university-wide coordinator. Unique experiences and successes have been noted in all types of agencies serving the eight societal groups. There have been very few problems with agencies. Two reasons for the success with agencies may be the inservices that were provided to agencies in the beginning and having community agencies as part of the program-development process.

VIII. Gaining Institutional Support

Utilizing a planning team that included faculty, staff, students, and community agencies established broad-based support. Establishing an advisory council of faculty and students in the College of Education gave credibility. Working cooperatively with departments across the university gained ultimate support of the president to institutionalize service-learning through establishing a university-wide coordinator position.

A recommendation: Involving new participants in the process gives new energy and broadens the support base.

IX. Special Characteristics/Financial Support

The College of Education joined with the College of Social and Behavioral Sciences along with Student Development to secure a grant. This was crucial to gain credibility and support within the university system at all levels.

X. Future Plans

A major step will be institutionalization through the support of the president of the university to establish a university-wide coordinator position.

XI. Contact

Darrol Bussler, Associate Professor, Educational Foundations, Mankato State University Box 52, Mankato, MN 56002-8400, ph 507/389-6222, fax 507/389-5854, *darrol_bussler@ms1.mankato.msus.edu*

Clemson University

I. Course/Program Title
Integrating Service-Learning Into Curricula

II. Category
Foundations/curriculum methodology course

III. Conceptual Framework/Objectives
This course provides opportunities for certified teachers to build competence in service-learning through personal participation in service and
reflection. Participants develop a plan to integrate service-learning into the
curricula of their school and/or district. This course provides knowledge and
experiences to enable participants to meet each of the following objectives:

1. define effective service-learning;
2. develop rationale for service-learning programs;
3. experience service-learning personally: preparation, participation,
and processing;
4. describe the service-learning cycle;
5. apply the principles of good practice for combining service and
learning;
6. experience guiding children in service-learning;
7. identify service-learning program organizational issues;
8. develop action plan for service-learning with children;
9. implement plan for guiding children in service-learning, postcourse,
at their school;
10. reflect on lessons learned through service-learning personally and
with children.

IV. Integration of Service-Learning Theory
Integrating Service-Learning Into Curricula is a master's-level course for certified teachers that also meets teacher recertification requirements. The
course is designed to prepare teachers to be able to integrate service-
learning into any academic curriculum in grades kindergarten through high
school. Not only does the course instruct in the methods of service-learning;
it also utilizes service-learning as a methodology in developing a true understanding of the concept.

Our philosophy is that class participants will best learn what service-
learning is by doing it themselves. After an introduction to service-learning
for the first week of classes, students experience service-learning through

the stages of preparation, action, reflection, and celebration by participating in an actual service project. In addition, students experience leading children in a service-learning project.

V. Service-Learning Assignments and Activities

Although students participate in all kinds of service (direct, indirect, and advocacy) during the course, the direct service experience has been the most meaningful. Their direct service is a one-time experience for students; therefore, it is most important that this experience be profound. Professors make initial contacts for site visits, modeling the role that teachers will take when they supervise service-learning for their students. Agency staff provide additional support.

Our most successful sites for our class participants have included Meals on Wheels, the local animal shelter, and a soup kitchen. These sites demonstrated real needs, some of which were met during the one-time experience. Participants were able to base much of their reflective journaling and class presentations on their vivid experiences.

An integral part of the course is a student-led service experience for children. In conjunction with a summer program for elementary children, the graduate students work with the summer program teachers to develop and implement a service-learning project with the children. Class participants make the necessary arrangements with the service site, work with the children to prepare them for service, and involve children as much as possible in preservice activities. They return to lead the service activity with the children and their teachers, guide their reflection, and celebrate their accomplishments.

Service sites and activities chosen by the teams of class participants, summer program teachers, and children have included cleaning up local parks and highways, doing plantings at a local botanical garden, and beautifying the school grounds. The common denominator for this one-time service activity has evolved to become the completion of a product that the children can point to with a certain amount of pride — where they can say, "We did it!" In addition, this experience with children provides class participants and the children's teachers with the opportunity to see at-risk children in an entirely new light. Children who have been the troublemakers in the regular classroom often have become the stars of the service-learning activities, leaving a profound effect on the class teachers and the children's summer program teachers. This is a significant reason why course participants become committed to implementing service-learning into their own teaching once school begins in the fall.

Other assignments have included class participants' contacting and interviewing local community-based agencies. This initial contact has in many cases become the first contact with a potential service site for the coming school year.

It is strongly recommended that instructors become well acquainted with agency personnel and the needs of that agency prior to service activities by the graduate students.

VI. Assessment

Grades are assigned based on (1) a contracted intent by the student to complete a differentiated level of requirements, and (2) an assessment by instructors of the quality of work completed by each student. Students are given opportunities to improve work if needed and/or when possible.

Follow-up of the first group of teachers who took the course revealed that all but one had implemented some type of service-learning activity by December of that school year.

Teachers from all three years have encouraged others in their schools to adopt service-learning. One school district has adopted service-learning as school board policy as an outgrowth of the commitment of several teachers who took the course. Many other teachers have become part of a Department of Education–sponsored cadre of service-learning trainers themselves, becoming leaders in the state movement to promote and expand service-learning.

The major challenge of preparing practicing teachers to return to their own classrooms utilizing service-learning as a teaching methodology is curriculum integration. Practicing teachers have to make a paradigm shift. They need to look at their curriculum, their students, and themselves in a different light. They have to understand that they can continue to teach toward the same educational goals but more effectively using service-learning.

This has proven to be a difficult concept to accept for many experienced teachers. We discovered this when students' presentations of their action plans have shown that although they understood community service, they haven't quite understood service-learning. We plan next time to play a greater role as facilitators and supporters while the plans are being developed, to assist them if needed in strengthening the service-learning component of their action plans. In addition, their perception that number of service hours is more crucial than the learning outcomes is changed through using focused exercises.

VII. Assessment of Service-Learning Placements

All participants in the process provide assessment of the service-learning sites. Each service group includes one of the instructors; thus, we have been able to assess the effectiveness of the service activity for our purposes firsthand. Secondly, we receive insights from the community agency personnel who administer the site. Finally, and very significantly, the reflection activity, both oral and creative (art, music, creative writing, etc.) of the graduate students truly tells us whether our goals have been reached.

Our most valuable placements for our graduate students have been ones where there was a real need. After three years of various site activities, our most successful ones have been Meals on Wheels, the local animal shelter, and a soup kitchen. For these experiences to be deeply felt, they need to have evident need, and the students need to feel strongly about their experience and about their contribution, especially since it is for a single visit. On the other hand, we do not recommend one-time placements in settings where only a long-term commitment would truly meet these goals, such as visits to nursing homes and middle-class day-care centers.

For the children's service activities, we have found that their physical proximity to a site is important for a one-time service activity. It is most effective to acknowledge their need to feel a sense of accomplishment, producing an obvious outcome, such as a park cleared of debris after a storm.

As in all effective service-learning activities, students, old and young alike, need to feel that their service is meaningful, and for a one-time experience, it is wise to offer an experience that is likely to provide a feeling of accomplishment.

VIII. Gaining Institutional Support

The major issues we have confronted in gaining institutional support include gaining formal university curriculum committee approval, gaining other faculty support, moving from the status of an elective to a required course, and institutionalizing within the undergraduate preservice program in addition to the graduate inservice program.

We presented the syllabus to the university curriculum committees at all levels — departmental, college, and university. The syllabus was approved at all three levels. It has been taught three times with teachers receiving recertification credit and, with approval from their committees, graduate program credit as an elective.

We realized that graduate-level courses weren't sufficient; we needed to prepare preservice teachers also. As a result of an invited seminar, student teachers in special education are required to complete a service-learning project as a team with their supervising teacher, therefore introducing the method into the school as well as preservice training. In addition, it has been implemented in three sections of the child development foundations course. Students identify needs and develop and implement group projects according to major.

IX. Special Characteristics/Financial Support

This course incorporates a great deal of reading into the curriculum, with opportunities for reflection in a journal. Class participants are encouraged to analyze these writings and their meaning related to the service-learning they experience as both servers and service-learning leaders.

In addition to the traditional readings, videos, and group activities undertaken in this course, a unique assignment has been to weave children's literature into all aspects of the participants' learning experiences. We demonstrate utilization of children's literature for all grade levels in all stages of the service-learning process. Class participants also are required to read a variety of children's books, developing strategies for incorporating these books into their curricula. Thought-provoking situations, age-old wisdom, and proverbial sayings are threaded throughout books that are written for children but by adults. The potential for this type of literature to enhance the learning in service-learning cannot be overemphasized.

The first offering of the course was sponsored by the State Department of Education, and students were able to attend tuition free. In subsequent years, a local school district has contracted with the university to have the course taught on site in its district. Students are given the opportunity to take the course tuition free.

X. Future Plans

The course has made significant impact on the institutionalization of service-learning within one of the local school districts. Increased efforts to contract with other school districts are currently under way. The next step is to have this course offered as one of two options for required methods courses at the graduate level.

At the undergraduate level, through the zero-based curriculum review process, the following recommendations have been made: "Additional opportunities for field experiences could come through service-learning projects. . . . All students could develop and implement service-learning projects for and/or with their students during the student teaching experience. . . . [Students] could design/create service-learning projects to carry out during their field experiences."

XI. Contacts

Carol Weatherford, Associate Professor, Department of Educational Foundations and Special Education, College of Health, Education, and Human Development, Tillman Hall, Clemson University, Clemson, SC 29634, ph 864/656-5117, fax 864/656-1322, *weather@clemson.edu*

Marty Duckenfield, Public Information Director, National Dropout Prevention Center, College of Health, Education, and Human Development, Clemson University, 205 Martin Street, Clemson, SC 29634-0726, ph 864/656-2599, fax 864/656-0136, *mbdck@clemson.edu*

Janet Wright, Service-Learning Coordinator, National Dropout Prevention Center, College of Health, Education, and Human Development, Clemson University, 205 Martin Street, Clemson, SC 29634-0726, ph 864/656-2599, fax 864/656-0136, *jw@clemson.edu*

Augsburg College

I. Course/Program Titles
EDU 265, Orientation to Education in an Urban Setting
EDU 282, Introduction to Special Education

II. Category
EDU 265 is a required foundations course; it is also open to noneducation majors as a general education perspectives course. EDU 282 is a required course for students seeking a special education minor. Both are at the introductory level and require no previous experience in education.

III. Conceptual Framework/Objectives
Augsburg College values service and service-learning. Institutional commitment to these concepts can be found in such places as the college's mission statement and in the college's financial support for the Office of Community Service and its director. Within this milieu, the Education Department integrates service-learning into the curriculum in two ways: (1) as a strategy that deepens learning by linking academic content and student experience within the context of the teacher education program; and (2) as a strategy to be studied and practiced in order to make it part of the skill-based repertoire possessed by beginning teachers leaving Augsburg's teacher education program.

In brief, this is accomplished in phases that can be graphically summarized as shown below:

> **PHASE I: EXPOSURE**
> - Goals: Develop basic familiarity with and exposure to SL
> - Occurs in first course in TE sequence

> **PHASE II: SKILL PLANNING**
> - Goals: To build familiarity with SL theory and to develop a SL lesson or unit
> - Occurs in basic methods

> **PHASE III: PRACTICE**
> - Goals: To allow student teachers to carry out an SL lesson
> - Occurs during student teaching placement, at the end of the TE sequence

(Erickson & Bayless, 1996)

The courses presented here are part of Phase I. As such, the goals are to use service-learning to promote academic learning while providing a service to children, teachers, and families and to build a beginning awareness of service-learning as a pedagogy.

EDU 265 is an introduction to the social foundations of education in an urban setting. This course considers the history of education in the United States, various philosophies of education, as well as laws, ethics, governance, and financial aspects of education. Specific objectives of EDU 265 as related to service-learning are to:

- help students evaluate their interest/suitability for a teaching career;
- provide students with experience working in an urban school within the framework of service-learning;
- encourage students to develop a respect for the pluralistic, multicultural urban environment, its people, and its schools;
- help students become critically aware of current problems and events in education.

EDU 282, Introduction to Special Education, is also a foundations course, offering an introduction to issues critical to the field of disabilities and specifically related to special education in the public school system. Most students are preservice regular education students. This course offers both a theoretical perspective as well as discussion of more practical issues that relate to the fields of disabilities. The course objective is to develop a knowledge base related to various types of disabilities. Students learn from a historical perspective about the pervasiveness and exclusionary practices that have and continue to exist for people with disabilities. It also deals with how teachers can work to include children with disabilities and their families in the regular educational setting.

IV. Integration of Service-Learning Theory

In EDU 265, service-learning provides the framework for a 30-hour field placement in which all students engage. Field placements are commonplace in education courses, but these placements cannot always be defined as service-learning. Often, the requirements for these placements are driven by training concerns, with limited room for those being served to contribute their expectations for how the time in the school will be spent. Because EDU 265 is a beginning education course that is also open to students outside the department, it has few specific requirements for the field experience component. Schools and teachers are able to help mold the experience around their needs, the needs of their K-12 students, as well as the needs of the college students from Augsburg.

Another reason that the field placement in EDU 265, Orientation to Education, functions as a service-learning placement is that a substantial reflection assignment is incorporated into the course. Students write three guided reflection papers during the last half of the course. In these papers, they are expected to tie their experiences to their text, to a nonfiction narrative book about schools and teaching, and to class discussions. They also discuss their reflection in small groups.

The connections between the K-12 classroom and student academic learning objectives are obvious and strong. With the addition of reflection and of the site-based input on the role of the Augsburg students in the K-12 classroom, this field experience becomes a genuine service-learning experience.

In EDU 282, Introduction to Special Education, students are afforded the opportunity to apply course content to a practical situation through connection with a family that has a child with a disability. Students are required to make visits to the family as well as to the school versus a specific number of hours in a classroom. This experience allows students the opportunity to meet the child and the parents in their natural environment and to contribute their insight to the overall planning of the child's individualized education plan (IEP). Through this experience, students are able to understand the issues from a parent's perspective versus the perspective they will typically have, that of a teacher. All students are assigned to a family that has a child with a disability. The types and degrees of the disability vary. The families involved sought out support services from a community agency in dealing with their child's school and the IEP process. The community agency, ARC of Hennepin County, is a parent-advocacy organization that works on a variety of issues for individuals with disabilities. The sites of the interactions are in the family home, the student's classroom, and at the IEP meeting.

V. Service-Learning Assignments and Activities

In EDU 265, students are placed in one of two sites. One is a public K-8 Montessori school; the other is a public K-10 community-based charter school. Both are in Minneapolis within walking distance of the Augsburg campus. In both placements, students act as tutors and classroom helpers. Students self-select their placements. Placements are made with the help of the community service–learning tutor coordinator and the volunteer coordinators at the respective schools.

Prior to the start of the service-learning placements, students read one of three nonfiction accounts of life in urban schools, write three reflection papers comparing their book with text-based materials, and participate in book discussion groups. With this as a base, the students are asked in their service-learning reflections to draw specific and defined comparisons among their experiences and the experiences and information found in their nonfiction book and their text. Students also meet three times in small groups to discuss their reflections and their experiences.

In EDU 282, all students are assigned to a family that has a child with a disability.

Once families contact ARC of Hennepin County, the coordinator and the professor teaching the course put the lists together. Students choose the family they are interested in working with based on location, the disability they may be interested in, and age of the child.

The course text deals not only with the disabilities that students have but also with issues parents and teachers must deal with in the education of the children with special needs. Students are also given supplemental readings that outline more specifically the IEP process and may use it as a reference in their work with the parents. They also become familiar with legal implications related to the process and the school's responsibility to serve children with special needs. In addition, the ARC coordinator provides an inservice on the IEP process.

Students are asked to complete an assessment and planning process entitled "McGill Action Planning System" (MAPS) (Vandercook and York 1989). Using the information they have gained about the family and student, they create a MAP that can offer additional information to the parent and the school to supplement the IEP. Students highlight the strengths, challenges, dreams, and fears of the child and the family, and attempt or offer creative alternatives. The complete MAPS process is given to the parents, and parents are also invited to class to participate in the process.

VI. Assessment

Learning in EDU 265 is assessed through a variety of means, including multiple-choice and essay quizzes, written reflections, and a major research paper. The service-learning component specifically is assessed through three written reflections tied to the experience and through successful completion of the experience. Successful completion is assumed upon the submission of a K-12 teacher evaluation of the Augsburg student. This component is an all-or-nothing grade; variations of performances at the service-learning site are not figured into "success." Criteria used to grade the written reflections are as follows: on time; on the topic (reflections are guided by particular questions each time); done thoughtfully with connections drawn among text, book, class discussion, and experience; mechanically accurate and word processed. Students must submit all three reflections and the teacher evaluation to receive a C or better on the assignment.

Student successes and challenges are apparent in each reflection and discussion. Because the goal is that students engage in and reflect on their experience, the quality of their services is not tied to their grade. Students are expected to give good measure to their K-12 teachers and students, but their grades — beyond completing the required hours — aren't tied to it.

In EDU 282, students are assessed on four levels related to the service-learning assignment. They are required to submit a paper on two visits in which they collected information on the family and the child. They are asked to submit an additional paper that describes the goals they developed with the family. Finally, they turn in their completed MAPS project as well as are asked to share this informally with the family.

The learning successes have been documented primarily through student and parent feedback as well as presentations of the MAPS process. Several examples that have illustrated success have come from both students and parents. One parent talked about how the student's new perspective allowed her to rethink what she had come to settle for when attending meetings at the school. The college student brought up issues to the teachers during the IEP meeting that she felt the student should be receiving based on what she knew of the legal responsibilities discussed in class. The parent said she had become so hardened to what she had been told she could not have for her son that she had stopped asking.

Through the MAPS process, students also helped develop portraits of the children with whom they were involved that added dimension to parents who typically receive a more clinical perspective on not only their child's disability but also his or her capability. These ideas in some cases were taken by the parent to the school and incorporated into the IEP. Overall, students felt they gained perspective on disability and special education they would not receive by simply viewing the situation from a teacher's perspectives. Some relationships remain ongoing.

VII. Assessment of Service-Learning Placements

In EDU 265, service-learning placements are evaluated formally and in writing by the students and informally by the instructor and the service-learning coordinator. Evaluations are shared with the volunteer coordinators on site. Placements can be at several sites or at only one or two sites; either seems to work for the Augsburg students. The former gives students more choices; the latter gives the site more familiarity with Augsburg. As an instructor, I prefer the latter because I have a better sense of what the Augsburg students are experiencing and can check in with the volunteer coordinators periodically. Placements to be avoided are those with teachers who expect Augsburg students to come in ready to take over their classes as full-fledged teachers. This is a bad placement in just about any field experience, not just for this course.

In EDU 282, placements are evaluated by students, families, and coordinators (college instructor and community agency) of the service-learning experience through written evaluations. Visiting the school placement offers perspective to students as well, though there is no formal assessment of school settings.

When students are asked how service-learning fits within their teacher education program, they have responded with the following comments:

- "Service-learning is providing help while gaining experience."
- "Service-learning is a hands-on type of learning outside of the classroom setting. By providing our services to the schools and the schools providing their services to us, a lot can be learned."
- "Service-learning means that I am giving my service to learn about teaching. I feel that is a good fit."
- "In thinking of this as a service-learning experience, I think of it like community service in that you are doing something to help someone else, except you are learning and getting something out of it also."
- "With service-learning we are actually contributing to the community."
- "Gained perspectives on disability and special education I would not have received by viewing the situation from just a teacher's perspective."
- "Helped me to see all what families deal with in schools."

VIII. Gaining Institutional Support

In terms of using service-learning in our two courses, we have experienced no need to wrestle for institutional support. Augsburg has an office for community service and has received several grants to promote the concept and practice of service-learning. Augsburg's mission statement includes the goal of " . . . providing service for the world. . . ." The pedagogy of service-learning fits well with institutional goals and practice. Augsburg also has developed strong community connections, which help us secure good placements for our students. Nevertheless, we do face critical issues in fully integrating service-learning into our teacher education curriculum, some of which are personal, some departmental. From a personal perspective, we have had to prove to ourselves that experiential learning actually does strengthen academic understanding, that it is not done just to appease students' needs for relevancy. Through students' reflections and follow-up discussions, we have realized how much the service-learning placement adds to students' knowledge base. They possess the authority of first-hand experience, and they speak from it. They also learn not to make hasty judgments about their experiences and their students — a tool essential to every good teacher.

On a broader basis, departmental issues faced in fully incorporating service-learning into our teacher education curriculum can be harder to overcome. First, our courses are already full of content. While service-learning can be added into the mix in a logical way, it can seldom be added without displacing something else. Varying levels of familiarity with and commitment to service-learning make it difficult to standardize the amount and quality of instruction our students receive in the pedagogy of service-learning.

Second, we cannot ensure that all our students will have field experiences with K-12 teachers trained in and using service-learning with their students. Not enough K-12 teachers are familiar with and committed to using the pedagogy of service-learning with K-12 students to ensure placements for our students. Thus, while we can work from our end to ensure exposure to and study of service-learning pedagogy, we cannot ensure that our students will have the chance to practice its use in a K-12 setting.

Third, as paradoxical as this might seem, some Augsburg students experience too much service-learning in their coursework. Individual students have found themselves with two and three service-learning requirements in a term — more than can be reasonably or productively accomplished. When this happens to students in Education Department courses, the placements can often be fairly easily combined. But when service-learning requirements are in courses from other academic departments, the goals can be different enough to make combining placements impossible. The community service office staff are currently working on a solution to this problem.

IX. Special Characteristics/Financial Support

EDU 265 was an existing course with an existing field experience that was transformed into a service-learning experience. EDU 282 was also an existing course. The service-learning component was a new addition to this course.

X. Future Plans

In terms of individual courses, the service-learning component of EDU 265 is at a good point. However, it would be interesting to experiment with a totally on-site course where class sessions met at the K-12 school site just before or after the classroom placement hours. This would allow the personnel of the K-12 school to become part of EDU 265 and to share their knowledge and perspectives. Space and schedule conflicts make this difficult to put in place, but it would be interesting to try.

Likewise, in EDU 282, it would be beneficial to get parents more involved in the course. The community agency has come to class and presented materials in preparation for the IEP process, but parent involvement, especially in structuring MAPS in class, would provide for a powerful link.

In terms of departmental issues, we continue taking small, gradual steps toward making service-learning an integral part of all our students' teacher education. With impetus from grants received by the Office of Community Service and with the leadership of the community service coordinator for tutoring programs, the department is holding discussions around issues related to more fully implementing our service-learning model. These discussions intensify the focus on where and how service-learning is being used, where and how we want it to be a part of our future program, and how to integrate the Office of Community Service into our field experience framework.

XI. Contacts

Vicki L. Olson, Associate Professor, Education Department, Augsburg College, 2211 Riverside Avenue S., Minneapolis, MN 55454, ph 612/330-1131, fax 612/330-1649, *olsonv@augsburg.edu*

Susan O'Connor, Assistant Professor, Education Department, Augsburg College, 2211 Riverside Avenue S., Minneapolis, MN 55454, ph 612/330-1494, fax 612/330-1649, *oconnors@augsburg.edu*

References

Erickson, J., and M.A. Bayless. (1996). "Integrating Service-Learning Into Teacher Education." In *Expanding Boundaries: Serving and Learning,* edited by B. Taylor. Washington, DC: Corporation for National Service.

Vandercook, T., and J. York. (1989). "The McGill Action Planning System (MAPS): A Strategy for Building the Vision." *Journal of the Association for Persons With Severe Handicaps* 14: 205-215.

University of Iowa

I. Course/Program Title
Elementary Teacher Education Program

II. Category
Comprehensive program (service-learning integrated into foundations course, social studies methods course, practicum, and student teaching).

III. Conceptual Framework/Objectives
The primary objective for the service-learning activities in the UI elementary teacher education program is to develop in preservice teachers the knowledge, skills, and attitudes necessary to implement service-learning as a teaching technique in the elementary classroom. This objective is approached in four phases. First, students are introduced to the concept of service-learning and its role in the socio-civic function of schooling in the Foundations of Education course. Second, students complete a service-learning project with elementary children in need as part of the requirements for the social studies methods course. The third component, concurrent with taking the social studies methods course, involves the students in working with Iowa City public school teachers and children in carrying out service-learning projects. Finally, students have the option to plan and conduct a service-learning project in their student teaching experience, with funding support from the Corporation for National Service. While all of these activities are vital to our objective, this description of our program will focus on the second and third components.

IV. Integration of Service-Learning Theory
The mission of social studies education is the development of informed and active citizens. Community service–learning is one type of civic behavior that calls upon citizens to care about their neighbors, to participate in making the community a better place to live, and to seek answers to the pervasive problems and needs in our society. The inclusion of service-learning in the social studies methods course thus serves to enhance preservice teachers' commitment to active citizenship. In addition, the community service–learning (CSL) project gives teacher education students opportunities to learn about community agencies and the services they provide to children in need; develop skills in planning, discipline, and time management; and investigate various social, environmental, political, and economic factors as they impact the lives of children and families.

The service-learning practicum (SLP), completed during the same semester as the CSL project, is also a requirement in the elementary education program and contributes 10 hours of student contact time toward the requirement for state teacher certification. The SLP focuses on how to implement service-learning with elementary students in a public school setting.

V. Service-Learning Assignments and Activities

The CSL project involves a wide variety of placements in schools and community agencies from which students may choose; all placements involve working with children who are in need (single-parent families, low income, learning disabilities, physical challenges, minority populations). Students may also choose a placement of their own as long as it involves one to two hours a week of direct contact with at least one elementary-age child in need. Students sign up for projects outside the professor's office and then attend orientations either on campus or at the community agency site before beginning their work with children. A graduate teaching assistant helps with contacting agencies, posting placements, collecting funds for police-record checks where needed, and helping students decide which CSL project is most suitable for them.

A general introduction to service-learning is provided in the social studies methods course before students begin the CSL project. Related assignments include readings on service-learning in the elementary school and the creation of a portfolio. The portfolio is designed to assist students in reflecting on their CSL experience and to provide them with a concrete product they can use in their future classrooms and in job interviews. The portfolio has five components: (1) a one-page introduction to their CSL project; (2) a few pages that illustrate their CSL activities (photos, drawings, memorabilia) and their reflections on their experience (journal entries, quotes from participants, essays, poems); (3) a few pages describing the community agency with which they worked and the services the agency provides to children and families; (4) a position paper on the role of service-learning in social studies education; and (5) a final letter reflecting on what they learned from their CSL project that will be useful to them as elementary school teachers.

Placements for the SLP are all in the Iowa City Community School District. Kindergarten through eighth grade public school teachers who wish to participate in the collaborative community service–learning program attend a day-long workshop in the summer and a midyear reflection session. They receive project supply funds ($100 per semester) along with the assistance of the teacher education students. A handbook is provided to each teacher education student and public school teacher in the program. The handbook lists the preservice teachers' five requirements for the practicum (observation, bulletin board display, whole-class lesson, assisting with the service activity, and reflection lesson) and provides pages for them to write lesson plans and reflect on their experiences. Two graduate students coordinate the scheduling and seminars for the practicum as well as observe each teacher education student teach once during the semester.

VI. Assessment

Learning from the CSL project is assessed through the completion of the portfolio, in-class discussions, reports from the agency members and families involved in the projects, and an individual conference with the professor or graduate teaching assistant at the end of the semester. Success is revealed when teacher education students' eyes are opened to the needs of children and the services community agencies can provide. Our greatest challenges involve occasional student resistance to putting time into getting involved in the community.

Learning from the SLP is assessed through the completion of the practicum requirements, completion of the handbook, attendance at two seminars, successful teaching during the observation, and a positive evaluation from the cooperating teacher. Research studies on these activities using both qualitative and quantitative data-collection methods (e.g., interviews, surveys, content analysis of written work) have also been conducted.

VII. Assessment of Service-Learning Placements

The placements for the CSL project are assessed through feedback from the teacher education students and the community agency members involved. On occasion, a project choice initiated by a student has become one of the placements for the course. Some placements have been modified significantly based on feedback from students and agency members.

The placements for the SLP are assessed through feedback from both teacher education students and public school teachers. While many teachers continue from semester to semester, others have tried service-learning and decided it was not for them. A few teachers have been asked to leave the program because they were not effective working with the teacher education students. We encourage both students and teachers to let us know early on about any problems or miscommunications so that we can assist in helping everyone have a productive experience. For example, if students tell us that their cooperating teacher is expecting them to plan and conduct the project all on their own, we call the teacher and reaffirm that the teacher education students are there to assist but that project ownership belongs to the classroom teacher and his or her students. Our successes are revealed when many of the teacher education students go on to plan and conduct quality service-learning activities in their student teaching experience. Our greatest challenges are dealing with teachers who are not taking their share of the responsibility or students who are not following through on the practicum requirements. On occasion, we have had students fail the practicum, which must then be repeated successfully before they go on to student teaching.

VIII. Gaining Institutional Support

We have gained institutional commitment to the service-learning activities through embedding them in existing required courses and practicums. We have also ensured their continuation through generating funding and personnel assistance at both the university and in the Iowa City Community School District.

IX. Special Characteristics/Financial Support

Initially, we had a Fund for the Improvement of Postsecondary Education (FIPSE) grant to support the CSL activities. We also have a Corporation for National Service grant to support our service-learning in student teaching component and some of the graduate student assistance described above.

X. Future Plans

Future plans include maintaining financial support for the program through the sale of our K-8 Joining Hands Service-Learning Resource kits and course materials and handbook described above. We are also conducting research on the graduates of our program who are now full-time teachers to discern what personal and environmental factors influence their decisions about implementing service-learning in the classroom.

XI. Contact

Rahima Wade, Assistant Professor of Elementary Social Studies, Lindquist Center N 291, The University of Iowa, Iowa City, IA 52242, ph 319/335-5118, fax 319/335-5608, *rahima-wade@uiowa.edu*

Seattle University

I. Course/Program Title
Community Service–Learning Partnership

II. Category
Comprehensive program (service-learning integrated into educational psychology course, service leadership course including practicum, a research project, and student teaching)

III. Conceptual Framework/Objectives
The focus on service that extends throughout the Master in Teaching (MIT) program is designed to facilitate prospective teachers' understanding of the benefits of expanding K-12 educational experiences to involve collaborative efforts with the larger community. To achieve this goal, students are educated in the use of service-learning as an instructional methodology, philosophy of learning, and a development strategy for schools and communities.

Service-learning is set in the context of the Jesuit tradition, Seattle University's mission, and the key beliefs and assumptions underlying the MIT program. The Jesuit educational tradition includes a vision of the nobility of the human person, who is understood as essentially a social being, relating to others through knowledge, love, and service. Seattle University attempts to embody the Jesuit vision by including a focus on the development of leaders for service. The service-learning strand also manifests the MIT program's first rationale, "The social responsibilities of teaching are of fundamental importance to the program. These social responsibilities guide teachers to connect the classroom with the school and community to allow students to apply their learning to address real issues related to justice and global human rights."

IV. Integration of Service-Learning Theory
Service-learning is initially presented to MIT students in the first quarter of the four-quarter MIT program. Here, service-learning is placed in the context of holistic education. The holistic paradigm focuses on relationship and integration of the inner qualities of human life with the outer physical world. Service-learning is offered to MIT students as one method for implementing holistic education in K-12 schools. Service-learning is described as especially productive because it can simultaneously facilitate engaged learning and provide an opportunity to increase one's sense of meaning and purpose in life. The goals of holistic education are fulfilled when, through participation

in service-learning activities, students develop a greater sense of who they are and the unique talents they possess.

MIT students participate in a group service-learning project as part of the 18 hours of in-classroom preparation they receive on the use of service-learning as a teaching method. This experience, combined with reflection activities, helps our preservice teachers realize the power of service-learning to enhance social justice, facilitate engaged academic learning, develop commitment to helping others, and experience greater meaning in their own lives.

V. Service-Learning Assignments and Activities

Service-learning preparation in the first quarter of the MIT program involves a variety of readings; however, primary emphasis is on two: *Enriching Learning Through Service* by Kate McPherson, and *Standards of Quality for School-Based and Community-Based Service-Learning* by the Alliance for Service-Learning in Education Reform (ASLER). [See p. 41 for a list of the 11 ASLER Standards.]

The McPherson text is short (53 pages) and includes numerous examples of a variety of service-learning projects linked to different academic subjects and conducted at all grade levels. The ASLER Standards set forth key principles to assist in the development of maximally successful service-learning projects. Much of the instruction is centered around explanation, examples, and case studies of how these principles can be applied in a K-12 setting.

The next focus on service-learning in the MIT program occurs in the second quarter. All students participate in a required, two-quarter-credit course called Service Leadership. This course consists of three primary components: (1) a 25-hour practicum performed in a K-12 setting working with a teacher experienced with service-learning; (2) regular reflection sessions, both at the university and at K-12 sites, to assist in managing problems that arise and linking service-learning experiences to the principles and theory presented previously; and (3) a final two-day service leadership conference at which MIT students, K-12 teachers and students, community agency personnel, parents, and service-learning guest speakers come together to celebrate service achievements, reflect, and develop ideas for more successful future projects.

MIT students choose to engage in the 25-hour service-learning practicum at one of approximately 20 different K-12 sites. Students work in groups of two to five with a K-12 teacher to learn about service-learning by providing service to K-12 students and teachers engaged in service-learning activities. MIT students engage in the following activities in their service-learning field placement sites: (1) assist teachers and students in contacting community agencies and resolving logistical problems, such as transportation; (2) monitor and work alongside K-12 students in performance of the service-learning project; (3) develop and lead in-class reflection sessions that highlight what has been learned through service; (4) design and teach whole-class lessons related to the service topic that focus on integration of service experiences and the academic curriculum; and (5) conduct school-wide inservice sessions to introduce K-12 faculty to service-learning. Since students frequently work in teams of four, they are able to give classroom teachers 100 hours of free support in the area of service-learning. Through participation in these activities, MIT students gain a practical understanding of how the principles of effective service-learning they study at the university can be applied in a K-12 setting.

All K-12 service-learning placements are arranged and nurtured by the MIT professor who teaches the service leadership course. This time-consuming task is made easier by the fact that there is a waiting list of K-12 teachers eager to work with MIT service-learning students. Service-learning field placement sites do not need to be practicing ideal models of fully developed service-learning projects. Most MIT students tell us they learn more about service-learning in new service projects where teachers are still grappling with initial start-up issues than in well-established projects.

All MIT students complete a group collaborative action research project that extends throughout all four quarters of the MIT program. During the past two years, approximately 25 percent of these groups have chosen to focus their research on some aspect of service-learning. Projects have ranged from K-12 students' social and psychological outcomes of service-learning participation to multicultural issues in service-learning to MIT graduates' use and experiences with service-learning during their first years of teaching.

MIT students complete a 12-week full-time student teaching placement during which many have the opportunity to implement a service-learning project. The group completing student teaching in March 1996 reported that 48 percent of them implemented a successful service-learning project. This included 55 percent of those teaching in elementary schools and 33 percent of those in secondary settings. The service-learning projects conducted included cross-age tutoring in reading and math, planning and conducting a Martin Luther King assembly for another school, writing letters to U.S. troops in Bosnia, conducting oral histories with senior citizens, and research and advocacy on issues ranging from dangerous street intersections to improved quality of school lunches.

VI. Assessment
Service-learning outcomes related to the 18 hours of instruction provided in the educational psychology course are assessed by evaluating the quality of

a student-created "service-learning action plan." The action plan can be completed by students individually or in pairs and involves the synthesis and application of students' knowledge of the principles of effective service-learning. The plan addresses all important elements of a service-learning project with sufficient detail to allow successful implementation. Finished plans are self-evaluated by students and graded by the course instructor. Students are strongly encouraged to create a plan they can actually implement in either their 25-hour service-learning field practicum or in their student teaching placement.

VII. Assessment of Service-Learning Placements

A variety of formal and informal instruments and techniques are used to evaluate outcomes of student participation in the service-learning course. Since a primary goal of the course is to help our preservice teachers understand the process and philosophy of service-learning and apply this knowledge to design and successfully implement service-learning projects with K-12 students, the major emphasis of our assessment is on the quality of service-learning projects completed by MIT students.

Students demonstrate how they have integrated principles of effective service-learning practice into their projects through their presentation at the service leadership conference. At this conference, each small group of MIT students who worked together in a K-12 school site has 45 minutes to present its service-learning project; the group members reflect on what they learned through the project, focus on K-12 student outcomes, and explain how they incorporated principles of effective practice into the project.

The ASLER Standards of Quality for School-Based and Community-Based Service-Learning were used to create an instrument to assess service-learning projects. Ten of the standards were incorporated in a rubric to assist in evaluating the project and MIT students' ability to successfully design and implement service-learning with K-12 students. If students did not incorporate a standard, they are expected to provide a convincing rationale for not fully addressing the standard or a discussion of how factors beyond their control inhibited their ability to meet the standard. If this is the case, they also need to explain the manner in which they would have addressed the standard if they had had the opportunity.

Other assessment strategies include the following:

1. An end-of-the-course reflection project in which individual students discuss what they learned from participation in the service leadership course, including the service-learning projects. These projects may be written papers, skits, collages, or other forms of expression.

2. A written feedback-and-evaluation form received from all K-12 teachers and community agency personnel who supervise MIT students in their

service projects. This form includes descriptions of student strengths and limitations, and suggestions for improvement for both individual students and the MIT program.

3. Informal assessment conducted in reflection sessions held throughout the course in which MIT students share critical incidents that occurred during their projects and write journal entries regarding their service projects. Sharing of journal entries is done on a voluntary basis.

4. An ongoing longitudinal study to examine the extent to which graduates of the MIT program actually implement service-learning as a teaching method in their own K-12 teaching. This involves surveying graduates during the fall of their second year of teaching.

There have been many successes experienced by the MIT students and K-12 teachers and students involved in the service leadership course. From 1993 through 1996, MIT students supported service-learning with 51 different teachers in 37 schools in the Puget Sound area. They helped improve the quality of service-learning experienced by more than 3,500 K-12 students.

VIII. Gaining Institutional Support

Institutional support for the service-learning component of the MIT program has gradually increased over the past five years. This is due to the fact that all eight full-time faculty members who teach in the MIT program and the dean of the School of Education recognize the value of service-learning in helping achieve program goals and Seattle University's mission. All eight MIT faculty participated in a full-day service-learning project at a Seattle homeless shelter. This hands-on experience was very successful in assisting them to understand the power of service-learning and why more time was necessary in the program in order to fully integrate service-learning.

The positive recognition received for initiating service-learning in our teacher education program has also been helpful in gaining increased institutional support.

IX. Special Characteristics/Financial Support

The service leadership course began without any outside funding. A grant from the Corporation for National Service has been valuable in helping to rapidly increase the quality and quantity of service-learning experiences in the MIT program.

X. Future Plans

We are working to create service-learning field placements that extend over a more substantial period of time. High-quality service-learning projects take time to plan and carry out, and relationships among teachers, students, and community members take time to blossom. We are currently developing a joint teacher education program with a Seattle-area school district in which service-learning field placement sites will also serve as student teaching placements.

We are also exploring methods to provide our recent graduates with the resources, technical assistance, and moral support needed to integrate service-learning into their teaching. This may involve inservice training, service-learning mentors, funds for project start-up, and support from AmeriCorps volunteers.

XI. Contact

Jeffrey B. Anderson, Associate Professor, School of Education, Seattle University, 900 Broadway, Seattle, WA 98122, ph 206/296-5754, fax 206/296-2053, *janderso@seattleu.edu*

Providence College

I. Course/Program Title
Elementary/Special Education Teacher Education Major/Public and Community Service Studies Minor

II. Category
Academic major and minor

III. Conceptual Framework/Objectives
At Providence College, students majoring in education graduate with dual certification in both elementary and special education. The program is committed to the development of teachers who are prepared to teach "all children" within an elementary school building, and department members view service-learning as a critical element in fostering meaningful involvement in activities that promote learning and cognitive development. Findings by researchers such as Conrad and Hedin (1991) indicate that service-learning has the potential to make instruction more worthwhile for students at risk, provide opportunities for students to develop problem-solving and decision-making skills, encourage students to develop closer ties and become part of the community, and develop a sense of self-esteem and self-worth. With this in mind, service-learning is being integrated into a number of courses in the program, and for a trial cohort of students, it forms the core of their preparation for teaching.

The goals of the service-learning strand are to prepare teachers who (1) can engage children in an inquiry-oriented curricular approach using community needs as the foundation; (2) provide meaningful learning experiences that foster civic responsibility, democratic values, and a sense of being an integral part of the community; (3) foster the development of a collegial environment within and among school, home, and community; and (4) address the needs of all children within the classroom curricular activities. A specific outcome of the strand is that students will develop projects in collaboration with classroom teachers and community agencies that meet a need in the school or community and integrate service with structured reflection and academic skills and content. Preservice teachers are introduced to the pedagogy of service through the following sequence of courses:

Year	Education Major	Public and Community Service Studies Minor
Sophomore 1		Introduction to Public and Community Service
Sophomore 2	Teaching of Math & Science/Practicum	Diversity, Community, and Service
Junior 1	Teaching Language Arts and Social Studies/Practicum	Ethics, Moral Leadership, and the Common Good
Junior 2	Teaching Reading/Practicum	Community Service in American Culture
Senior 1	Assessment and Curriculum for Students With Mild/Moderate Learning Problems/Practicum	Foundations of Organizational Service
Senior 2	Student Teaching: Elementary and Special Education	Independent Study

Concurrently, students pursue a minor in public and community studies through Providence College's Feinstein Institute, which supports their knowledge about the cultural diversity of their students, the community, and the school's place in society.

IV. Integration of Service-Learning Theory

Each methods course has a field component, or practicum, that enables the preservice teacher to integrate theory and practice in actual classrooms. In collaboration with elementary teachers from two partner urban elementary schools, practicum students' experiences are structured in a way that permits them to become more familiar with the community, participate in the development of service-learning projects, and integrate curriculum into service activities. For example, at the beginning of each practicum, students are provided with an orientation to the school and the surrounding community. As students explore theory and develop skills to teach reading, math and science, language arts, and social studies, they are provided with opportunities to plan and implement lessons that meet specific learning outcomes, both for themselves and the elementary students, within the project activities. In their final methods course, one that addresses the issue of meeting the needs of students with learning difficulties, objectives are broadened to ensure that all students, including students with special needs, participate in service-learning projects and become active and contributing members of the school community.

V. Service-Learning Assignments and Activities

As a component of their public and community service studies minor, the education majors are enrolled in courses that involve them in service in a variety of community agencies and settings. Some examples of placements might include an AIDS hospice, a neighborhood soup kitchen, a homeless shelter, or a home health agency. Recently, students worked with a community center to develop an after-school program for neighborhood children and are directing and staffing the program. Course and placement offerings are coordinated by education and public and community service studies faculty to assure that college students have experiences that will enhance their knowledge and understanding of the communities in which the schools are situated and broaden their view of the opportunities for service activities.

Since the courses and activities in the public service minor address readings and experiences related to the theory and knowledge of service-learning, course readings and assignments in the methods courses are directed more toward the use and implementation of service-learning as an inquiry-oriented curricular approach, and the focus is on the infusion of service-learning pedagogy and projects into the elementary school curricular framework. For example, in the science and math methods course, the service-learning project is used as the tool to introduce the students to the National Council of Teachers of Mathematics *Standards* related to problem solving, integration, communication, and meaningfulness. In the reading methods course, college students must connect their service-learning activities to district literacy outcomes and identify performance opportunities to document attainment of those outcomes within service projects.

VI. Assessment

Assessment and evaluation have been carefully considered, and methods are currently being developed and field tested. Assessment of college students is achieved through the development of a portfolio that is specifically related to the service-learning strand and program outcomes. Program faculty are currently constructing a matrix of program outcomes, standards, and criteria that will enable faculty and students to align outcomes to specific program courses and projects. For example, for the inquiry-oriented outcome defined earlier, students might document that they had engaged children in an inquiry activity to assess community needs and to determine a specific project to meet those needs.

VII. Assessment of Service-Learning Placements

Assessment of the strand itself and the service-learning practicums is achieved in a number of ways. First, college students keep a weekly reflective log, which enables them to reflect on the school, community, service, and the teaching/learning process. Faculty observe college students at the practicum sites and meet with them and the project school teachers weekly to monitor project progress and facilitate project implementation. At the end of each school year and prior to the beginning of the new school year, college faculty and project school teachers meet to review the year's activities and plan for the upcoming academic year.

VIII. Gaining Institutional Support

A project such as this is time and labor intensive. It requires collaboration among college faculty from different departments, the staff and administrators of local schools, and community organizations. Both college and school district administrators need to approve agreements, and college faculty curriculum committees need to be made aware of and approve additions of or changes to course sequences and credits. Teachers and college faculty need to be recruited to participate in the program and then to become comfortable with using and teaching the pedagogy and working closely with school and community partners. This year we have learned that a key component of preparing the school teachers to more meaningfully collaborate around service projects and preservice teacher preparation is for the teachers themselves to dialogue with college faculty on service-learning. These dialogues occur in two ways. First, college and school faculty, graduate interns, and practicum students meet weekly to discuss their projects, and, second, a three-credit graduate professional development course on service-learning is offered to partner school participants. This course provides opportunities for teachers, faculty, and administrators to explore theory and practice, work out problems that arise during the development and implementation of service projects, and reevaluate outcomes for preservice teachers.

IX. Special Characteristics/Financial Support

The development of this program is funded by a Learn and Serve America Higher Education Grant, currently in its second year. In addition, Providence College was the recipient of a substantial grant to develop a public and community service studies major in 1993. Both of these grants have contributed valuable resources in terms of expertise, encouragement, materials, and funding to free busy faculty and teachers from their daily schedules and provide time for thinking and working together.

X. Future Plans

Future plans include refining the competencies, standards, and criteria we expect our preservice teachers to meet, developing assessment strategies for measuring the impact of the project on children, developing a more extensive professional development partnership with the two elementary schools (one school has identified service-learning as its school improvement focus), and developing a series of graduate courses to assist teachers in using service-learning pedagogy in their classrooms and schools as a vehicle for school reform.

XI. Contacts

Jane Callahan, Assistant Professor, Education Department, Providence College, Providence, RI 02918-0001, ph 401/865-2501, fax 401/865-2057, *jcalahan@providence.edu*

Lynne Ryan, Associate Professor, Education Department, Providence College, Providence, RI 02918-0001, ph 401/865-2504, fax 401/865-2057, *lynnryan@providence.edu*

Reference

Conrad, D., and D. Hedin. (1991). "School-Based Community Service: What We Know From Research and Theory." *Phi Delta Kappan* 72(10): 743-749.

Service-Learning and Teacher Education

by Jane Callahan

Instructor Readings

Allam, C., and B. Zerkin. (1993). "The Case for Integrating Service-Learning Into Teacher Preparation Programs." *Generator* 13(1): 11-13.

Allam and Zerkin suggest that teachers need to create classrooms that nurture all aspects of the student, social and personal as well as intellectual. Service-learning may be used to enhance such development, thereby improving community life. Service-learning should be incorporated into teacher preparation to create teachers who will provide opportunities for moral and intellectual development for their students. (T)

Anderson, C.S., and J.T. Witmer. (Fall 1994). "Addressing School Board and Administrative Concerns About Service-Learning." *Democracy & Education* 9(1): 33-37.

Concerns, fears, and misconceptions accompany service-learning because of a lack of understanding of this alternative approach to education. This essay acknowledges the concerns of school boards and gives suggestions to supporters of service-learning on how to handle some common concerns. Some issues addressed in the article are validity, staffing, student maturity, and liability. (P)

Anderson, J., N. George, S. Hunt, D. Nixon, and R. Ortiz. (1995). *Beginning Teachers' Perceptions and Use of Community Service-Learning as a Teaching Method.* Philadelphia, PA: National Service Learning Conference.

The authors compare and contrast two groups of teachers and their attitudes toward both community service and service-learning. One group participated in a community service internship as part of their master in teaching program, while the other group completed the standard program. The authors examine the question, "Does participation in community service as part of teacher preparation affect attitudes toward and implementation of service-learning?" (R)

Legend for codes: (T) = Theory-oriented article; (P) = Practitioner-oriented article; (R) = Research-oriented article.

Anderson, J., and K. Guest. (1995). "Linking Campus and Community: Service Leadership in Teacher Education at Seattle University." In *Integrating Service Learning Into Teacher Education: Why and How?* pp. 11-30. Washington, DC: Council of Chief State School Officers.

The authors describe Seattle University's initiative to establish an ethos of community service and commitment to service-learning in graduates of its master in teaching program. They discuss development of service leadership and provide detailed descriptions of service leadership, assessment strategies, and community and student outcomes. Suggestions are offered for implementing community service–learning experiences in other teacher education programs. (P)

Bayless, M.A., and J.A. Erickson. (1996). "Integrating Service-Learning Into Teacher Education." *Building Connections* 1(1): 10-13.

Bayless and Erickson state that, in schools, modifications must be made in order to tend to changing school communities. Service-learning aids necessary changes by providing a challenging academic experience, which allows for development of higher-order thinking skills. Universities and colleges can participate in this reform by including service-learning courses in their teacher training programs and by placing student teachers in schools interested in service-learning. (P)

Boyte, H. (June 1991). "Community Service and Civic Education." *Phi Delta Kappan* 72(10): 765-767.

The author suggests that community service is the wrong route to cure political apathy among young people today. He claims people too often participate in community service for personal reasons and fail to truly draw attention to the community at large. Instead, educators might use service-learning as a vehicle to provide students with opportunities to solve problems independently, to increase interest, and to improve skills necessary for good politics. (T)

Brooks, J.G., and M. Brooks. (1993). *In Search of Understanding: The Case for Constructivist Classrooms.* Alexandria, VA: Association for Supervision and Curriculum Development.

This text provides practical strategies for development of classrooms that enhance educational reforms through student learning and understanding. It details a new set of images that emerge from student engagement, interaction, reflection, and construction, and offers suggestions for administrators, teachers, and policymakers moving toward school reform while viewing the student as a thinker, creator, and constructor. (P)

Cohen, D., M. McLaughlin, and J. Talber, eds. (1993). *Teaching for Understanding*. San Francisco, CA: Jossey-Bass.

> The editors suggest that moving practice, research, and policy in directions that can enable and support the vision of practice is called "teaching for understanding." This requires breaking out of routines to transform routine ways of administering schools and classrooms, as well as formulating education research and policy. (T)

Conrad, D., and D. Hedin. (1991). "School-Based Community Service: What We Know From Research and Theory." *Phi Delta Kappan* 72(10): 743-749.

> Conrad and Hedin point out that John Dewey laid a foundation for service-learning by advocating student growth through actions that would improve the welfare of others. Service-learning has emerged from this philosophy and now encourages the reform of education and youth. Because of the recent surge of service-learning, both qualitative and quantitative studies need to be undertaken to ensure that the strategy does improve both academic and personal growth. (R)

Council of Chief State School Officers. (1995). *Integrating Service Learning Into Teacher Education: Why and How?* Washington, DC: CCSSO.

> This essay establishes the rationale for the inclusion of service-learning in the teacher education program at six different higher education institutions across the country. It contains the description of the service-learning components, such as activities, community outcomes, and personal benefits, and provides suggestions for teacher education programs that include service-learning activities and a list of curriculum resources. (R)

Darling-Hammond, L. (June 1993). "Reframing the School Reform Agenda." *Phi Delta Kappan* 74(10): 753-761.

> The author proposes that this century's movement into a high-technology Information Age demands a new kind of education and new forms of school organization. She argues that students are not standardized and therefore teaching should not be routine, and that effective teaching strategies require variety to meet the needs of individual students. Reframing of schools must seek to develop communities of learning grounded in communities of democratic dialogue. (T)

Eland, W.M., and R.C. Wade. (Fall 1995). "Connections, Rewards, and Challenges." *National Society for Experiential Education Quarterly* 21(1): 4-27.

> Skill, knowledge, and creativity of the classroom teacher play a major role in the ultimate success of a service-learning project. Primary

responsibilities of teachers are to guide their students in serving the community and learning from the process of doing so. Placing teachers in a position to carry out service-learning activities requires important consideration for motivating teachers; connecting service-learning to their values, beliefs, and personal life experiences; rewarding or problematic issues of service-learning; and challenges of service-learning. (T)

Eyler, J., and D. Giles. (Fall 1994). "The Theoretical Roots of Service-Learning in John Dewey: Toward a Theory of Service-Learning." *Michigan Journal of Community Service–Learning* 1(1): 77-85.

    The authors suggest that it is necessary and desirable for service-learning to develop theory both as a body of knowledge and as a guide for pedagogical practice. Compiling research about service-learning requires a basis of theory that may be developed and refined. They review John Dewey's educational and social philosophy as it relates to learning, as well as pose key questions for development. The article concludes that by determining a call for research leads to a call for theory. (T)

Giles, D., E. Honnet, and S. Migliore, eds. (1991). *Research Agenda for Combining Service and Learning in the 1990s*. Raleigh, NC: National Society for Experiential Education.

    The editors set forth a framework for research, five categories of research questions, and methodological issues. They also suggest the formation of a partnership between researchers and practitioners to improve practice as well as theory. (R)

Jacoby, B., and Associates. (1996). *Service-Learning in Higher Education*. San Francisco, CA: Jossey-Bass.

    This collection of essays reviews the practice of service-learning in higher education. The contributors include many of the most prominent higher education service-learning practitioners in the nation. The book is divided into three parts. Part One reviews service-learning foundations and principles. Part Two identifies specific designs for service-learning in colleges and universities. Part Three discusses several organizational, administrative, and policy issues regarding implementing and sustaining service-learning in higher education institutions. (T,P)

Kahne, J., and J. Westheimer. (May 1996). "In the Service of What? The Politics of Service-Learning." *Phi Delta Kappan* 77(9): 593-599.

> The authors promote the uniting of learning and service in America's classrooms. Current goals of curricular-reform efforts include development of students' self-esteem, higher-order thinking skills, and opportunities for authentic learning experiences. Challenges in the moral and political domains that need to be considered are presented. (T)

Kennedy, E. (June 1996). "National Service and Education for Citizenship." *Phi Delta Kappan* 77(10): 771-773.

> The author suggests that young Americans have been losing sight of the hallmark of America, commitment to public service. He reminds the nation that to increase participation, we need to ask for it and that the National Community Service Act of 1990 invites Americans, especially young citizens, to reinstate their commitment to community service. (T)

Kielsmeyer, J., and J. Nathan. (June 1991). "The Sleeping Giant of School Reform." *Phi Delta Kappan* 72(10): 739-742.

> The authors believe youths are an alienated group in society, resulting in part from adults' perception of them as problems. They believe that service-learning has the potential to turn this viewpoint around and place youth in the role of valued citizens, while improving education and providing an immediate reason to learn. (T)

Knapp, M.S., P.M. Shields, and B.J. Turnbull. (June 1995). "Academic Challenges in High Poverty Classrooms." *Phi Delta Kappan* 76(10): 770-776.

> The authors of this article maintain that high-poverty classrooms that implement meaningful learning activities yield results superior to those of a more traditional approach. When teachers place advanced skills as a top priority and teach for meaning and understanding, they reinforce instruction by linking it to students' existing knowledge base. As a result, when properly executed, meaningful learning experiences allow the mastery of basic skills as well as higher-order thinking skills. (T)

Kolb, D. (1984). *Experiential Learning: Experience as the Source of Learning and Development*. Englewood Cliffs, NJ: Prentice-Hall.

> This book describes in detail a theoretical model of experiential learning that is explained as a continuous cycle that includes experience, reflection, generalization, and application of theory to new experi-

ence. It emphasizes that those who advocate community service and are concerned about learning dimensions must ensure that programs include opportunities for reflection and generalization for participants. (T)

Kraft, R.J., and M. Swadener, eds. (1994). *Building Community: Service Learning in the Academic Disciplines*. Denver, CO: Colorado Campus Compact.
This book is especially written for teachers and professors wishing to institutionalize service-learning. It offers program descriptions, practical help, theoretical foundations, examples of service-learning in teacher training, and a review of research and evaluation. (P)

Lawson, H. (1994). "Toward Healthy Learners, Schools, and Communities." *Journal of Teacher Education* 45(1): 62-70.
Lawson argues that social systems currently neglect the importance of prevention methods when aiding social problems, considers the current system one that can actually contribute to problems associated with youth at risk, and urges collaboration among social systems to create healthy school environments and healthy learners. (T)

Louis, K.S., S.D. Kruse, and Associates. (1995). *Professionalism and Community: Perspectives on Reforming Urban Schools*. Thousand Oaks, CA: Corwin Press.
The authors propose a framework for thinking about teachers' work that focuses on two key aspects related to current pressures for educational reform. They emphasize professional community and suggest that unless teachers are provided with more supportive and engaging work environments, they cannot be expected to concentrate on increasing their abilities to reach and teach today's students effectively. School, rather than the individual or small group, is the critical unit for change. (T)

Retish, E., D.I. Yoder, and R. Wade. (Summer 1996). "Service-Learning: Meeting Student and Common Needs." *Teaching Exceptional Children* 28(4): 14-18.
Students with learning disabilities and those with various cultural backgrounds can benefit from service-learning by taking on new roles as service providers in their own communities. Special education and ESL teachers in this study use service-learning to encourage more meaningful interaction among students. They explain critical steps of a successful project and note benefits of increased self-esteem and self-knowledge among students. (P)

Root, S. (1994). "Service-Learning in Teacher Education: A Third Rationale." *Michigan Journal of Community Service Learning* 1(1): 94-97.

> The author examines altered responsibilities of teachers due to the changed social context of schooling. She also considers service-learning an opportunity to reform education and presents the need to include preservice teachers in service-learning projects to create more learner-centered classrooms. She says that service-learning will encourage a change in school environments. (T)

————, A. Moon, and T. Kromer. (1995). "Service-Learning in Teacher Education: A Constructivist Model. In *Integrating Service Learning Into Teacher Education: Why and How?* pp. 31-40. Washington, DC: Council of Chief State School Officers.

> The authors compare and contrast several rationales for including service-learning in teacher education curriculum. They describe a project that utilized recent findings from research in the area of effective inservice training. The article concludes that there is a need to prepare preservice and inservice teachers. (R)

Sergiovanni, T.J. (1994). *Building Community in Schools.* San Francisco, CA: Jossey-Bass.

> The text is a guide for principals, superintendents, and teachers who believe that community building must become the heart of any school-improvement effort. It suggests the possibility that we might better understand schools as social organizations rather than formal ones and that, in particular, they might be viewed as communities. (T)

Course Readings

Bellah, R., R. Madsen, W. Sullivan, A. Swidler, and M. Tipton. (1985). *Habits of the Heart.* Berkeley, CA: University of California Press.

> This book discusses the conflict between our strong sense of individualism and our undeniable need for community. After five years of intensive research, the authors conclude that, as Americans, we no longer have the language necessary to make solid moral judgments and that our individualism prevents us from committing ourselves to others. *Habits of the Heart* offers clear insight into our times and lives as Americans. (T)

Campbell, P., S. Edgar, and A. Halstead. (October 1994). "Students as Evaluators: A Model for Program Evaluation." *Phi Delta Kappan:* 160-164.

The authors believe that teachers and administrators must give students opportunities to evaluate programs. These opportunities allow students a chance to develop responsibility, community, and skills in logic as well as provide teachers information on their programs. With careful guidance from staff, the process can have a strong impact on all involved. (P)

Cohen, E. (1986). *Designing Groupwork: Strategies for the Heterogeneous Classroom.* New York, NY: Teachers College.

The author discusses how students can more actively contribute, share, and, most important, learn when groupwork is part of their schooling. The book combines easy-to-follow theory with examples and teaching strategies that are adaptable to any situation. It portrays the advantages and dilemmas of groupwork and its use in multi-ability and bilingual classrooms, and describes step-by-step approaches to successful planning, implementation, and evaluation of groupwork activities. (P)

Corporation for National Service. (1985). *National Service Resource Guide: Strategies for Building a Diversified Funding Base.* Washington, DC: Corporation for National Service.

This paper proposes that a well-thought-out fundraising plan and strong community support are essential to building and sustaining high-quality community service programs. It suggests that service organizations think on a strategic level about forming innovative partnerships and soliciting community resources. It also focuses on successful fundraising with a comprehensive fundraising plan, convincing evidence of effectiveness, active engagement of supporters, and development of community relationships. (P)

Dauber, S.L., and J.L. Epstein. (1993). "Parent Attitudes and Practices of Involvement in Inner-City Elementary and Middle Schools." In *Families and Schools in a Pluralistic Society,* edited by N.F. Chavkin, pp. 53-71. Albany, NY: State University of New York Press.

This comprehensive volume features substantial material from the nation's most renowned research projects on parent involvement. In addition to a section on research, the book includes a section on practice that presents research-tested strategies on working with minority parents. The book concludes with a section on future challenges that educators must confront and appendices on promising national programs and helpful resource materials. (R,P)

Fullan, M.G. (1991). *The New Meaning of Educational Change*. New York, NY: Teachers College Press.
> The author shares experiences of the most powerful lessons about how to cope with and influence educational change. If reforms are to be successful, individuals and groups must find meaning concerning *what* should change as well as *how* to go about it. Theory and practice explaining why change processes work as they do and identifying ways of improving success rates are presented. (T)

Goodlad, J. (1984). *A Place Called School*. New York, NY: McGraw-Hill.
> In this comprehensive study of secondary schools in America, Goodlad examines the organizational structure, curriculum, and culture of high schools. He suggests that to improve our schools, fundamental changes must occur, including how schools are organized; how long students must be engaged in formal curriculum; and providing alternative settings for learning about work, community, and life skills. Goodlad recommends that students should be free, at age 16, to participate in more activities outside of school that include a "combination of work, study, and service conducted within an educational ethos." (R,T)

Hedin, D. (1987). "Students as Teachers: A Tool for Improving School Climate." *Social Policy* 17(3): 42-47.
> The author presents peer and cross-age tutoring as a useful instructional resource and examines psychological and intellectual benefits for tutors and tutees as well as for teachers. The article outlines and offers possible solutions to problems of using tutoring in schools. (P)

Hollender, J. (1990). *How to Make the World a Better Place: A Guide to Doing Good*. New York, NY: Quill-Morrow.
> This guide offers more than 120 specific actions that will make a difference, from recycling tips and conservation techniques to tips on financial investment. The author provides a complete guide with phone numbers and addresses, background statistics, and quotable information, which might generate thought and stimulate service projects. Each action is designed to generate the greatest impact in the least amount of time. (P)

Honnet, E.P., and S.J. Poulsen. (1989). *Principles of Good Practice for Combining Service and Learning.* Wingspread Special Report. Racine, WI: The Johnson Foundation.

> The authors suggest that, when properly combined, service and learning bring about benefits superior to either one used alone. Participants, however, are cautioned to include specific elements to create a successful project. The report details these necessary elements for success. (P)

Hoose, P. (1993). *It's Our World, Too! Stories of Young People Who Are Making a Difference.* Dubuque, IA: Little, Brown.

> This is a clear-headed, good-hearted guide to help young people empower themselves. It includes stories about youth activists throughout history and dramatic photographs of activists in action, and provides profiles of young people taking a stand today against problems in the world. It also offers "ten tools for change": how to write "power letters," raise funds, and more. (P)

Jacobi Gray, M. (Spring 1996). "Reflections on Evaluation of Service-Learning Programs. *NSEE Quarterly* 21(3): 29-31.

> The author suggests that many challenges face those interested in evaluating service-learning programs. Three issues in particular tend to pose problems to evaluators: (1) unclear goals of projects, (2) tension stemming from traditional approaches to evaluation, and (3) unrealistic expectations of use of findings. Jacobi Gray concludes that evaluation remains a concern for practitioners and should be approached with care and thoughtfulness. (T)

Kinsley, C., and K. McPherson. (1989). *Enriching the Curriculum Through Service-Learning.* Vancouver, WA: Project Service Leadership.

> This book includes 21 descriptions of various aspects of service-learning that demonstrate how it enhances curriculum. This is a practical guide for practitioners to gain understanding and strategies to implement service-learning to improve student learning. It responds to educators in their efforts to reform schools and improve education, and describes specific service-learning projects used to enhance curriculum in schools while improving student learning. It presents ideas from literature to social studies, as students participate in conflict-resolution programs to peer tutoring, so as to make learning "real." (P)

Lawson, H. (1994). "Toward Healthy Learners, Schools, and Communities." *Journal of Teacher Education* 45(1): 62-70.

> Lawson states that crises are rampant in American families, schools, and our health-care system, and believes that all are failing children. Part of the problem stems from the human services focusing on crisis-oriented policies instead of on prevention programs. These shortcomings mar America's communities. To rectify this situation, the author suggests that schools can link themselves to families and communities to break cycles of failure. (T)

MacNichol, R. (1993). "Service-Learning: A Challenge to Do the Right Thing." *Equity and Excellence in Education* 26(2): 9-11.

> This article explores why community service–learning (CSL) is the right thing to do for professional renewal, enrichment, and meaning. Examples are given from Gig Harbor High School (Washington). The role of community service–learning in changing school cultures is also examined. It suggests that service-learning is a path to more effective education. (T)

Myers, C. (1995). "Service-Learning: A Teaching and Learning Strategy." In *Integrating Service Learning Into Teacher Education: Why and How?* pp. 1-10. Washington DC: Council of Chief State School Officers.

> Myers describes service-learning as a dynamic and powerful instructional strategy. She addresses many of the obstacles teachers and their students face today and suggests that service-learning is so powerful because it develops diverse facets of students, motivates, and responds to all learning styles. (T)

Parsons, C. (1991). *Service Learning From A to Z*. Chester, VT: Vermont Schoolhouse Press.

> Teachers, administrators, counselors, and education faculty all want community service programs that enhance students' educations while developing civic pride and values. This book provides the means to help students on their way to becoming hands-on members of society. Parsons demonstrates how to steer students toward lives as participating, caring citizens. She assists in designing projects that will enrich curriculum, produce involved and voting citizens, enliven the meaning of democracy, encourage active teaching and learning, and bring schools, families, and communities together. (P)

Prowat, R.S. (April 1992). "From Individual Differences to Learning Communities: Our Changing Focus." *Education Leadership* 49(7): 9-13.

The article establishes a time line of teaching and learning and its drastic changes in the past 30 years. The emerging picture of learning communities and teaching and learning contrasts dramatically with that of the recent past. The author suggests that many reformers believe that the creation of school-wide learning communities is a necessary condition for the creation of classroom learning communities. This sets the stage for service-learning within a school. (T)

Rousculp, E., and G.H. Maring. (1992). "Portfolios for Community Learners." *Journal of Reading* 35(5): 17-19.

The authors of this article believe course content is best learned in a classroom environment where learners work in partnership and collaboration. They describe how they created such a learning community in their reading methods course to better teach this concept of "community of learners" to their students. (P)

Sagawa, S., and S. Halperin, eds. (1993). *Visions of Service: The Future of the National and Community Service Act.* Washington, DC: National Women's Center and American Youth Policy Forum.

This publication contains 36 short essays on the reauthorization of the National and Community Service Act. It begins with two introductory papers, "Visions of Service: The Future of the National and Community Service Act" and "Historical Background: An Overview," and continues with a comprehensive overview of the service movement in the United States. (T)

Serow, R.C. (1990). "Volunteering and Values: An Analysis of Students' Participation in Community Service." *Journal of Research and Development in Education* 23(4): 198-203.

This study examines the value patterns of students in light of the community service movement on campuses throughout America. Serow concludes that community service is a result of forces in one's background as well as educational experiences. (R)

Silcox, H.C. (1993). *A How-to Guide to Reflection: Adding Cognitive Learning to Community Service Programs.* Holland, PA: Brighton Press.

This book examines the movement in service-learning where academic learning extends to the community to encourage more meaningful forms of education. Silcox expertly describes the use of reflective teaching methodology. It provides a resource for teachers working with students of various ages. (P)

Zahorik, J.A. (1995). *Constructivist Teaching.* Bloomington, IN: Phi Delta Kappa Educational Foundation.

The author examines many faces of constructivist teaching theory and practice and suggests how teachers can decide what form of constructivist teaching they might want to use. Teaching elements, basic types, beliefs, and importance of constructivist teaching are presented. Threats and future challenges of the implementation of constructivist teaching are proposed. (T,P)

Curriculum Resources

Alliance for Service-Learning in Education Reform. (1993). *Standards of Quality for School-Based Service-Learning.* Chester, VT: ASLER.

The Alliance for Service-Learning in Education Reform has outlined 11 crucial components for successful service-learning projects. A sample of these components includes opportunity for students to learn new skills, thoughtful preparation and reflection, high level of student participation, service that is meaningful to the community, and support from staff as well as others. (T,P)

Cairn, R., and T.L. Coble. (1993). *Learning by Giving: K-8 Service-Learning Curriculum Guide.* St. Paul, MN: National Youth Leadership Council.

The four main parts of this curriculum guide offer definitions and rationale for using service-learning, programmatic and logistical suggestions for development or expansion of service-learning programs, sample lesson plans, and an annotated list of national resources. Part I, "Service-Learning," describes the what and why of service-learning. Part II, "Nuts & Bolts," answers how to get started, offering project ideas and examples, cooperative group initiative games, and handouts and assessment forms. Part III, "Samples," includes 15 sample lesson plans for grades K-2, 3-5, and 6-8. Part IV, "Resources," describes National Youth Leadership Council's national programs, videos, and training programs, along with NYLC regional centers. Additional national organizations and resources are listed by issue area. An annotated bibliography of books for grades K-8 by area is included. (P)

Corporation for National Service. (1996). *Expanding Boundaries: Serving and Learning.* Columbia, MD: Cooperative Education Association.

Both educational reform and educational reconstruction stress the importance of a school-community link. Service-learning can play a central and powerful role toward achieving that link. This book presents a forum at which to highlight the successes as well as the mistakes of service-learning, while inspiring a goal of higher quantity and quality of learning. It establishes a goal that every student in America should view service as a common expectation and common experience. (P)

Council of Chief State School Officers. (1993). *Service-Learning Planning and Resource Guide*. Washington, DC: Council of Chief State School Officers.
This is a two-part funding and resource guide. The funding guide offers detailed guidelines for applications to federal funding sources to support a variety of activities necessary to develop, promote, or expand service-learning initiatives. It includes funds that support planning, project grants, research, training, technical assistance, curriculum development, administration/staffing, evaluation, staff development, and dissemination. Two types of assistance include formula grants and competitive or discretionary grants. The resource guide is designed to help teachers, colleges and universities, and other public and private agencies locate resources to help them design and implement service-learning initiatives. Resources include ideas for training, publications, curriculum materials, resource guides, technical assistance, membership services, program manuals, and databases. (P)

Dunlap, N.C., S.F. Drew, and K. Gibson. (1994). *Serving to Learn: K-8 Manual*. Columbia, SC: South Carolina Department of Education.
This volume is part of a three-volume set of content-specific ideas for integrating active, service-learning experiences into the curriculum. The ideas are cross-referenced by course, grade level, and type of service. Each activity describes student goals, resources needed, and preparation for service activity, reflection, and celebration. The references include a bibliography and listing of local and national service-learning organizations. The appendix includes transparencies defining service-learning, the steps for implementing service, South Carolina Youth Service Network, and a Service-Learning Leadership award. The other two volumes are references for high school and adult education. (P)

Follman, J. (1994). *Learning by Serving: 2,000 Ideas for Service-Learning Projects*. Harrisburg, PA: Penn-SERVE.
Defining service-learning as the formal integration of service into student instruction and learning, this guide provides teachers with ideas for narrowing the gap between what students do in school and what

they will do after they leave school. The example activities, derived from actual projects, demonstrate the nearly limitless range of possibilities for service-learning. The guide is divided into four sections. The first section provides examples of interdisciplinary projects, by grade level. The second section offers single-discipline projects, by subject and grade level. The third section offers practical information on the steps involved in establishing a service-learning program. The fourth section contains descriptions of useful publications on service-learning and annotated lists of organizations at the local, state, regional, and national levels that can provide information and resources to people interested in initiating or expanding service-learning. (P)

Kinsley, C., ed. (1991). *Whole Learning Through Service: A Guide for Integrating Service Into the Curriculum K-8*. Springfield, MA: Community Service Learning Center.
This curriculum presents community service–learning models based on five themes: intergenerational, homeless/hungry, citizenship, community health awareness, and environmental. The authors, teachers who have practiced the lessons in the manual, organized model units of study for the classroom, school, or community using themes to demonstrate how the service experience becomes the core of a unit. Two lesson plans, many service experiences, and types of resources are identified for each theme. Although it is written for the Springfield public schools and Springfield, Massachusetts, it is easily adaptable to other communities. (P)

Laplante, L.J., and C.W. Kinsley. (1995). *Things That Work in Community Service–Learning*. Springfield, MA: Community Service Learning Center.
This guide is a compilation of 15 curriculum units that illustrate the many ways in which community service–learning can be infused into secondary education. The case studies in this volume resulted from a minigrant program in which teachers facilitated service-learning projects and then documented the process for this publication. Each unit outlines the academic connections to service projects and steps for connecting with the community. Proceeds from this manual will be used to fund future minigrants. (P)

Manson, R. (1996). *Where Do I Begin? A Resource for Initiating Service-Learning*. Providence, RI: Feinstein Institute for Public Service, Providence College.
The author presents strategies for initiating, planning, and executing a service-learning project within a classroom or school. The book

serves as a "working notebook," where any project may be placed into the basic framework of the guide and be developed through following sequential steps. It provides samples of projects as they span across the curriculum, along with worksheets. The guide examines two school sites with differing service-learning projects and provides insight into issues that impact success. (P)

Maryland Student Service Alliance. (1995). *Maryland's Best Practices: An Improvement Guide for School-Based Service-Learning.* Baltimore, MD: Maryland Department of Education.

Based on interviews with 80 Maryland teachers who use service-learning as a teaching method, this guide gives experienced service-learning teachers concrete ways to evaluate and to improve their service-learning practice. Seven best practices for school-based service-learning are (1) to meet a recognized need in the community, (2) to achieve curricular objectives through service-learning, (3) to reflect throughout service-learning, (4) to develop student responsibility, (5) to establish community partnerships, (6) to plan ahead for service-learning, and (7) to equip students with knowledge and skills needed for service. Each of these seven practices includes two to three approaches to implement the practice. Pitfalls and safety nets and a glossary of terms are included. (P)

National Youth Leadership Council. (September 1994). *Route to Reform: K-8 Service-Learning Curriculum Ideas.* St. Paul, MN: National Youth Leadership Council.

Teachers from the Generator School Project and the WalkAbout summer program present their ideas regarding service-learning as a method of instruction that can improve student achievement and catalyze other school-improvement strategies, such as interdisciplinary instruction, team teaching, and block scheduling. The descriptions of year-round service-learning projects offer ideas meant to be adapted across settings, seasons, and time lines. Each Generator School project description includes school/community profile, project description, time line, project scheduling, additional funding, and equipment needed, as well as contact information, grade level, and academic focus. Each WalkAbout summer program includes a project description, time line, scheduling, funding, safety/liability, equipment needed, educational strategies, academic outcomes, personal growth outcomes, community involvement, reflection activities, means of assessment, and hurdles encountered. (P)

Parsons, C. (1995). "Serving to Learn, Learning to Serve." In *Civics and Service From A to Z*. Thousand Oaks, CA: Corwin Press.

This article is a practical guide for teachers, administrators, counselors, and education faculty members wanting service-learning programs as a foundation for good teaching and learning. It presents a design for projects that enrich the curriculum, produce citizens who vote, bring schools, families, and communities together, enliven the meaning of democracy, and encourage active teaching and learning. (P)

Acknowledgment

The author would like to acknowledge the substantial contributions of Susan Hammond, Jennifer Toland, Stephanie Springer, and Paula Eaton to the development of this annotated bibliography.

Service-Learning Resources

Organizations

Alliance for Service-Learning in Education Reform (ASLER)
c/o Close Up Foundation
44 Canal Center Plaza
Alexandria, VA 22314-1592
703/706-3640
fax 703/706-0001
cufmail@ixnetcom.com

American Association for Higher Education
One Dupont Circle, NW, Suite 360
Washington, DC 20036-1110
202/293-6440
fax 202/293-0073
info@aahe.org

AmeriCorps (see Corporation for National and Community Service)

Campus Compact
c/o Brown University
Box 1975
Providence, RI 02912
401/863-1119
fax 401/863-3779
campus@compact.org

Campus Outreach Opportunity League (COOL)
1511 K Street, NW, Suite 307
Washington, DC 20005
202/637-7004
fax 202/637-7021
homeoffice@cool2serve.org

Corporation for National and Community Service
1201 New York Avenue, NW
Washington, DC 20525
202/606-5000
fax 202/565-2781
TDD 202/565-2799

Feinstein Institute for Public Service
Providence College
549 River Avenue
Providence, RI 02918-0001
401/865-1204
fax 401/865-1206
kmorton@providence.edu

Learn and Serve: Higher Education (see Corporation for National and Community Service)

National Dropout Prevention Center
College of Health, Education, and Human Development
Clemson University
205 Martin Street
Clemson, SC 29634-0726
864/656-2599
fax 864/656-0136
mbdck@clemson.edu

National Information Center for Service-Learning
University of Minnesota
R-290 VoTech Education Building
1954 Buford Avenue
St. Paul, MN 55108-6197
800/808-SERVE
fax 612/625-6277
serve@maroon.tc.umn.edu

National Society for Experiential Education
3509 Haworth Drive, Suite 207
Raleigh, NC 27609
919/787-3263
fax 919/787-3381
info@nsee.pdial.interpath.net

National Youth Leadership Council (NYLC)
1910 West Country Road B
Roseville, MN 55113
612/631-3672
fax 612/631-2955
nylcusa@aol.com

Partnership for Service-Learning
815 Second Avenue, Suite 315
New York, NY 10017-4594
212/986-0989
fax 212/986-5039
pslny@aol.com

Service Learning 2000 Center
School of Education
Stanford University
Stanford, CA 94305-3096
415/322-7271
fax 415/328-8024
don.hill@forsythe.stanford.edu

Youth Service America
810 18th Street, NW, Suite 705
Washington, DC 20006
202/783-8855

Networked Resources on the World Wide Web

AmeriCorps:
http://www.cns.gov/americorps.html

Campus Outreach Opportunity League (COOL):
http://www.COOL2SERVE.org/cool/home.html

Contact Center Network:
http://www.contact.org

Corporation for National Service:
http://www.cns.gov/

Learn and Serve: Higher Education:
http://www.cns.gov/ls-hed.html

National Service-Learning Cooperative Clearinghouse:
http://www.nicsl.coled.umn.edu/intros/geninfo.html

National Service Resource Center:
http://www.etr-associates.org/nsrc/

Service-Learning Home Page:
http://csf.colorado.edu/sl/

Service-Learning Discussion Groups (Listservs)

Several service-learning listservs (email discussion groups) have been established at the University of Colorado at Boulder. One is the moderated *Journal of Service-Learning*, which means the email items are selected and edited before being sent to subscribers. A general-interest *unmoderated* listserv on service-learning (i.e., the email items are not selected or edited prior to being distributed to subscribers) is also maintained at this site. Another unmoderated group maintained at this site is the *Learn and Serve: Higher Education* listserv.

To subscribe to the *Journal of Service-Learning,* send the command:
     sub jsl Yourfirstname Yourlastname
to
     listproc@csf.colorado.edu

To subscribe to the general-interest service-learning listserv, send the command:
     sub service-learning Yourfirstname Yourlastname
to
     listproc@csf.colorado.edu

To subscribe to the Learn and Serve: Higher Education listserv, send the command:

> *sub lshe Yourfirstname Yourlastname*

to

> *listproc@csf.colorado.edu*

For more information about these listservs, you should browse the Service-Learning Home Page at the University of Colorado at Boulder: *http://csf.colorado.edu/sl/*

Contributors to This Volume

Volume Editors

Jeffrey B. Anderson is associate professor of education at Seattle University. He received his Ph.D. in curriculum leadership from the University of Denver and has been involved in teacher education for nine years. During his 10 years as a high school social studies and special education teacher, he regularly engaged with his students in service-learning and school-to-work projects. Anderson received the 1995 Washington State Award for Excellence in Teacher Preparation for his work in integrating service-learning into teacher education at Seattle University. He also directs the Seattle Community Service Learning Partnership, an organization working to enhance K-12 and teacher education through service-learning. He has published in the areas of service-learning, supervision of instruction, and teacher self-assessment.

Joseph A. Erickson is an assistant professor in the education department at Augsburg College in Minneapolis, Minnesota. Since graduating from the University of St. Thomas in 1979, he has worked as a secondary school teacher and licensed psychologist. In 1985, he began working with the Minneapolis-based Search Institute, with which he has collaborated on a number of youth- and family-related research projects, and has published several articles in the areas of religious measurement and faith development. He earned his doctorate in educational psychology at the University of Minnesota in 1990. Starting in 1991, he has studied and promoted service-learning in K-12 and postsecondary schools, focusing on various ways to integrate service-learning into teacher education programs. Some of his other interests include educational computing, instructional evaluation, recruitment and retention of teachers of color, and the promotion of healthy communities in fostering positive youth development.

Authors

Jose Arredondo is coordinator of multicultural education and assistant professor of education at Valparaiso University in Valparaiso, Indiana. Before coming to Valparaiso University, Arredondo was assistant superintendent of schools in East Chicago, Indiana, director of development at Calumet College, county sheriff, county auditor, state representative, and principal and teacher in the Gary, Indiana, school system. He is the founder and director of Ballet Folklorico and Mariachi Acero, a nonprofit organization that collaborates with Valparaiso University to develop various projects.

Darrol Bussler is associate professor of educational foundations for Mankato State University in Mankato, Minnesota. He is a former secondary teacher and former community education director. One of his primary interests is democratizing education, which includes an initiative to involve youth in policy-making bodies such as school boards and city councils. He is currently serving as chair of the Society for Educational Reconstruction and views educational reconstruction philosophy as a base for service-learning.

Jane P. Callahan is assistant professor of education at Providence College in Providence, Rhode Island. She received her doctorate from the University of Idaho. She has worked extensively in the public schools and, as a faculty member and educational consultant, has developed programs that involve preservice and practicing teachers in the areas of collaboration and working with students with special needs and their families. During the past three years, she has been involved with the Institute for Public and Community Service, developing curriculum, teaching in the program, and coordinating a Learn and Serve America Higher Education Grant focused on integrating service-learning pedagogy into the teacher education program.

Carole A. Cobb is director of service-learning at Kentucky State University in Franklin, Kentucky, and director of federal, state, and special programs for the Franklin County schools. She received her Ph.D. in curriculum and instruction from Wayne State University. She has been a teacher and assistant principal at the middle and high school levels. She is the winner of the National Library of Poetry contest and is on Detroit's Black Women's Honor Roll.

William H. Denton is professor of educational leadership at Clark Atlanta University, where he specializes in community education. As director of the Institute for Community Educational Leadership, he developed Culture for Service, CAU's program of academically based service, and currently serves as principal investigator for the Atlanta University Center Service Learning Collaborative funded by the Corporation for National Service.

Marty Duckenfield is public information director at the National Dropout Prevention Center at Clemson University and the coordinator of the university's Service-Learning Collaborative. A former public school teacher, she has cotaught a master's-level course, Integrating Service-Learning Into Curricula. In addition, Duchenfield is coauthor of *Service Learning: Meeting the Needs of Youth at Risk,* and she edits the newsletter *Learning and Serving.*

Diane Fuqua is an associate professor in the School of Education at James Madison University in Harrisonburg, Virginia. In addition to her teaching duties in the early childhood program, she served two years as faculty coordinator of the Center for Service-Learning, now a part of the Madison Leadership Center at James Madison. Her research and teaching interests, in addition to community service, include multicultural education, classroom climate, and creativity.

John Guffey was formerly the Turtle Island Project director for the National Indian Youth Leadership Project. Guffey received a bachelor's degree in biology and worked for the U.S. Forest Service before becoming a teacher. After two years of teaching in Kuwait, Guffey returned to the United States and earned a master's degree in religious studies from Earlham School of Religion and an Ed.S. in multicultural education from Indiana University. His involvement with NIYLP is rooted in native (Iowa) ancestry and interest in indigenous cultural perspectives as they apply to education and human development.

Don Hill serves as director of the Service Learning 2000 Center at the Stanford University School of Education. His service-learning work at the Corporation for National Service Higher Education Learn and Serve project includes coteaching a service-learning course for preservice teachers; facilitating workshops for more than 1,000 K-16 teachers, administrators, and community workers; and designing a variety of service-learning instructional materials. Before coming to Stanford in 1988, Hill taught high school social studies for 27 years.

Joseph F. Keating was a K-12 science and math teacher for 25 years. He received his Ph.D. in multicultural science education from the University of New Mexico. He was the recipient in 1993 of both the Presidential Award for Excellence in Secondary Science Teaching and the New Mexico Academy for the Advancement of Science Teacher of the Year Award. He is assistant professor of science education at California State University at San Marcos.

Christine Hunstiger Keithahn has been involved with service-learning since 1991. In her 10-year teaching career, she has taught grades one through six in public schools in Los Angeles and Seattle. She currently teaches at Hawthorne Elementary School in Seattle. Her education includes a B.A. in sociology and psychology from Occidental College and an M.Ed. in governance policy and administration from the University of Washington. She lives in Seattle with her husband, grandmother, and daughter.

Theresa J.H. Magelssen received her bachelor of arts degrees in English and elementary education at Augsburg College. She and her husband live in Minneapolis, where she teaches a first and second grade combination classroom at Marcy Open School in southeast Minneapolis.

Gerald H. Maring earned his Ph.D. in reading education in 1977 from the University of Missouri after teaching in junior and senior high schools for eight years. At Washington State University, his work focuses on literacy development, K-12. Since 1992, he and his students have been developing instructional units and projects that integrate content, content literacy, and service-learning. Maring's forthcoming text for teachers, published by Wadsworth, is entitled *Content Literacy: A Community-of-Learners Approach*.

Carol Myers is a youth development and school improvement consultant. She assists K-12 and postsecondary schools to integrate service-learning into core academic curricula.

Mary J. Syfax Noble is an elementary school administrator in the Minneapolis Public Schools. In addition, Noble is a member and vice chair of the Minnesota Commission on National and Community Service. She received two master of arts degrees from Xavier University in Cincinnati, Ohio, and a B.S. degree from The Ohio State University. She has taught elementary grades one through eight and has written many articles and contributed to several books about service-learning.

Susan O'Connor is an assistant professor of education at Augsburg College. She is also the coordinator of the department's special education minor. Her focus within the field of disability is on creating inclusive schools and communities for people with disabilities and their families. She is also interested in multicultural education.

Carolyn R. O'Grady is assistant professor of education at Gustavus Adolphus College in St. Peter, Minnesota, and a frequent workshop facilitator for schools and small organizations on issues of diversity, including race, gender, and sexual orientation. Her research interests include education as social change, spirituality in education, and the intersection of multicultural education and service-learning.

Vicki L. Olson is an associate professor of education at Augsburg College, where she teaches a variety of courses, primarily in the area of elementary education. She is also an active volunteer in her youngest daughter's school and in her church.

Vito Perrone is a faculty member in the Harvard Graduate School of Education, where he is also director of programs in teacher education. He has written extensively about such issues as educational equity, curriculum and progressivism in education, and testing and evaluation. His recent books are *A Letter to Teachers* (Jossey-Bass, 1991) and *Expanding Student Assessment* (ASCD, 1992). His book on Leonard Covello will be published by Teachers College Press in fall 1997. Perrone has been a public school teacher and a university professor of history, education, and peace studies and dean of the New School and the Center for Teaching and Learning at the University of North Dakota. He has served for 26 years as coordinator of the North Dakota Study Group on Evaluation and is actively engaged in the life of elementary and secondary schools.

Terry Pickeral is assistant director of the Campus Compact National Center for Community Colleges at Mesa Community College, Arizona. He directs a national program to advance service-learning on community colleges through faculty development. He has developed several K-12 service-learning programs to meet local, state, and national initiatives. He also is manager of the Corporation for National Service Learn and Serve America Teacher Education Affinity Group and is involved in research on the integration of service-learning by novice teachers.

Denise Clark Pope has served for the past three years as research director at the Service Learning 2000 Center at the Stanford University School of Education, where she has conducted qualitative studies of K-12 service-learning in action. She is currently pursuing a doctoral degree at the School of Education in the curriculum and teacher education program. As a former high school and college English teacher, Pope is interested in students' curricular experiences, high school–reform issues, and adolescent development.

Susan C. Root is chair of the Education Department at Alma College in Alma, Michigan, where she teaches educational psychology, growth and development, and early childhood education, and supervises student teachers. Root was coauthor of a W.K. Kellogg Foundation grant to support the development of a service-learning program at Alma. She is chair of the Michigan Campus Compact Curriculum Subcommittee and cochair of Alma College's service-learning task force.

Lynne Ryan is chair of the Education Department at Providence College. She received her doctorate from the University of Connecticut and has been at Providence College since 1980. She works extensively with school districts in Rhode Island and the Rhode Island Department of Education on topics related to the education of all children in inclusive educational settings. In addition to service-learning and inclusive education, her other research interests are in the areas of teacher education and assessment.

Janet Salo is an advocate for a primary focus on preserving and enhancing the educational rights of children who have developmental disabilities. She works at ARC of Hennepin County as a family support coordinator by empowering, informing, and connecting families with information, resources, and support options in order to improve the quality of life for the family and the individual who has a developmental disability. She lives in Minneapolis, Minnesota, with her son, Evan.

Robert Shumer is director of the National Service-Learning Cooperative Clearinghouse at the University of Minnesota and codirector of the Center for Experiential Education and Service-Learning. Shumer has conducted research on service-learning and developed service-/community-based learning programs across the country. He teaches courses on experiential and service-learning as well as on research, youth development, and school-to-work issues. He has had experience at the K-12, undergraduate, and graduate levels in California and Minnesota.

Julie A. Stoffels is associate professor of education at Alverno College in Milwaukee, Wisconsin, and coordinator of its secondary education program. She graduated from Monmouth College, Illinois, and received her M.A.T. in English from Northwestern University. Stoffels taught high school English for six years in Arlington Heights, Illinois, District 214, and in Arlington, Virginia. Her Ph.D. is in curriculum and instruction from Marquette University. Currently, she serves as president of the Association of Independent Liberal Arts Colleges for Teacher Education.

Rahima C. Wade is assistant professor of elementary social studies at the University of Iowa. She coordinates the Iowa Service-Learning Partnership, a network of school districts and area educational agencies involved with service-learning in Iowa's public schools. Wade is editor of *Community Service-Learning: A Guide to Including Service in the Public School Curriculum* (State University of New York Press, 1997) as well as numerous publications about service-learning in educational journals.

Carol Weatherford is an associate professor at Clemson University in the Department of Educational Foundations and Special Education. She developed and taught a course for master's-level teachers called Integrating Service-Learning Across Curricula. Weatherford served on the Clemson University Service-Learning Committee and currently serves on the Clemson University Service-Learning Collaborative. She provided leadership in the development, implementation, and evaluation of Visions for Youth, a program that involves high-risk preadolescents in service-learning activities.

Janet Wright is currently the service-learning coordinator at the National Dropout Prevention Center at Clemson University. Her role includes co-facilitation of the Southern Regional Technical Assistance Center for the National Service Learning Cooperative and other service-learning initiatives. Wright frequently presents on the topic of service-learning and has cotaught three graduate courses at Clemson University regarding integrating service-learning into the curriculum. Prior to coming to Clemson, Wright spent 21 years in the public schools as a teacher, central office administrator, and elementary principal.

Series Editor

Edward Zlotkowski is professor of English at Bentley College. Founding director of the Bentley Service-Learning Project, he has published and spoken on a wide variety of service-learning topics. Currently, he is also a senior associate at the American Association for Higher Education.

About AAHE

AAHE's Vision AAHE envisions a higher education enterprise that helps all Americans achieve the deep, lifelong learning they need to grow as individuals, participate in the democratic process, and succeed in a global economy.

AAHE's Mission AAHE is the individual membership organization that promotes the changes higher education must make to ensure its effectiveness in a complex, interconnected world. The association equips individuals and institutions committed to such changes with the knowledge they need to bring them about.

About AAHE's Series on Service-Learning in the Disciplines

The Series goes beyond simple "how to" to provide a rigorous intellectual forum. *Theoretical essays* illuminate issues of general importance to educators interested in using a service-learning pedagogy. *Pedagogical essays* discuss the design, implementation, conceptual content, outcomes, advantages, and disadvantages of specific service-learning programs, courses, and projects. All essays are authored by teacher-scholars in the discipline.

Representative of a wide range of individual interests and approaches, the Series provides substantive discussions supported by research, course models in a rich conceptual context, annotated bibliographies, and program descriptions.

Visit AAHE's website (www.aahe.org) for the list of disciplines covered in the Series, pricing, and ordering information.